# LANGUAGE FOR DAILY USE

## *Phoenix Edition*

 *Orange*

**Curriculum and Instruction**

**Dr. Dorothy S. Strickland**
Professor of Education
Department of Curriculum and Teaching
Teachers College, Columbia University

**Consulting Educators**

Dr. Richard F. Abrahamson, Consultant for Literature
Professor of Education
Department of Curriculum and Instruction
College of Education, University of Houston

Lexis Allen
Language Arts Curriculum Consultant
Clark County School District
Las Vegas, Nevada

Nola Bacci
Principal
West End Elementary School
Lynbrook, New York

Jennifer Better
Curriculum Coordinator
Cupertino Union School District
Cupertino, California

Dr. Barbara Burke
Assistant Director
Language Education Department
Detroit Public Schools
Detroit, Michigan

Dr. Therese J. D'Abre
Communicative Arts Coordinator, K–12
Dennis/Yarmouth Regional School District
South Yarmouth, Massachusetts

Betty Gould
Learning Development Specialist
Sachem Central School District
Holbrook, New York

Hildagarde Gray
Librarian
St. John the Baptist School
Pittsburgh, Pennsylvania

Elizabeth Handford
Curriculum Coordinator
Southside Christian School
Greenville, South Carolina

Helen Levy
Librarian
Springdale Elementary School
Princeton City School District
Cincinnati, Ohio

Dr. Ewald J. Scharrschmidt
Fourth-Grade Teacher
Lincoln Elementary School
Wausau, Wisconsin

David Zaslow
Writer-in-Residence
South Oregon Public Schools
Ashland, Oregon

*Phoenix Edition*

# LANGUAGE FOR DAILY USE

**Harcourt Brace Jovanovich, Publishers**

**Orlando    New York    Chicago    Atlanta    Dallas**

## ACKNOWLEDGMENTS

For permission to reprint copyrighted material, grateful acknowledgment is given to the following sources:

*Atheneum Publishers:* "Our Washing Machine," in *The Apple Vendor's Fair.* Copyright © 1963 by Patricia Hubbell (New York: Atheneum, 1963).

*The Christian Science Publishing Society:* First verse of "Post Early for Space" by Peter Henniker-Heaton from *The Christian Science Monitor* © 1957 by The Christian Science Publishing Society. All rights reserved.

*Delacorte Press:* Untitled poem excerpted from the book *Poems From Sharon's Lunch Box* by Alice Gilbert. Copyright © 1972 by Alice Gilbert.

*Doubleday & Company, Inc.:* "Split Pea Soup" excerpt adapted from *Paul Bunyan and His Great Blue Ox by* Wallace Wadsworth. Copyright 1926 by Doubleday & Company, Inc.

*E. P. Dutton, Inc.:* Proverb by Bella Coola Indians from *Whirlwind Is a Ghost Dancing* by Natalia Belting. Copyright © 1974 by Natalia Belting. First stanza of poem, "Galoshes" from *Stories to Begin On* by Rhoda W. Bacmeister. Copyright 1940 by E. P. Dutton & Co., Inc. Renewal copyright © 1968 by Rhoda W. Bacmeister.

*Edwina Fallis and the Association for Childhood Education International, 3615 Wisconsin Avenue, N.W., Washington, D.C.:* First verse of "September" by Edwina Fallis from *Sung Under the Silver Umbrella.* Copyright by the Association.

*Aileen Fisher:* "Skins" by Aileen Fisher from *That's Why,* published by Thomas Nelson & Sons, New York, 1946. Copyright renewed 1974.

*Harcourt Brace Jovanovich, Inc.:* Pronunciation key and entries reprinted and reproduced from *The HBJ School Dictionary,* copyright © 1977 by Harcourt Brace Jovanovich, Inc.

*Harper & Row, Publishers, Inc.:* Text of "It's Dark in Here" from page 21 of *Where the Sidewalk Ends: The Poems and Drawings of Shel Silverstein.* Copyright © 1974 by Shel Silverstein. Text of "Waves of the Sea" from *Out In the Dark and Daylight* by Aileen Fisher. Text copyright © 1980 by Aileen Fisher. Accents added for emphasis. Text of "Sitting in the Sand" from *Dogs & Dragons, Trees & Dreams: A Collection of Poems* by Karla Kuskin. Poem copyright © 1958 by Karla Kuskin. Accents added for emphasis.

*Holt, Rinehart and Winston, Publishers:* "The dark gray clouds...," from *The Sun Is a Golden Earring* by Natalia M. Belting. Copyright © 1962 by Natalia Belting.

*Houghton Mifflin Company:* "Apple Song" from *Pool in the Meadow* by Frances Frost. Copyright 1933 by Frances Frost. Copyright renewed 1961.

*Bertha Klausner International Literary Agency, Inc.:* "Funny the Way Different Cars Start" by Dorothy W. Baruch.

*Alfred A. Knopf, Inc.:* "April Rain Song" from *The Dream Keeper and Other Poems* by Langston Hughes. Copyright 1932 by Alfred A. Knopf, Inc. and renewed 1960 by Langston Hughes.

*J. B. Lippincott, Publishers:* Complete, adapted text of *Wesley Paul, Marathon Runner* by Julianna A. Fogel. Text copyright © 1979 by Julianna A. Fogel.

*The Literary Estate of Irene Rutherford McLeod and Chatto & Windus Ltd.:* First verse of "Lone Dog" from *Songs to Save a Soul* by Irene Rutherford McLeod.

*Macmillan Publishing Co., Inc.:* "Night" from *Collected Poems* by Sara Teasdale. Copyright 1930 by Sara Teasdale Filsinger, renewed 1958 by Guaranty Trust Company of New York, Executor. "The Hills" from *Poems* by Rachel Field. (New York: Macmillan 1957).

*National Wildlife Federation:* "Dew" by Mark Warner from *Ranger Rick's Nature Magazine,* © June 1979.

*Barbara S. Neelands:* "The Good Luck Bogle" by Barbara Neelands. Copyright 1980.

*Plays, Inc.:* "The Turtle Who Changed His Tune," adapted by Claire Boiko, reprinted by permission from *Plays, The Drama Magazine for Young People.* Copyright © 1980 by Plays, Inc., Publishers. This play is for reading purposes only. For permission to produce this play, write to Plays, Inc., 8 Arlington Street, Boston, MA 02116.

*Philomel Books, a Division of the Putnam Publishing Group:* Excerpt from "Joe Magarac in *The Rainbow Book of American Folk Tales and Legends* by Maria Leach. Copyright © 1958 by Maria Leach.

*G.P. Putnam's Sons:* Adapted from *Jane Goodall* by Eleanor Coerr. Copyright © 1976 by Eleanor Coerr.

*C. Walter Ruckel:* First verse of "Abraham Lincoln" by Mildrew Plew Meigs in *Child Life* magazine.

*Scholastic Inc.:* "The Fox and the Goat" from *Aesop's Fables* retold by Ann McGovern. Copyright © 1963 by Scholastic Inc.

*Troll Associates, Mahwah, New Jersey:* From *Francis Drake* by David Goodnough, copyright © 1979.

*Bryna Untermeyer:* For Louis Untermeyer's versions of "The Fox and the Grapes" and "The Boastful Bullfrog and the Bull" from *Aesop's Fables* illustrated by A. & M. Provenson, published by Golden Press, copyright © 1965 by Western Publishing Co.

*Harriet Wasserman Literary Agency as agent for Mary Ann Hoberman:* "The Folk Who Lived in Backward Town" in *Hello and Goodbye* by Mary Ann Hoberman. Copyright © 1959 by Mary Ann Hoberman

PRINTED IN THE UNITED STATES OF AMERICA
ISBN 0-15-317005-0

# CONTENTS

## UNIT 4   125

## UNIT 5  161

*x*

1

# LANGUAGE
## Learning About Sentences

# STUDY SKILLS
## Using the Library

# COMPOSITION
## Writing Sentences

# LITERATURE
## Reading Poetry

When you first began to speak, you used simple words. *More, up,* and *no* are three favorite words of young speakers. Can you think of other easy first words?

As you grew older, you had more to say. One word at a time was not enough. You began to speak in sentences. Of course, you did not know what a sentence was then, but you probably do now!

Now you speak in sentences all the time. You write sentences too. Do you remember the different kinds of sentences? In this unit you will learn about the four kinds. You will learn to write and edit these kinds of sentences. You will also find out how libraries are organized, and you will discover new things about poetry.

Look at the pictures on the opposite page. What is happening? Make believe you are one of the people in the picture. Make up some sentences you might say.

# LANGUAGE

## Lesson 1: Understanding Sentences

Sentences can be found all around us. You can find them in a library book. You can see them written in a letter from your uncle. Can you think of other places where you can find sentences used?

### Think and Discuss

Some sentences give information.

1. I found a butterfly.

Some sentences ask questions.

2. Do you know what kind it is?

Some sentences command.

3. Don't hurt the butterfly.

Some sentences exclaim.

4. How beautiful the butterfly is!

To be a sentence, a group of words must state a complete thought. Pick out the sentence in these groups of words.

5. Some insects are pretty.
6. Some pretty butterflies.

Group 5 is a sentence. It expresses a complete thought. Group 6 is not a sentence. Can you think of some words to add to make it a sentence?

How does each sentence begin and end?

> ● A **sentence** is a group of words that states a complete thought. It begins with a capital letter and ends with a mark of punctuation.

## *Practice*

**A.** Write the groups of words that are sentences.

1. Do you know where to look for insects?
2. Under leaves.
3. Under logs and rocks.
4. Dead trees are a good place to find insects.
5. Take off the bark and see what you find.
6. Some beetles make their homes there.
7. What a strange beetle that is!
8. Bees, wasps, and butterflies.
9. Swimming in ponds.
10. Another good place to find insects is near a light.
11. Many insects are attracted to light.
12. Many kinds of moths.
13. You can catch water bugs along the pond's edge.
14. Pick up a stone in a brook.

**B.** Add words of your own to each group of words. Write the complete sentences.

15. look for insects
16. my friends and I
17. in my back yard
18. three red ants
19. told me about insects
20. a butterfly collection

## *Apply*

**C. 21.–25.** Write five sentences of your own telling about insects. Make sure each group of words you write is a complete thought.

# Lesson 2: Using Declarative and Interrogative Sentences

**Kate:** 1. Did you know the museum got a new mummy?
**Nick:** 2. Yes, I read about it in the newspaper.
**Kate:** 3. Would you like to go with me to see it?
**Nick:** 4. We could go tomorrow afternoon.

When Kate and Nick talked to each other on the telephone, they used two different kinds of sentences. What does each kind of sentence do?

## Think and Discuss

The kind of sentence Nick used is called a **declarative sentence.** A declarative sentence makes a statement. It tells something. Find the sentences Nick used. How do these sentences end?

Kate's sentences ask questions. That kind of sentence is called an **interrogative sentence.** What punctuation mark ends an interrogative sentence?

Now read these sentences. Which is a declarative sentence? Which is an interrogative sentence? How do you know?

**Kate:** 5. Where was the mummy found?
**Nick:** 6. It came from Egypt.

What begins each declarative and interrogative sentence? Remember that the first word of *every* sentence begins with a capital letter.

> ● A **declarative sentence** makes a statement. It ends with a period (.).
> ● An **interrogative sentence** asks a question. It ends with a question mark (**?**).

## Practice

**A.** Copy the sentences. Decide what kind of sentence each one is. Write *declarative sentence* or *interrogative sentence* after it.

1. Have you been to this museum before?
2. I was here once with my brother.
3. My fourth-grade class visited the museum last year.
4. Did you see the dinosaurs?
5. We saw the collection of moon rocks.

**B.** Write each sentence correctly. Then write *declarative sentence* or *interrogative sentence* to tell the kind of sentence.

6. the mummies were found in Egypt
7. some were found in pyramids
8. have you seen pictures of pyramids
9. they were built with huge blocks of stone
10. what else was found in the pyramids
11. masks of gold and precious stones often were found buried with the mummies
12. how did the Egyptians use these beautiful masks
13. each mummy was placed in the tomb with a mask covering its head
14. the masks were brightly colored, and some were covered with gold flakes
15. do you have any idea which exhibit you would like to see next

## Apply

**C. 16.–25.** Write five declarative sentences about the pictures. Write five interrogative sentences you might ask about them.

# Lesson 3: Using Imperative and Exclamatory Sentences

Read these sentences about a math contest.

1. Get ready for the math contest.
2. Please wait for your turn.
3. How happy I am!
4. What a great team we have!

## Think and Discuss

Sentence 1 gives a command, and sentence 2 makes a request. Such sentences are called **imperative sentences.** What mark ends each imperative sentence?

A sentence that shows strong feeling is called an **exclamatory sentence.** Which are exclamatory sentences? How do they end? How do both imperative and exclamatory sentences begin?

Now read these sentences. Which is an imperative sentence? Which is an exclamatory sentence? How do you know?

5. What a contest that was!
6. Return to class now.

> • An **imperative sentence** gives a command or makes a request. It ends with a period (.).
> • An **exclamatory sentence** shows strong feeling or surprise. It ends with an exclamation point (!).

## Practice

**A.** Write the sentences. After each sentence write *imperative sentence* or *exclamatory sentence.*

1. What a pretty painting that is!
2. Turn on the lights.

3. Get ready for the race.

4. What a team we have!

5. Inés, come here.

6. How quickly you came!

7. Ring the bell for recess.

8. Wow, the fire alarm is ringing!

9. Please bring your paper to me.

10. What excellent work you did!

**B.** Write each sentence correctly. Then write *imperative sentence* or *exclamatory sentence* to tell the kind of sentence.

11. how quickly the day passed

12. get ready to go home now

13. water the plants on the windowsill

14. how big those plants have grown

15. please close the windows now

16. fix the papers on the bulletin board

17. don't let the door slam

18. wow, that slamming door really scared me

19. find the hamster that is lost

20. great, I found it

## Apply

**C. 21.–30.** Imagine your class is taking a trip to an amusement park. Write five commands you might hear. Write five exclamations you or others might say.

## A Challenge

There are three different ways to put this set of words in order. Make a declarative, an interrogative, and an imperative sentence. You will have to leave some words out to make an imperative sentence.

the    you    cave    should    leave    now

# Lesson 4: Forming Questions and Answers

Every day in school you must answer questions. Did you ever notice how questions begin? Questions often begin with the words *who, what, when, where, why,* or *how.* Look at some questions that begin with these words.

1. <u>Who</u> was Ben Franklin?
2. <u>When</u> did he live?
3. <u>Where</u> was he born?
4. <u>Why</u> is he famous?
5. <u>What</u> are some of his inventions?
6. <u>How</u> did he help our country?

## Think and Discuss

Do you know how to answer a question correctly? Always answer a question in a complete sentence.

Read how these questions were answered.

7. Who <u>was</u> <u>Ben</u> <u>Franklin</u>? <u>Ben</u> <u>Franklin</u> <u>was</u> a famous American.
8. When did <u>he</u> <u>live</u>? <u>He lived</u> from 1706 to 1790.

Some words from the questions were borrowed to begin each answer. In question and answer number 7, which words are the same? Which words are the same in question and answer 8?

Now you do the changing! Read questions 4–6 at the start of this lesson. Think of a way to begin the answer to each one.

## Practice

**A.** Answers are given for each question. Write the answer in a complete sentence. Remember to use words from the question in your answer.

1. Why is Ben Franklin famous? (as an author, an inventor, and a statesman)

**2.** When did he begin printing *Poor Richard's Almanac?*
(in 1733)

**3.** What are some of his inventions? (bifocal glasses, the
Franklin stove, and a clock)

**4.** How did he discover that electricity and lightning were
the same? (with his kite experiment)

**5.** Where did he travel to make friends for our country?
(in America and Europe)

## *Apply*

**B. 6.–15.** Write five questions someone might ask you
about yourself. Begin each question with one of these
words: *who, what, when, where, why,* and *how.* Then write
the answers to your questions in complete sentences.

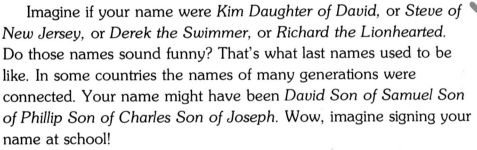

## HOW OUR LANGUAGE GROWS

Imagine if your name were *Kim Daughter of David,* or *Steve of New Jersey,* or *Derek the Swimmer,* or *Richard the Lionhearted.* Do those names sound funny? That's what last names used to be like. In some countries the names of many generations were connected. Your name might have been *David Son of Samuel Son of Phillip Son of Charles Son of Joseph.* Wow, imagine signing your name at school!

Last names have interesting histories. Some come from a place where your relatives lived (such as *Greenfield*). Some names come from the career of your ancestor (such as *Baker*).

**1.** Do you know what your last name means? Talk about it with your class.

**2.** Careers have changed quite a lot over the last few hundred years. Make up 10 names that could come from modern careers (*Stacy Stockbroker,* for example).

# Lesson 5: Understanding Complete Subjects and Predicates

Which group of words below expresses a complete thought?

1. the girl
2. fixes broken toys
3. The girl fixes broken toys.

## Think and Discuss

Only the third group of words expresses a complete thought. How does this group of words begin? How does this group end? Now read these.

4. Mr. Alves
5. works in a bank
6. Mr. Alves works in a bank.

If you put the words in groups 4 and 5 together, you end up with the words in group 6. There is a difference. Only group 6 is a sentence. Why?

Every sentence is made up of two parts.

> - The **complete subject** is all the words that make up the subject. The subject of the sentence is the part about which something is being said.
> - The **complete predicate** is all the words that tell something about the subject.

Subjects and predicates go together to make sentences. Read these complete subjects and predicates.

| Complete Subjects | Complete Predicates |
| --- | --- |
| 7. Ruth Morgan | come to her office. |
| 8. Her telephone | is a doctor. |
| 9. Many patients | rings day and night. |

Make sentences by matching each complete subject with the correct complete predicate. Read the sentences.

## Practice

**A.** Write the sentences. Draw one line under the complete subject and two lines under the complete predicate.

1. That man sells giant balloons in the park.
2. Herb drives a taxicab.
3. Bret organizes garage sales.
4. Evan sells lemonade at a stand.
5. Mrs. Dennis picks apples at an orchard.
6. Jackie makes handmade holiday cards.
7. Jane's mother makes films for television.
8. Rita Blake runs a neighborhood car wash.
9. Our next-door neighbor raises collies.
10. Three of my friends baby-sit.

**B.** Make up a complete predicate to go with each complete subject or a complete subject to go with each complete predicate. Write your new sentences.

| | | | |
|---|---|---|---|
| 11. the doctor | | 12. that great musician |
| 13. an author | | 14. reports the news |
| 15. farms the land | | 16. the road crew |
| 17. Luisa | | 18. works at the zoo |
| 19. delivers messages | | 20. teaches at a college |

## Apply

**C. 21.–25.** The sentences in this lesson tell about people who have jobs. Write five sentences about people you know who work. Be sure that each sentence has a complete subject and predicate.

## Sentences   pages 2–3

Decide which groups of words are sentences. Write them correctly.

1. squirrels live in this tree
2. from branch to branch without falling
3. my sister and I saw them yesterday
4. nest inside the trunk each spring
5. squirrels eat nuts
6. do you see those squirrels
7. chasing each other among the branches
8. squirrels have claws to help them climb

## Declarative and Interrogative Sentences   pages 4–5

Write each sentence correctly. Then write *declarative sentence* or *interrogative sentence* to tell the kind of sentence.

9. Are you going to the library after our science class
10. They know how to play this game as well as you do
11. Am I first or second in this race
12. Do you think we will win next Tuesday
13. She is a fast runner but not as fast as Barbara
14. Our team has practiced for two weeks
15. Should we continue to practice
16. Our gym teacher has arranged these games

## Imperative and Exclamatory Sentences   pages 6–7

Write each sentence correctly. Then write *imperative sentence* or *exclamatory sentence* to tell the kind of sentence.

17. My, this meal looks delicious
18. Please pass the butter to your sister
19. Put some gravy on your meat and potatoes
20. Ouch, these potatoes are really hot

21. What a meal we had tonight
22. Use good manners when you eat
23. Clear the plates from the table

## Questions and Answers   pages 8–9

Answers are given for each question. Write the answer in a complete sentence. Remember to use words from the question in your answer.

24. What is the name of our galaxy? (the Milky Way)
25. When was the telescope invented? (in the 1600's)
26. Where is the Andromeda galaxy? (in the constellation Orion)
27. Who was Galileo? (an early astronomer)
28. Why do we use a telescope? (to magnify distant stars)
29. What is another name for the Big Dipper? (the Great Bear)

## Complete Subject and Predicate   pages 10–11

Copy the sentences. Draw one line under the complete subject. Draw two lines under the complete predicate.

30. I love winter weather.
31. Deep snow is fun.
32. We throw snowballs.
33. My best friend can ski.
34. We race down the hill.
35. Bert forgot his mittens.
36. Many people skate.
37. She has a blue snowsuit.
38. Carlos slips on the ice.
39. That family looks cold.

## Applying Sentences

Make each group of words into a complete sentence. Write at least one of each of the four kinds of sentences—declarative, interrogative, imperative, and exclamatory.

40. yesterday when Mr. Rámirez went fishing
41. many kinds of fish in the sea
42. as big as a whale
43. difference between an octopus and a squid
44. looking for seashells at the beach
45. can find beautiful stones

# STUDY SKILLS

## *Lesson 6: Understanding the Organization of the Library*

Linda is writing a report about George Washington. She visited the library to find information. When she arrived at the library, she spoke first with Mr. Dawson, the librarian. Mr. Dawson helped Linda to find the information she needed.

### Think and Discuss

Mr. Dawson explained that libraries have different kinds of books. Each is found in a different section of the library.

**Fiction** books are stories that are all or partly imaginary.

**Nonfiction** books tell facts about real people, things, or events.

**A biography** is a nonfiction book that tells about the life of a real person.

**Reference** books are nonfiction books used to find facts about many different topics. The encyclopedia, atlas, and dictionary are reference books.

What other materials can you find in a library? Mr. Dawson showed Linda pictures, films, records, cassettes, magazines, newspapers, and artwork. All these are also kept in many libraries. Most of these materials can be borrowed just like a book. Mr. Dawson told Linda she might find information on her topic in these sources too.

## Practice

**A.** Read the list of books. For each, write *fiction, nonfiction, biography,* or *reference* to tell the kind of book. The words in parentheses ( ) will help you decide.

1. *World Book Encyclopedia*
2. *Cathy Rigby on the Beam*   (true-life story of a champion gymnast)
3. *Beginning Stamp Collecting*   (how to start a stamp collection)
4. *The Mystery of the Fat Cat*   (a mystery story)
5. *Webster's New World Dictionary*
6. *Kit Carson and the Wild Frontier*   (the true story of a frontier cowboy)
7. *The Story of Snakes*   (facts about snakes)
8. *Your Skin Holds You In*   (the skin and its qualities)
9. *Rand McNally Road Atlas*
10. *Mr. Bass's Planetoid*   (space fantasy)

**B. 11.–15.** Write five things other than books that you can find in a library.

## Apply

**C. 16.** Draw a map of your school or town library. Show these sections of the library on the map.

| | | |
|---|---|---|
| fiction | biography | records |
| nonfiction | reference | films |

Linda decided to look for books about George Washington. There are thousands of books in the library. Luckily, there is an easy way for Linda to find the books she wants.

## Think and Discuss

A **card catalog** is a set of small cards. These cards list every book in the library. There are three kinds of cards in the card catalog: title, author, and subject cards. The cards are kept in drawers. On the outside of the drawers are guide letters. These tell the first letter of the authors, titles, and subjects in that drawer. The cards are arranged in alphabetical order.

Now look at the cards below. The **title card** lists the title of the book first. *A, an,* and *the* are not used when the book title is alphabetized. The **author card** lists the author's last name first. The **subject card** lists the subject of the book first.

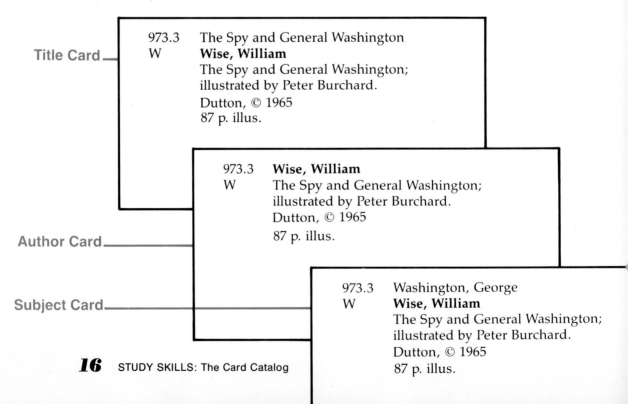

Title Card

973.3    The Spy and General Washington
W        **Wise, William**
         The Spy and General Washington;
         illustrated by Peter Burchard.
         Dutton, © 1965
         87 p. illus.

Author Card

973.3    **Wise, William**
W        The Spy and General Washington;
         illustrated by Peter Burchard.
         Dutton, © 1965
         87 p. illus.

Subject Card

973.3    Washington, George
W        **Wise, William**
         The Spy and General Washington;
         illustrated by Peter Burchard.
         Dutton, © 1965
         87 p. illus.

What is the title of this book? What is the author's name? What is the subject of the book?

In which drawer of the card catalog on this page would you find the title card for this book? In which drawer would you find the author card?

## Practice

**A.** On what type of card would you find each book? Write *subject card*, *title card*, or *author card*.

1. a book by Arthur Shay
2. a book about airplanes
3. a book called *My Friend Kim*
4. a book about ducks
5. a book called *Clue in the Antique Clock*

**B.** Look at the card catalog in your library. In what drawer would you find each book? Write the letters of the drawer.

6. a book called *Alma's Lion*
7. a book by Ruth Robbins
8. a book by Robert Lawson
9. a book about insects
10. a book called *The Emperor and the Drummer Boy*

## Apply

**C.** Write two words you could use to find each book in the card catalog.

11. *Akavak: An Eskimo Journey*, by James Houston
12. *The Skates of Uncle Richard*, by Carol Fenner
13. *Football Fugitive*, by Matt Christopher
14. *Chester*, by Mary Shura
15. *Stuart Little*, by E. B. White

# COMPOSITION

## Lesson 8: Combining Sentences with *and, but,* or *or*

Jimmy is writing about ants. He wrote several sentences. Read them.

1. Some ants eat seeds.
2. Other ants eat mushrooms.
3. Some ants eat seeds, **and** other ants eat mushrooms.

### Think and Discuss

When you write several short sentences about a topic, try to combine some of them. Two short sentences can sometimes be combined into one longer sentence. This makes your sentences more interesting to read.

Read these sentences. Notice how two short sentences have been combined.

4. Ants collect flower nectar.
5. They kill other insects for food.
6. Ants collect flower nectar, **or** they kill other insects for food.

7. Ants will eat almost anything.
8. They like their food moist.
9. Ants will eat almost anything, **but** they like their food moist.

What three words were used to combine the shorter sentences? Find the words *and, but,* and *or* in the longer sentences. What mark do you see in front of these connecting words?

> ● Use a comma before the words *and*, *but*, and *or* when two sentences are combined.

## Practice

**A.** Combine each pair of sentences. Use the words in parentheses ( ) to connect them. Remember to use commas.

1. Ants are interesting insects. There are many different kinds. (and)
2. Ants are usually brown or black. One type is green. (but)
3. Their bodies are covered by hard shells. They can still move easily. (but)
4. Ants have three pairs of legs. Some have wings. (and)
5. Their large jaws can cut up leaves. They can snatch food. (or)
6. Ants' jaws are able to tunnel into wood. They can dig in the ground. (and)
7. Ants live together in a colony. Their home is called a nest. (and)
8. Some colonies live under stones. Others nest under the bark of trees. (but)

**B. 9.–13.** Listen while your teacher dictates some sentences to you. Write the sentences. Be sure to use commas correctly.

## Apply

**C. 14.–18.** Write five pairs of short sentences about insects. Then combine each pair, using *and, but,* or *or.* Write the five new sentences. Check to be sure they make sense. Remember to use commas before the words *and, but,* and *or.*

# Lesson 9: Writing Sentences

Read these sentences about careers.

There are many interesting jobs to think about if you like plants. Botanists may work to develop new kinds of plants. They want to grow strong and unusual plants. If you like to care for plants, you could be a nursery worker. Nursery workers water plants. They put the plants in bigger pots as the plants grow. Do you like people as well as plants? If so, be a florist. Florists sell plants and flowers to people. Do you like large plants? Do you want to work outdoors? Then the job of a forest ranger is for you! Forest rangers help care for the plant life in our national parks. They also teach other people about wild plants.

## Think and Discuss

Remember these points about writing sentences.

- A sentence is a group of words that expresses a complete thought. It always begins with a capital letter. It always ends with a punctuation mark.
- Use a question mark at the end of an interrogative sentence.
- Use an exclamation point at the end of an exclamatory sentence.
- Use a period at the end of a declarative or imperative sentence.

Did each sentence about careers follow all these rules? Find an example of each type of sentence among the sentences about careers.

## Practice

**A.** Use the ideas in the sentences you read on page 20, or use your own ideas. Add the subject or predicate to these sentences. Write the complete sentences.

1. A botanist _____.
2. _____ sells plants and flowers.
3. Forest rangers _____.
4. Forest rangers also _____.
5. Do _____ help care for plants?

**B.** These sentences do not follow the rules on page 20. Add capital letters, punctuation, subjects, or predicates where they are needed. Write the sentences correctly.

6. our city park has many workers
7. Would you like to work in a park
8. Try to get a summer job there
9. runs the merry-go-round.
10. the zoo keeper and the park ranger

## Apply

**C. 11.–15.** Think of a job done by someone you know, or think of a job you would like to do. Write five sentences about the job. Tell such things as:

What is this job called?
What do you need to learn if you want this job?
What are some exciting parts of this job?
What are some difficult parts of this job?
Why would you like this job?

# Lesson 10: Editing Sentences

Mario wrote some sentences about his mother's job. Read the sentences.

*1. my mother is a nurse.*
*2. She works at Dover Hospital.*
*3. She went to school to learn this job.*
*4. Many nurses work at the hospital.*

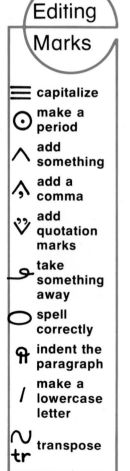

### Editing Marks

≡ **capitalize**

⊙ **make a period**

∧ **add something**

⌄ **add a comma**

⌄⌄ **add quotation marks**

**take something away**

◯ **spell correctly**

**indent the paragraph**

/ **make a lowercase letter**

∼ **transpose**
tr

When Mario checked his work, he found two mistakes in capitalization and punctuation. Did you find them too?

## Think and Discuss

After you write something for the first time, it is a good idea to read your work over. You may find mistakes. You may find ideas you want to change. Making corrections and changes improves your writing.

Mario used editing marks to show his mistakes. This mark ≡ under a small, or lowercase, letter will remind Mario to make a capital letter. He used this mark ⊙ to show where a period was needed. Then he was ready to write his sentences again, correctly this time.

Look at the editing marks Mario used. Review what each one means.

## Practice

**A. 1.–5.** Copy Mario's sentences. Make all the changes and corrections he wanted to make.

## Apply

**B. 6.–10.** Reread the sentences which you wrote about a job in Lesson 9. Did you begin each sentence with a capital letter? Did you end each with a punctuation mark? If you did not, use the editing marks. Correct your work. Then copy your sentences again correctly.

# MECHANICS PRACTICE

## Writing Sentences

- Begin a sentence with a capital letter.
- Use a period at the end of a declarative or imperative sentence.
- Use a question mark at the end of an interrogative sentence.
- Use an exclamation point at the end of an exclamatory sentence.

Write the sentences correctly. Use capital letters and punctuation marks where they are needed.

1. noisy parrots were screeching
2. a hungry tiger growled angrily
3. in the trees several monkeys chattered
4. two huge snakes hissed
5. can you hear their noise
6. an elephant lifted its trunk and trumpeted
7. suddenly the noise stopped
8. how quiet the jungle became
9. why do you think the noise stopped
10. a man walked along the narrow path
11. in his hands he carried a camera
12. what wonderful pictures he took
13. bring this roll of film to the man
14. he will take more pictures for his book
15. when will he leave for home

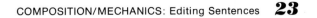

# LITERATURE

## Lesson 11: Understanding Rhythm and Rhyme in Poetry

It is fun to read poems silently, but the real joy comes when poetry is read out loud. Poets try to use words that will sound interesting when they are read out loud.

As you read these poems, listen for the sound of the words. Feel the rhythm of the ocean as you read.

### Sitting in the Sand

Sitting in the sand and the sea comes up
So you put your hands together
And you use them like a cup
And you dip them in the water
With a scooping kind of motion
And before the sea goes out again
You have a sip of ocean.

*Karla Kuskin*

## Waves of the Sea

Waves of the sea
make the sound of thunder
when they break against rocks
and somersault under.
Waves of the sea
make the sound of laughter
when they run down the beach
and birds run after.

*Aileen Fisher*

## Think and Discuss

One way to make a poem interesting is to use words
that **rhyme.** When lines of poetry have the same last
sounds, the lines rhyme. Poets also use words that give a
poem a beat, like the beat of a song. This beat is the
**rhythm** of the poem. A poem's rhythm often fits the topic
of the poem.

Look back at the poems that begin the lesson. What
lines rhyme in these poems? Sometimes a poet makes pairs
of lines rhyme. Sometimes every other line rhymes. There
are many ways to use rhyme patterns in poems.

Look at the marks over some words. These mark the
strong beats in each line of the poem. The strong beats
show you where to make your voice louder when you
read the poem aloud. They show the rhythm of the poem.
How many strong beats does each line have in "Waves
of the Sea"?

## Practice

**A.** **1.–4.** Find two pairs of rhyming words in each poem. Write the words.

**B.** Pretend you are a poet. Write a word that rhymes with these words from the poems.

**5.** sand      **6.** wave      **7.** beach

**8.** sea      **9.** sound      **10.** shore

## Apply

**C.** **11.** Riddles are fun to try to answer. Many riddles make use of rhyming words and rhythm. See if you can guess the answer to this riddle.

> There is a star that gives no light.
> It's seen by day and sleeps at night.
> It does not call the sky its home
> But rests beneath the ocean's foam.

Try to write a riddle of your own. Use a pattern of rhythm and rhyme. Ask a friend to guess the answer to your riddle.

### To Memorize

Nothing great was *ever* achieved without enthusiasm.

*Ralph Waldo Emerson*

What does the word *enthusiasm* mean? Is enthusiasm needed to attain greatness? Use your own words to explain what this quotation means.

# Lesson 12: Understanding Sound in Poetry

A poem paints a picture with the sound of its words. Rhythm and rhyme are two special sounds in poetry. Poets have other ways of using sound. Sometimes they use words that name sounds. Words such as *buzz, crack, sizzle, boom,* and *hiss* make poems come alive with sounds. What are some other sound words? A poet may also use the same sound over and over. Repeating a sound adds to the rhythm of a poem.

## Think and Discuss

Listen for sound words and repeated sounds in this poem.

### Our Washing Machine

Our washing machine went whisity whirr
Whisity whisity whirr
One day at noon it went whisity click
Whisity whisity whisity click
Click grr click grr click grr click
Call the repairman
Fix it. . . . Quick!

*Patricia Hubell*

Which words imitate washing machine noises? Words such as *whisity* and *whirr* are sound words.

In "Our Washing Machine" the poet uses many words that begin with the sound of /w/. Which words in the poem begin with this sound? Repeating the same beginning sound is called **alliteration.**

Read these poems. Listen for sound words and alliteration.

## Funny the Way Different Cars Start

Funny the way
Different cars start.
Some with a chunk and a jerk,
Some with a cough and a puff of smoke
Out of the back,
Some with only a little click—with hardly any noise.

Funny the way
Different cars run.
Some rattle and bang,
Some whirrr,
Some knock and knock.
Some purr
And hummmmm
Smoothly on with hardly any noise.

*Dorothy W. Baruch*

I made a machine for making fuzz,
The most marvelous machine that ever was.
It put fuzz on the ceiling, and fuzz on the walls,
And covered the floor with fuzzy fuzz balls.

*Alice Gilbert*

## Practice

**A. 1.** List two sound words from "Funny the Way Different Cars Start." Next to each, name something else that could make that sound.

**B.** Name one or more things that could make these sounds.

    **2.** grr      **3.** click      **4.** thump      **5.** crash

**C.** Write the sentences that have alliteration.

   **6.** There once was a wizard with a wonderful wand.
   **7.** The cat meowed and the dog barked.
   **8.** The shop for shoes was shut.
   **9.** Patty Potter put purple potatoes in the pan.
   **10.** Do you know the new neighbor?

## *Apply*

**D.** Add words to show alliteration. Then use each group of words in a complete sentence.

   **11.** a happy, humming _____
   **12.** the wild, woolly, wonderful _____
   **13.** a _____, _____ lawn mower
   **14.** a _____, _____ toaster
   **15.** the _____, _____, _____ computer

---

# A BOOK TO READ

Title: **Where the Sidewalk Ends**
Author: Shel Silverstein
Publisher: Harper & Row

   I am writing these poems
   From inside a lion,
   And it's rather dark in here.
   So please excuse the handwriting
   Which may not be too clear. . . .

   Whether he is inside a lion, fixing a crocodile's toothache, or turning into a television set, you will love Shel Silverstein. He can create a ghastly, ghostly, or gorgeous rhyme about anything! This book of hilarious poems will brighten up your dullest day.
   Travel to "where the sidewalk ends," a place of joy and laughter where the grass grows white, the sun burns bright, and the cool wind smells like peppermint candy.

# 1 UNIT TEST

● **Sentences**   pages 2–3

In each set write the letter of the group of words that is *not* a sentence.

**1.** a. Sam met Jose.
   b. They played ball.
   c. Jogged up the hill.
   d. The boys walked home.

**2.** a. We fished at camp.
   b. One day we hiked.
   c. We swam in Red Lake.
   d. Ghost stories at night.

**3.** a. Kara bought a ticket.
   b. Some popcorn and candy.
   c. She sat down.
   d. The movie started.

**4.** a. Al did homework.
   b. He studied spelling.
   c. Heard a funny story.
   d. He worked ten problems.

**5.** a. Dan rode a ferry.
   b. Cars and people rode.
   c. Chains held the cars.
   d. Across the lake.

**6.** a. Those three cookbooks.
   b. Mom made eggplant.
   c. Cookbooks are helpful.
   d. Follow the recipes.

● **Declarative and Interrogative Sentences**   pages 4–5

Copy these sentences. Use a question mark or a period at the end of each sentence.

**7.** Are you going to meet the train at the station

**8.** Aunt Freda will be on it

**9.** What time is it now

**10.** I think you had better leave soon

**11.** You wouldn't want to be late

**12.** Where should I wait

**13.** When does Aunt Freda expect us

**14.** She will arrive this afternoon

**15.** How long will she stay with us

## ● Imperative and Exclamatory Sentences   pages 6–7

Copy the sentences. Label each one *imperative sentence* or *exclamatory sentence.*

16. What a strange-looking package!
17. Don't shake it.
18. Don't cut the strings.
19. Unwrap it carefully.
20. Why, it's a tiny puppy!
21. What a nice surprise!
22. How small and soft it is!

## ● Questions and Answers   pages 8–9

Answers are given to each question. Write the answers in complete sentences.

23. Who was Amelia Earhart?   (an American airplane pilot)
24. When was she born?   (in 1898)
25. Why was she famous?   (first woman to fly alone over the Atlantic Ocean)
26. What happened to her later?   (lost on an airplane flight)
27. Where was she lost?   (over the Pacific Ocean)

## ● Complete Subjects and Predicates   pages 10–11

Copy each sentence. Draw one line under the complete subject. Draw two lines under the complete predicate.

28. Mr. Fazio owns an apple orchard.
29. Stacy and her father picked apples there.
30. They gathered three bushels of shiny red apples.
31. Stacy's father heaved them onto his truck.
32. The beautiful apples would make delicious pies.
33. Stacy showed her brother the apples.
34. Each apple was cut and peeled.
35. The Fazio family made ten quarts of applesauce.

## The Library   pages 14–15

Copy each sentence. Write the correct answer in the space. Use these words: *biography, fiction, reference, nonfiction,* and *librarian.*

1. A _____ is the person in charge of a library.
2. _____ books tell facts about the lives of real people.
3. _____ books are imaginary stories about people or things.
4. _____ books tell facts about real people, things, or events.
5. _____ books such as encyclopedias contain information on many different subjects.

## The Card Catalog   pages 16–17

Use this card from a card catalog. Answer the questions using complete sentences.

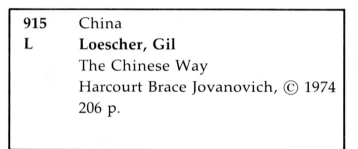

```
915     China
L       Loescher, Gil
        The Chinese Way
        Harcourt Brace Jovanovich, © 1974
        206 p.
```

6. Would you find this card in the drawer marked *A–D, H–J,* or *S–T?*
7. What is the title of the book?
8. Who is the author?
9. What is the subject of the book?
10. Is this an author, subject, or title card?

## Combining Sentences with *and, but,* or *or*   pages 18–19

Combine each pair of sentences. Use the word in parentheses ( ). Write the sentences.

1. Lisa is making a mask.
   Gary is helping her.   (and)
2. The mask will be made of paper.
   A face will be painted on it.   (and)
3. Lisa will draw the eyes.
   Gary will make the nose and mouth.   (but)

**4.** The mask that Lisa is making may be silly.
It might be scary.   (or)

**5.** The mask may be difficult to make.
It will be fun to do.   (but)

● **Writing and Editing Sentences**   pages 20–23

Write a sentence telling about each of these jobs. Then edit the sentences for capital letters and punctuation marks.

**6.** builder   **7.** taxi driver   **8.** teacher
**9.** fire fighter   **10.** singer

● **Rhythm and Rhyme in Poetry**   pages 24–26

Read the poem.

### The Folk Who Live in Backward Town

The folk who live in Backward Town
Are inside out and upside down.
They wear their hats inside their heads
And go to sleep beneath their beds.
They only eat the apple peeling
And take their walks across the ceiling.

Mary Ann Hoberman

**1.** Write the pairs of words that rhyme.
**2.** Write the number of strong beats in line 1.

● **Sound in Poetry**   pages 27–29

**3.** Copy this part of a poem. Underline the words that show alliteration. Circle the sound words.

### Galoshes

Susie's galoshes
Make splishes and sploshes
And slooshes and sloshes,
As Susie steps slowly
Along in the slush.

Rhoda W. Bacmeister

# LANGUAGE
## Learning About Nouns

# STUDY SKILLS
## Summarizing

# COMPOSITION
## Writing Book Reports

# LITERATURE
## Reading a Biography

Have you ever used a camera? Perhaps you have taken pictures of places you have visited and things you have seen. Maybe you have taken pictures of people too. Look at the pictures on page 34. What people do you know?

Words as well as pictures can tell us about people. We can name them—a man, a woman, a grandfather. We can tell what they do—a swimmer, a carpenter, a president. We can give them titles—Senator Smith, Doctor Seng, Governor Jackson.

In this unit you will find out about words that name. You will learn about writing book reports. You will also learn how to use facts and opinions in book reports. You will read an exciting passage about a famous person.

# LANGUAGE

## *Lesson 1: Understanding Nouns*

Read this poster. Notice the underlined words.

### *Think and Discuss*

Some words name people. Some words name places or things. The words *acrobats* and *jugglers* name people. *Galesburg Fairgrounds* are words that name a place. Which words name things?

Words that name are called **nouns.** Nouns can name people, places, or things.

Read these sentences. Find the nouns.

1. The clown performed.
2. The big, brown tent was filled.
3. I won a stuffed giraffe.

Which noun names a person? Which noun names a place? Which noun names a thing?

> ● A **noun** is a word that names a person, place, or thing.

## Practice

**A.** Copy the sentences. Underline each noun.

1. Many people come to Galesburg.
2. Meda and Masako travel from Benhaven to get to the fairgrounds.
3. The boys see a high-diver climb a tall ladder.
4. The woman dives into a bathtub filled with sponges.
5. Then a juggler begins to twirl balls, blocks, and rings.
6. Soon the acrobats tumble and toss without hitting the ground.
7. Suddenly, sixteen clowns appear from an automobile.
8. A fire-eater lights a torch.
9. The man swallows the flames and smoke.
10. Lemonade and ice cool his hot meal.

**B.** **11.–20.** Write three nouns that name people who went to the fair. Write three nouns that name places where a fair can be held. Write four nouns that name things you can find at a fair.

## Apply

**C.** **21.–25.** Write five sentences of your own. Use nouns that name people, places, and things. Underline the nouns in your sentences.

# Lesson 2: Understanding Singular and Plural Nouns

Read these sentences. Find the nouns.

1. Today we found a frog
2. Now we have two frogs.

Which noun names one frog? Which noun names more than one frog?

## Think and Discuss

Nouns name persons, places, or things. Some nouns name *one* person, place, or thing. These nouns are **singular.** Some nouns name *more than one* person, place, or thing. These nouns are **plural.** The noun *frog* in sentence 1 is singular. In sentence 2 the noun *frogs* is plural. What letter was added to *frog* to make it plural?

Now read these sentences.

3. We saw a praying mantis.
4. We watched two praying mantises.
5. We saw a butterfly.
6. We collected more butterflies.

Which nouns are singular? Which are plural? Notice the spelling of each plural noun. The plural noun in sentence 4 ends in *es.* With what two letters does *butterfly* end? What happens to the *y* in *butterfly* to make *butterflies*?

> - To form the plural of most nouns, add *s.*
> - To form the plural of nouns ending in *s, x, ch,* or *sh,* add *es.*
> - To form the plural of nouns ending with a consonant and *y,* change the *y* to *i* and add *es.*

## Practice

**A.** Write the plural form of each noun.

**1.** bear **2.** fox **3.** walrus **4.** pony **5.** alligator
**6.** canary **7.** dog **8.** fly **9.** daisy **10.** horse
**11.** rose **12.** branch **13.** beach **14.** rabbit **15.** grasshopper

**B.** Write the sentences. Use the plural form of each noun in parentheses ( ).

**16.** The people on our block have many _____. (hobby)
**17.** The _____ had a hobby show. (neighbor)
**18.** We set up some _____ so that the audience could sit. (bench)
**19.** Odessa brought her three _____ in a tank. (guppy)
**20.** Po Lan brought his pictures of _____. (bird)
**21.** Maxine arrived carrying a lot of _____. (box)
**22.** She had a collection of _____ to show. (insect)
**23.** Michael brought cups and _____. (dish)
**24.** He had packed picnic _____ for everyone. (lunch)
**25.** There were _____ and apples. (sandwich)

## Apply

**C.** Write the plural form of these words. Then use each plural in a sentence.

**26.** tree **27.** bush **28.** ax **30.** cabin **30.** family

# Lesson 3: Forming Plural Nouns

Read these sentences. Notice the underlined nouns.

1. The <u>deer</u> is feeding.
2. Some <u>deer</u> are feeding.
3. The <u>goose</u> is flying.
4. Five <u>geese</u> are flying.

Which nouns are singular? Which are plural?

## Think and Discuss

You have learned about plural nouns that end in *s* and *es*. Some nouns do not add *s* or *es* to make their plural forms. Look back at sentences 1 and 2. Notice that the noun *deer* is the same in each sentence. In which sentence is the noun *deer* plural? *Deer* is a noun that has the same singular and plural forms.

Now look at sentences 3 and 4. How does the spelling of goose change to make its plural form?

Look at this chart. Study the plural nouns.

| Singular | Plural | Singular | Plural |
|----------|--------|----------|--------|
| sheep | sheep | woman | women |
| deer | deer | man | men |
| elk | elk | child | children |
| moose | moose | foot | feet |
| trousers | trousers | ox | oxen |
| pants | pants | mouse | mice |

## Practice

A. **1.–12.** Study the chart of plural nouns. Then close your book. Write each noun that your teacher says.

B. Write each sentence. Use the correct plural form of the noun in parentheses ( ).

**13.** Some _____ from a farm walked across the United States.   (child)

14. All they carried were their magical _____.  (glass)
15. On their trip they met some talking _____.  (deer)
16. They met large _____ that gave them rides.  (goose)
17. They met two _____ who played magical flutes.  (man)
18. They saw some _____ in a gingerbread house.  (woman)
19. They bought some _____ in a store.  (trousers)
20. When they returned to the farm, they told all the _____ about their adventure.  (ox)

## Apply

C. Copy these words. Next to each write its plural form. Then use the plural form in a sentence.

21. tooth    22. sheep    23. elk    24. moose    25. grandchild

---

### To Memorize

#### Abraham Lincoln

Remember he was poor and country-bred;
His face was lined; he walked with awkward gait.
Smart people laughed at him sometimes and said,
"How can so very plain a man be great?"

*Mildred Plew Meigs*

What do you think makes a person great? Does it have to do with where the person lives or how the person looks?

# Lesson 4: Understanding Common and Proper Nouns

Kito took a trip. He visited many places and saw many people and things. Read the sentences Kito wrote about his trip. Notice the underlined nouns.

1. Philadelphia is a beautiful city.
2. One landmark we saw was the Liberty Bell.
3. Our guide was Ms. Jacobs.
4. The best day of the trip was Tuesday.

## Think and Discuss

You know that nouns name persons, places, or things. Some nouns name *any* person, place, or thing. These nouns are called **common nouns.** Common nouns begin with a small letter. What are the common nouns in sentences 1, 2, 3, and 4? Other nouns name a *particular* person, place, or thing. These nouns are called **proper nouns.**

Look at sentence 1. The noun *Philadelphia* is a proper noun. What kind of letter begins *Philadelphia?* What are the proper nouns in sentences 2, 3, and 4?

Look at this chart. It shows some common and proper nouns.

| Common Nouns | Proper Nouns |
| --- | --- |
| person | Kito |
| day | Tuesday |
| month | April |
| holiday | Thanksgiving |
| canyon | Grand Canyon |
| statue | Statue of Liberty |
| mountains | Rocky Mountains |
| state | Alabama |
| desert | Sahara Desert |

> - A **common noun** names any person, place, or thing. It is a general word that begins with a small letter.
> - A **proper noun** names a particular person, place, or thing. A proper noun begins with a capital letter.

## Practice

**A.** Make two columns. Write *Common Nouns* at the top of one. Write *Proper Nouns* at the top of the other. Put each word in the correct column.

1. Mississippi River
2. Illinois
3. river
4. desert
5. Houston
6. country
7. Lake Erie
8. Ed Jones
9. United States
10. Wednesday
11. city
12. Gobi Desert
13. tower
14. day
15. state
16. tourist
17. lake
18. Coit Tower

**B.** Rewrite these sentences. Capitalize the proper noun in each sentence. Underline the common noun.

19. We flew on an airline called airways america.
20. The state we visited is new mexico.
21. The most interesting day was saturday.
22. We went to the town of truth or consequences.
23. Very far away loom mountains called the san mateo mountains.
24. I climbed a tall peak called horse peak.
25. We drove to chaco canyon, a canyon nearby.

## Apply

**C.** Write a proper noun to match the common nouns listed. Use each pair of nouns in a sentence.

26. state
27. city
28. store
29. airport
30. landmark

# Lesson 5: Writing Names and Titles of People

Read the names in this list of important American women.

1. Doctor Margaret Mead
2. Dr. Margaret Mead
3. Governor Ella Grasso
4. Gov. Ella Grasso

All the names begin with capital letters. Do you know why?

## Think and Discuss

The names of the women begin with capital letters because they are proper nouns. The women's names also have titles before them. Read the four titles. Notice that each title also begins with a capital letter. When a title comes before a person's name, it begins with a capital letter.

Two titles in the list at the top of the page are written as **abbreviations.** An abbreviation is a short way to write a word. Find the abbreviations. Do the abbreviations begin with capital letters? What mark of punctuation follows the abbreviations?

Here is a chart of titles. Notice what the titles mean.

| | |
|---|---|
| **Mr.** | title for an unmarried or married man |
| **Ms.** | title for an unmarried or married woman |
| **Mrs.** | title for a married woman |
| **Miss** | title for an unmarried woman |
| **Dr.** | title used before the name of a doctor |
| **Gov.** | title of the highest state official |
| **Sen.** | title of a United States senator |

Initials are another kind of abbreviation. An initial is the first letter of a name. An initial is followed by a period.

Read this name. Notice the initials

7. Susan Brownell Anthony    8. S. B. Anthony

- Begin each part of the name of a person with a capital letter.
- Begin the title of a person with a capital letter.
- Use a period after an abbreviation of an initial or title.

## Practice

**A.** Write these names and titles correctly. Use abbreviations for titles.

**1.** mister premo             **2.** doctor susan ling
**3.** senator james           **4.** governor ralph j stevens

**B.** Write these sentences correctly.

**5.** mrs harriet tubman helped slaves escape from the South.
**6.** Another important woman was martha washington.
**7.** A famous Indian named pocahontas helped the Virginia settlers.
**8.** fannie m farmer wrote a new kind of cookbook.
**9.** miss susan b anthony fought for women's rights in the United States.
**10.** marion anderson was the first black singer at the Metropolitan Opera.

## Apply

**C.** Write the names and titles of these persons correctly. Use some abbreviations and initials.

**11.** your mother    **12.** your father    **13.** your teacher
**14.** your doctor    **15.** your principal

# Lesson 6: Writing Names of Places

Powa Tome received a letter from his pen pal Richard Booth. Richard lives in the country of Australia. Look at the envelope.

*Richard Booth*
*33 Rose St.*
*Melbourne, Victoria*
*Australia*

*Powa Tome*
*6 Maple Ave.*
*Lexington, Kentucky 40504*
*United States of America*

The names of streets are capitalized. The cities, states, and countries are capitalized also. Do you remember why?

## Think and Discuss

All important words in the names of streets, cities, states, and countries begin with capital letters. These words are proper nouns. What word in Powa's address is not capitalized? Why not?

When words such as *street* or *avenue* are part of a name, they are often abbreviated. Find the abbreviation of *street* in Richard's address. Read the abbreviation for *avenue* in Powa's address. How do the abbreviations begin? How do they end? Here are some common abbreviations.

Perry Street/Perry **St.**          Pike Boulevard/Pike **Blvd.**
Post Road/Post **Rd.**              Loring Place/Loring **Pl.**
Green Avenue/Green **Ave.**         Ocean Highway/Ocean **Hwy.**

> - Begin each important word in the name of a town, city, state, and country with a capital letter.
> - Begin each important word in the names of streets and their abbreviations with capital letters.
> - Use a period after an abbreviation of a place name.

## Practice

**A.** Write these sentences correctly.

1. Tisa lives on orange avenue in chicago, illinois.
2. She is moving to brisbane, australia.
3. There she will live on pratt boulevard.
4. Australia is 6,000 miles from the united states.
5. The capital city of australia is canberra.
6. The two largest cities are sydney and melbourne.
7. Australia exports beef to great britain.
8. The national animal of australia is the kangaroo.
9. Australian wool is bought by japan and france.
10. Australia's koala bears live in new south wales.

## Apply

**B.** Write these names and addresses.

11. Write your name and address.
12. Write the name and address of your school.
13. Write the name and address of someone you know who lives in another town or country.
14. Write the name and address of a restaurant near you.
15. Write the name and address of a store near you.

### A Challenge

Look in an atlas. List five examples of countries and cities in different parts of the world. Do research on one of them. Write some sentences about that city or country.

# Lesson 7: Using Possessive Nouns

Read these sentences.

1. Susie lives next door.
2. Susie's cat is brown.
3. My neighbor is a truck driver.
4. My neighbor's hamster is cute.

Which sentences show that someone owns something?

## Think and Discuss

You have learned that nouns name persons, places, or things. Nouns can also show ownership or possession. Such nouns are called **possessive nouns.** Read the sentences again. Which sentences have possessive nouns? What pet does Susie own? What pet does the neighbor own? *Susie's* and *neighbor's* are possessive nouns.

Notice the punctuation mark in the words *Susie's* and *neighbor's.* It is called an **apostrophe.** What letter follows the apostrophe? The possessive nouns in sentences 2 and 4 are singular possessive nouns. They are formed by adding an apostrophe and *s* (**'s**) to singular nouns.

Read sentence 5. The possessive noun is underlined.

5. The <u>boys'</u> rabbit is tame.

The noun *boys* is plural. With what letter does it end? Notice the apostrophe. The possessive noun in sentence 5 is a plural possessive noun. It is formed by adding an apostrophe (') to a plural noun that ends in *s.*

You know that some plural nouns do not end in *s.* Some of these nouns are *men, women, children,* and *geese.* Notice how the plural possessive noun is formed in sentence 6.

6. The <u>children's</u> pets are playing.

**48** GRAMMAR/MECHANICS: Possessive Nouns

What is added to *children* to make it possessive?

Use this chart to help you form possessive nouns.

| Noun | | Possessive Noun |
|---|---|---|
| Singular | boy | boy's |
| Plural ending in *s* | girls | girls' |
| Plural not ending in *s* | women | women's |

Spell the possessive form of each noun.

7. The (bear) fur is thick.
8. The (walruses) tusks are long.
9. The (mice) teeth are sharp.

- To form the possessive of a singular noun, add an apostrophe and an *s.*
- To form the possessive of a plural noun ending in *s* or *es*, add only an apostrophe.
- To form the possessive of a plural noun that does not end in *s*, add an apostrophe and an *s.*

## Practice

**A.** Write the sentences. Underline the possessive nouns. If the possessive noun is singular, write *singular possessive.* If the possessive noun is plural, write *plural possessive.*

1. Julian's class had a pet show.
2. Have you seen Janice's iguana?
3. The children's pets were all given prizes.

**4.** The iguana won all of the judges' votes.

**5.** The winners' prizes were blue and red ribbons.

**B.** After each sentence is a singular or plural noun. Copy the sentences using the correct possessive form.

**6.** Many _____ defenses are powerful.   (animals)

**7.** Snapping _____ jaws bite forcefully.   (turtles)

**8.** A _____ claws will strike at an enemy.   (bear)

**9.** Animals scatter at a _____ smell.   (skunk)

**10.** _____ teeth can tear apart an animal.   (Leopards)

**11.** An invader can be slapped by a _____ tail quills. (porcupine)

**12.** An _____ tentacles squeeze the enemy.   (octopus)

**13.** _____ tusks can stab other animals.   (Elephants)

**14.** The _____ great speed is its protection.   (dolphin)

**15.** The _____ hisses scare away their enemies.   (geese)

**C.** Copy each sentence. Use the singular or plural possessive form of the nouns at the end of each sentence.

**16.** The _____ talons are sharp.   (eagle, singular)

**17.** The _____ hands shoot rocks at enemies.   (baboon, plural)

**18.** The _____ sting protects them.   (bee, plural)

**19.** Poisonous bites come from the _____ fangs. (centipede, plural)

**20.** The _____ tentacles sting an attacker.   (jellyfish, singular)

**21.** Water squirts from marine _____ mouths.   (iguana, plural)

**22.** Invaders are fought by an _____ long, sharp antlers. (antelope, singular)

**23.** A black widow _____ bite can kill a person. (spider, singular)

**24.** _____ feet kick and jab other animals.   (kangaroo, plural)

**25.** The _____ sharp teeth are their protection.   (fox, plural)

## Apply

**D. 26.–30.** Write five sentences of your own. Use a possessive noun in each sentence. Use both singular and plural possessive nouns.

## HOW OUR LANGUAGE GROWS

Native Americans have lived in this land for thousands of years. They named their tribes, rivers, and lands with beautiful words. The European settlers borrowed many of their words to name our streets, cities, counties, and states. It is exciting to learn the poetry of these names.

Look at the list of names of states. Can you match them with a Native American word?

| State | Native American Spelling | Meaning |
|---|---|---|
| Alabama | Oyerungen | place of plenty |
| Connecticut | Alibamu | I clear the thicket |
| Idaho | Ouiscousin | meeting of the rivers |
| Mississippi | Eda-hoe | light on the mountain |
| Oregon | Quonecktacut | river of pines |
| Texas | Tejas | allies |
| Wisconsin | Maesi-sipu | fish river |

**1.** Look at a map of your state. Can you guess what names come from the Native Americans?

**2.** Use the encyclopedia. Find the Native American names for Illinois and Massachusetts.

# LANGUAGE REVIEW

## Nouns   pages 36-37

Copy the sentences. Underline the nouns.

1. The circus is coming to our town.
2. I like watching the clowns drive funny cars.
3. Sam and Tina sat in the front row.
4. The trained bears ride bicycles around the ring.
5. Lorenzo Delano used to be a clown.
6. Brady likes the popcorn and apples best.

## Singular and Plural Nouns   pages 38-39

Write the plural form of each noun.

| | | | |
|---|---|---|---|
| 7. kitchen | 8. dish | 9. olive | 10. table |
| 11. recipe | 12. peach | 13. bunch | 14. meat |
| 15. grape | 16. turnip | 17. radish | 18. perch |
| 19. cereal | 20. lunch | 21. lime | |

## Plural Nouns   pages 40-41

Write the plural form of each noun.

| | | | |
|---|---|---|---|
| 22. fairy | 23. child | 24. family | 25. woman |
| 26. cherry | 27. foot | 28. baby | 29. moose |
| 30. man | 31. lady | 32. firefly | 33. scissors |
| 34. berry | 35. mouse | 36. tooth | 37. lily |
| 38. reindeer | 39. guppy | | |

## Common and Proper Nouns   pages 42-43

One word in each item is a proper noun. Write the proper noun correctly.

| | | | |
|---|---|---|---|
| 40. summer | november | weekend | month |
| 41. desert | country | park | ms. lassen |
| 42. world | south america | city | valley |
| 43. tuesday | week | month | holiday |

| 44. | doctor | brother | mr. parnes | artist |
|-----|--------|---------|------------|--------|
| 45. | new york | river | village | state |

## Names and Titles of People    pages 44–45

Copy the sentences. Write the proper nouns correctly.

46. They received an invitation from mr and mrs j wong.
47. It was addressed to carol l and bill r langstrom.
48. Our daughter, miss suzanne t bonardi, is invited.
49. Will leroy be able to baby-sit?
50. Maria and victoria are too young to be left alone.

## Names of Places    pages 46–47

Copy the sentences. Write the proper nouns correctly.

51. We lived on saw mill river rd until last year.
52. Professor lang moved from topton ave to our street.
53. He grew up in geneva, switzerland, near france.
54. Is geneva closer to lausanne or bern in switzerland?
55. He also taught in santa barbara, california.

## Possessive Nouns    pages 48–51

After each sentence is a singular or plural noun. Rewrite each sentence, using a possessive noun.

56. _____ Pet Shop is my favorite store.   (Warren)
57. The _____ cages are always very clean.   (animals)
58. The _____ teacher bought a hamster.   (children)
59. This _____ eyes are a beautiful color.   (kitten)
60. _____ father owns the pet store.   (Randy)

## Applying Nouns

Write the proper nouns correctly. Make up a complete sentence for each one.

61. governor winter
62. toronto, canada
63. mrs c p white
64. old farm rd
65. miss t s salina
66. high cliffs blvd

# STUDY SKILLS

## Lesson 8: Finding the Main Idea

If you had lived around 1800, you might have met John Chapman. All the sentences in this passage tell about him. As you read ask yourself, "What is the most important thing the passage tells about John Chapman?"

It was a lucky day in 1801 when John Chapman first came to the Ohio Territory. Pioneers there called him Johnny Appleseed. That's because he spent 46 years of his life planting apple seeds. Because of his work, Ohio and Indiana bloomed with hundreds of thousands of apple trees.

### Think and Discuss

Look away from your book and think about the passage. What one important idea do all the sentences tell about? That is the **main idea.**

Imagine that you have just read an article in a magazine. Someone asks, "What was it about?" Your answer should tell the one main idea of the whole article.

### Practice

**A.** Write the sentence that best states the main idea of each passage.

**1.** Agatha Christie was a writer of mystery stories. In all, she wrote 83 books, 17 plays, and 9 volumes of stories. Her books have sold over 400 million copies.

   **a.** Agatha Christie was an actress.

**b.** Agatha Christie wrote a lot.

**c.** Agatha Christie was mysterious.

2.    There once was a man called John Montagu. He was also known as the Earl of Sandwich. During a card game in 1762, Montagu got very hungry. But he couldn't bear to stop playing cards and use both hands to eat. So he asked someone to bring him a slice of meat between two pieces of toast. That way he could eat with one hand and play cards with the other. That is how the first sandwich got its name.

**a.** The sandwich was invented by John Montagu.

**b.** Montagu liked roast beef.

**c.** Montagu lived in the 1700's.

3.    Jacques Cousteau is an underwater diver and explorer. In 1943 he made his first undersea test of the aqualung. Using the air tank, Cousteau explored a cave 60 feet down. He brought up lobsters for dinner. Since then Cousteau has explored the deep waters of the Earth hundreds of times. His findings have helped people know more about the fascinating underwater world.

**a.** Cousteau likes to eat lobster for dinner.

**b.** Cousteau has spent much of his life exploring the underwater world.

**c.** Cousteau tested the aqualung in 1943.

## *Apply*

**B.** Read a passage in a favorite book. Tell the main idea of the passage.

# Lesson 9: Reading for Details

Yolanda is reading about George Washington. She found a passage that gives many details about Washington's horses. Read the passage. It is packed with facts.

George Washington was a rider of many years' experience. He rode two horses. One was Blueskin. The other was Nelson. He said that Nelson was his favorite. That's because he was so sure and steady during battle.

## Think and Discuss

A statement of fact tells about something that can be checked or proved. When you read a passage, you learn many facts or details. Look for key words that answer questions such as these: *Who* is the passage about? *What* is happening? *Where* does the passage take place? *When* does it take place?

Now read the passage about George Washington again. How many horses did Washington ride? Which sentences tell what their names were? Did Washington have a lot of experience as a rider? Which sentence tells that?

Details can tell about what color something is, or how old it is, or what size it is. When you read for information, read carefully. Look for key words that give you the details in the passage.

## Practice

**A.** Read each passage. Write two details that you find in each.

1.   Maria Martinez was an expert potter. The designs for her pottery are based on ancient Pueblo designs. Major museums in the United States and Europe exhibit her pottery.

2.   Marian Anderson was a great concert singer. She was popular in the 1940's and 1950's. In 1955 she became the first black artist to sing with the Metropolitan Opera Company.

3.   Some famous people have animal nicknames. One was the "Iron Horse." He was better known to his fans as Lou Gehrig. Gehrig played in 2,130 baseball games. He was a player for the New York Yankees.

4.   Do you think a woman will soon be President? Women have run in national elections for President of the United States. In 1884 Belva Ann Lockwood ran. Victoria Woodhull Martin ran in 1892. Several others have run too. No woman has won this election yet.

5.   Franz Liszt was a famous pianist. He lived in the 1800's in Hungary. Liszt once played a difficult piano piece with two glasses of water balanced on the back of his hands. He never once spilled a drop.

## Apply

**B. 6.–10.** Choose a topic. Write five sentences that give details about the topic.

**Topics:** My School Day       My Favorite Animal
A Store I Like       A Person I Admire
A Walk Through My Neighborhood

# Lesson 10: Telling Fact from Opinion

Read these two sentences about the Beatles. Think about what each one tells you.

1. The Beatles were musicians.
2. There were never musicians better than the Beatles.

## Think and Discuss

The first statement about the Beatles is a **statement of fact.** A statement of fact tells about something that can be checked and proved.

The second sentence is a **statement of opinion.** A statement of opinion tells what a person thinks or believes. It is not based on what is certain. Someone else may disagree or have a different opinion.

Now read some more sentences about the Beatles.

3. John Lennon, Paul McCartney, Ringo Starr, and George Harrison were members of the Beatles.
4. The Beatles' music is just a lot of noise.
5. Ringo Starr's real name is Richard Starkey.

Which of the sentences give information that can be proved or checked? These are statements of fact. Which of the sentences tells what someone believes or thinks? Could this statement of opinion be proved?

## Practice

A.  Two Beatles fans are talking. Read the sentences. Write *statement of fact* next to the sentence when the speaker states a fact. Write *statement of opinion* when the speaker states an opinion.

1. "I Want to Hold Your Hand" was a Beatles song.
2. The Beatles sold over 200 million records.

3. The Beatles wrote more great songs than anyone else.
4. John Lennon and Paul McCartney wrote many songs together.
5. The four Beatles were the best-looking musicians that ever appeared.

**B.** Write the sentence in each pair that states an opinion.

6. The Beatles were the greatest rock 'n' roll band ever to appear.
   The Beatles were very popular.
7. Rock 'n' roll is awful.
   Some people don't like to listen to rock 'n' roll.
8. There are three radio stations in our town that play rock 'n' roll.
   Too many radio stations play rock 'n' roll.
9. Classical music is much better than rock 'n' roll.
   Some people like classical music better than they like rock 'n' roll.
10. Beatles fans were the most enthusiastic group that ever came to see a concert.
    Many rock 'n' roll fans are enthusiastic.

## *Apply*

**C. 11.–15.** Think of a record or song you like. Write two statements of fact and three statements of opinion about the music.

# COMPOSITION

## Lesson 11: Writing a Book Report

Did you ever read a book because your best friend read it and told you how good it was? It's fun to share good books with your friends.

### Think and Discuss

One way to share a book is to write a book report. You can tell interesting facts from the book. You can also give your opinion about the book. Read the book report that Jennifer wrote.

**Title** *Why Don't You Get a Horse, Sam Adams*
**Author** *Jean Fritz*
**Summary** *This book tells about the life of Samuel Adams. He lived in the early days of America. He wanted our country to be free from England. Sam Adams couldn't ride a horse. With his dog, Queue, he walked everywhere to talk to people about freedom. He had many adventures as he worked to make our country free.*
**Opinion** *I thought the book was fun to read. It told interesting things about Sam Adams and his dog, Queue.*

What is the title of Jennifer's book? The first word, the last word, and all the important words in the title are capitalized. Small words such as *a, an, the,* and *of* are not capitalized unless they are the first word in the title. Notice that the title is underlined.

After the title, Jennifer listed the author's name. Then she wrote a summary of the book. She wrote the main idea first. Then she wrote some details and her opinion of the book. Name some details from Jennifer's report.

---

**How to Write a Book Report**
1. **Write the title of the book.**
2. **Tell the author's name.**
3. **Write a summary of the book. Include the main idea and some interesting details.**
4. **Tell your opinion of the book.**

---

## Practice

**A.** Terry gathered this information for a book report. Write the book report. Follow the form on page 60.

The author of the book is Eloise Greenfield.

I thought the book was interesting because it told the things Mary McLeod Bethune did to help black people.

The title of the book is *Mary McLeod Bethune.*

This book is about the life of a black woman named Mary McLeod Bethune. No one in her family could read. Mary wanted to learn. She did learn to read. She became a teacher. She started her own school for black children.

## Apply

**B.** Read a biography about a famous person. Then write a book report about the book.

# Lesson 12: Editing a Book Report

Read this book report Jason wrote. Notice the changes he has made.

**Title** The Champion of merrimack county

**Author** Roger W. drury

**Summary** This story is about a mouse named O Crispin. He is a champion bicycle rider. When o crispin practiced for the state championship in mr. berryfield's old bathtub, he smashed his bicycle. Do you think he gets the bicycle fixed in time for the race? Read the book and find out.

**Opinion** ^[I thought the book was funny.] It made me believe that O crispin was real.

**Editing Marks**

- ≡ capitalize
- ⊙ make a period
- ∧ add something
- ∧, add a comma
- ∨ add quotation marks
- take something away
- ○ spell correctly
- ¶ indent the paragraph
- / make a lowercase letter
- ∾ tr transpose

## Think and Discuss

When he read over his report, Jason noticed some mistakes in capitalization. What words will he capitalize? What editing mark did he use to show this?

When he wrote his opinion of the book, Jason forgot something. What words did he add? Jason used this mark ∧ to show where words were added.

## Practice

**A.** Copy Jason's book report. Make all the corrections and additions shown.

## Apply

**B.** Look at the book report you wrote in Lesson 11. Did you tell some interesting details? Did you use capital letters correctly? Did you tell your opinion of the book? Edit your book report. Then copy it neatly.

# MECHANICS PRACTICE

### Writing Names

- Begin each part of the name of a person with a capital letter.
- Begin titles of a person such as *Ms.*, *Mrs.*, *Mr.*, and *Dr.* with a capital letter.
- Always capitalize the word *I*.
- Begin the names of pets with a capital letter.
- Use a period after an initial.
- Use a period after an abbreviation of a title.

**A.** Write these names of people and pets correctly.

1. princess alicia
2. gov ellen stein
3. dr ralph burrows
4. rover
5. squeeky
6. mrs m t lopez
7. mr yoshi hirami
8. sen coretta jackson
9. ms w d evans
10. franklin
11. bruce t richards
12. eli klein
13. rep sarah chase
14. president reagan

**B.** Write the sentences correctly. Use capital letters and periods where they are needed.

15. mrs baños was walking her dog cleo.
16. He was taking his cat fluff to the animal doctor.
17. The animal doctor is dr r o lupo.
18. She has cared for my dog rascal.
19. She said i should bring rascal back soon.
20. Her helper, tony roncelli, will be there.

# Lesson 13: Giving a Book Talk

Besides writing a book report, there is another way to share a good book with your friends. You can give a book talk. In a book talk you talk about a book instead of writing about it. Here is a book talk Marsha gave.

I just read an exciting book called *Help! I'm a Prisoner in the Library* by Eth Clifford. It's about two girls. They are trapped in an old library during a blizzard. When the lights go out during the snowstorm, the library seems haunted. A strange, talking bird flies through the darkness. Then the girls hear a loud thud and moaning from upstairs. Is someone else in the library with them? Read the book and find out.

## Think and Discuss

What did Marsha tell first in her book talk? After the title and author, she told what the book was about. In a book talk you can tell about the characters in the book. You can tell an exciting part, a funny part, or a sad part. The important thing is to tell something interesting. Then everyone will want to read the book. Be careful not to tell too much or you will give the story away.

Here are some things to remember when you give a book talk.

> **How to Give a Book Talk**
> 1. **Stand up straight and look at your audience.**
> 2. **Speak clearly and slowly.**
> 3. **Give the title and the author of the book.**
> 4. **Say what the book is about or tell what kind of book it is.**
> 5. **Tell an interesting part of the book.**

When the other students give their book talks, remember to listen carefully and quietly. Then you are sure to hear about some good books to read.

## Practice

**A.** Think of a book that you would like to share with the class. Plan your book talk. Remember to follow the directions in the chart on this page. Then practice your book talk. Tell it to one other person. Practice using a tape recorder, if you can.

## Apply

**B.** Give your book talk for the class. You may also want to do one of these things to make your talk more interesting.

Illustrate one of the scenes from your book. Show your drawing during your book talk.

Make a book jacket for your book. Show the book jacket when you give your talk.

Pretend you are on television. Write a commercial to "sell" your book.

# LITERATURE

## *Lesson 14: Reading a Biography*

It is interesting to read about the lives of people you admire. You can learn about their childhoods. You can learn about how they became good at what they do. Think about a famous person you admire. Perhaps it is a famous explorer or scientist. Maybe it is an athlete or a singer. Do you remember what kind of book tells about the life of a famous person?

### *Think and Discuss*

A book about the life of a famous person is called a **biography.** Here is part of a biography. It is about the famous scientist Jane Goodall. Jane studied wild chimpanzees in Tanzania, Africa. When she first went to Africa, her mother went with her.

### *Jane Goodall*

*by Eleanor Coerr*

Jane Goodall wanted to study wild chimpanzees in Tanzania, Africa. She spent months raising enough money for equipment and supplies. The government of Tanzania would not let her go alone into the jungle. None of Jane's friends wanted to live in such a wild, faraway place. Finally her mother came to Jane's rescue. Mrs. Goodall would go with her daughter.

Jane began her long and rewarding adventure in 1960. She and her mother bounced over 800 miles of rough roads. Then a boat had to take them the last 12 miles of their

journey. Finally they reached the area where many chimpanzees lived.

Day after day Jane got up before dawn and hiked for miles without getting close to a single chimpanzee. Sometimes Jane heard their loud hooting or saw one vanish into the bush. Even when she climbed to her lookout spot, the Peak, Jane saw no chimps. She was puzzled. What was she doing wrong? Would she never get close enough to study them?

Mrs. Goodall was a great help during those difficult weeks. She kept the camp neat and running smoothly. She added to Jane's collection of insects and plants. Most important, she gave Jane hope and encouragement. If she found jungle life hard, she never said so.

One day Jane finally got a close look at chimpanzees. She climbed to the Peak, and several groups paid her a visit. It was the turning point for Jane. The next morning she carried a small tin trunk up to her lookout. It contained some coffee, a kettle, cans of beans, a sweater, and a blanket. Whenever the chimps slept in the trees near the Peak, Jane spent the night there, too.

As the weeks went by, the chimpanzees began to accept the slim blonde young woman who liked to sit near them so quietly. Rain or shine, Jane studied the chimpanzees. She made some important discoveries. She was the first person to see wild chimps eat meat and use "tools." They stripped twigs and stuck them into termite mounds to pull out the tasty insects. They made sponges out of leaves to sop up water from a hollow place. Jane was especially interested to see how mother chimps raised their young.

Living in the jungle was not always pleasant. Jane had to endure insect bites. Poisonous snakes, hungry leopards, and angry male chimpanzees sometimes frightened her. She accepted the hardships and danger. They were part of the life she had chosen.

By 1965 Jane's work had become so important that a permanent camp was built at Gombe. Scientists and students traveled there to work and study. Today it is a busy research center. Thanks partly to Jane's efforts, the chimpanzee area was made a national park. Jane hoped that her animal friends would always have a safe place to live.

A biography has a **main character.** This is the person about whom the biography is written. Who is the main character of the biography you read? As you read a biography, you get to know the main character very well. You may learn facts about the main character. You may see him or her in action. Parts of the biography may tell how the person solves problems or acts toward others.

Some characters in a biography are people who have helped the main character in some way. Parents, teachers, and close friends are often such characters. Who was another character in the story about Jane Goodall?

## *Practice*

**A.** Answer the questions using complete sentences.

1. What is a biography?
2. Who is the main character in this biography?
3. Who is the other character in the biography? How does she help the main character?
4. List three facts the author tells you about the main character.
5. Why is the main character interesting?

**B.** Read these sentences about Jane Goodall in action.
For each, write another sentence to describe her.

6. As soon as Jane could walk, she brought things into
   the house to show her mother.
7. Once Jane helped a farm for old horses.
8. Jane finished high school with honors.
9. Every day Jane worked long hours in a restaurant.
10. Rain or shine, Jane studied the chimpanzees.

## *Apply*

**C.** Pretend you are writing a biography. It is about
someone in your family. Choose details that show why
this person is special. Show your character in action.

# A BOOK TO READ

Title: **Arthur Mitchell**
Author: Tobi Tobias
Publisher: T. Y. Crowell

Arthur Mitchell grew up in a large family. There were always
jobs to do. Even the hard tasks could not keep Arthur from smiling,
dancing, and making a show out of work.

Arthur had a talent for dancing. This talent and many years of
hard work gave him the chance he wanted. He was asked to
become a member of the New York City Ballet. He knew that
dancing was one of the most demanding careers in the world. He
also knew that it was what he most wanted to do.

Arthur's dancing career was a success. He danced in many
starring roles. He also helped other black people become
professional dancers. You will see what he did to help when you
read his exciting biography.

# 2 UNIT TEST

● **Nouns**     pages 36–37

Write the letter of the word in each sentence that is a noun.

**1.** The children made a mural in art class.
 a     b       c               d

**2.** Tim and Tara sketched some trees and hills.
 a    b            c        d

**3.** Janice drew two rabbits and a deer.
              a     b     c      d

**4.** Jack painted people on the drawing.
          a        b      c   d

**5.** Three children hung the mural on the wall.
 a                    b                c        d

● **Singular and Plural Nouns**     pages 38–39

Read the nouns. If the noun is singular, write its plural form. If the noun is plural, write its singular form.

**6.** fish          **7.** tire          **8.** wish          **9.** mystery
**10.** witch        **11.** stories      **12.** ax           **13.** bike
**14.** jet          **15.** business     **16.** dishes       **17.** bus
**18.** ponies       **19.** hobbies      **20.** horse

● **Plural Nouns**     pages 40–41

Copy each sentence. Use the plural form of the noun in parentheses ( ).

**21.** Three _____ hiked in the woods.   (woman)
**22.** Four _____ joined them by the pond.   (child)
**23.** A flock of _____ flew overhead.   (goose)
**24.** One boy ripped his _____ on a prickly bush.   (trousers)
**25.** Everyone's _____ hurt at the end of the day.   (foot)

## Common and Proper Nouns   pages 42–43

Copy each sentence. Capitalize the proper noun and underline the common noun in each sentence.

**26.** My best friend is rosita.

**27.** She moved to the town of canterbury.

**28.** She lives on a street named mulberry lane.

**29.** Nearby is a store called sue's sweet shop.

**30.** It opens in the morning on monday.

## Names and Titles of People   pages 44–45

Copy these sentences. Use abbreviations for any titles. Use initials for the first and middle names.

**31.** My sister's name is Doctor Colleen Mulligan.

**32.** My uncle is Mister Michael Joseph Eden.

**33.** Miss Eleanor Wright is my aunt.

**34.** My grandfather is Senator Steven Paul Gold.

**35.** He is a friend of Governor James Rose.

## Names of Places   pages 46–47

Rewrite these sentences correctly.

**36.** Mrs. Peterson visited us from germany.

**37.** We went to see her in a hotel on park st.

**38.** She used to live in the united states of america.

**39.** She has traveled to australia and south america.

**40.** She has even gone on safari in africa.

## Possessive Nouns   pages 48–51

After each sentence is a singular or plural noun. Complete the sentence using the correct possessive form of the noun.

**41.** Pete borrowed _____ book.   (Jane)

**42.** _____ book was filled with pictures.   (Pete)

**43.** One picture showed some _____ tools.   (carpenters)

**44.** Another displayed _____ clothing.   (women)

**45.** _____ furniture was on another page.   (Babies)

## Main Idea    pages 54–55

Write the main idea of each paragraph.

1.    Houses can be made of many different building materials. In Massachusetts there is a house built entirely of paper. It is called the Paper House.

2.    Do you know what the oldest living thing on Earth is? It is a bristlecone pine tree growing in California. This tree is more than 4,800 years old.

3.    There are many kinds of flags. Nations of the world have their own flags. Some flags stand for groups such as the Red Cross. States and cities also have flags. Flags are even used to send messages.


## Details    pages 56–57

Copy each paragraph. Underline the detail sentences.

4.    The alligator is an interesting reptile. It is amphibious and lives mostly in rivers and large swamps. Alligators eat frogs, fish, and snakes for food.

5.    A squirrel monkey is one of the tiniest monkeys. Its body length is 9 to 14 inches. As an adult it weighs only 13 to 38 ounces.

6.    A flying squirrel can glide through the air. It has a fold of skin on each side of its body. The folds of skin form "wings." The squirrel uses its broad, flat tail to guide itself.


## Fact and Opinion    pages 58–59

Read each sentence. Write *statement of fact* if the sentence states a fact. Write *statement of opinion* if the sentence states an opinion.

7. I think the camel is odd looking.
8. The letter *e* is the most often used letter in the alphabet.
9. Cream cheese is better than jelly on bread.
10. The hottest city in the world is Timbuktu in Africa.
11. Chicken noodle soup is the best kind of soup.
12. In Coloma, a town in Chile, it has never rained.
13. Our alphabet contains 26 letters.

## ● Writing and Editing a Book Report     pages 60–63

**1.** Write a book report about a book that you have read recently. Then edit the book report for capital letters and punctuation marks. Check to see that you have included facts and opinions in your report.

## ● Giving a Book Talk     pages 64–65

Write *true* or *false* to show if the sentence tells something you do when you give a book talk.

**2.** Stand up straight and look at your audience.
**3.** Speak slowly and clearly.
**4.** Give the title of the book.
**5.** Say the author's name.
**6.** Tell the whole story.

## ● Reading a Biography     pages 66–69

Read this paragraph from a biography about Francis Drake, an explorer.

Drake had red hair and a bright red beard. His eyes were blue, and he was known for his cool, steady gaze. The men who sailed with Drake had learned to fear that gaze. His queen, Elizabeth I, had learned to respect it.

David Goodnough

Answer these questions in complete sentences.

**1.** What is a biography?
**2.** Who is the main character in this biography?
**3.** Who is another character in the book?
**4.** What did Drake look like?
**5.** What kind of person do you imagine him to be?
**6.** Did some people fear him? Write the sentence in the story that proves your answer.
**7.** Do you think the story of Francis Drake's life will be exciting? Give a reason for your answer.

# MAINTENANCE and REVIEW

**Sentences**  pages 2–3

Add words to make complete sentences. Copy correctly the groups of words that already are complete sentences.

1. I work in a pet store after school until six.
2. Howling, barking, and chattering all afternoon.
3. In the puppy section two afternoons a week.
4. Can you guess my favorite animal in the store?
5. One day my friends Elizabeth and Lionel.
6. They wanted to buy a pet.
7. Looked at goldfish, turtles, and lizards.
8. They bought two little green turtles.

**Kinds of Sentences**  pages 4–7

Write each sentence correctly. Then write *declarative, interrogative, imperative,* or *exclamatory* to tell the kind of sentence.

9. do you like to ski in the winter
10. don't forget to wear an extra pair of socks
11. many ski areas make their own snow
12. wow, look at that great jump
13. lock your skis if you go inside the lodge
14. this ski area has three chair lifts
15. what a steep slope that is
16. will you help me ski down safely

**Complete Subject and Predicate**  pages 10–11

Copy each sentence. Draw one line under the complete subject. Draw two lines under the complete predicate.

17. Mark hit the ball.
18. Mark ran to first base.
19. Lois pitched a curve.
20. The players took the field.
21. Jan caught a fly ball.
22. Ali threw it to Ken.

**23.** The umpire called an out.  **24.** That small boy plays well.
**25.** The fans cheered.  **26.** My mom and dad came.

## Nouns   pages 36–37

Write the sentences. Underline the nouns.

**27.** At this store you can buy fruit and vegetables.
**28.** People shop here for meat and fish.
**29.** These shelves are lined with boxes of cereal.
**30.** On this row you will find bread and rolls.
**31.** Many families push carts.
**32.** Does the store sell food for pets?

## Plural Nouns   pages 38–41

Write the plural form of each noun.

**33.** child  **34.** family  **35.** moose  **36.** peach
**37.** brother  **38.** puppy  **39.** fox  **40.** sheep
**41.** scissors  **42.** goose  **43.** ox  **44.** tooth

## Common and Proper Nouns   pages 42–43

Write the sentences correctly.

**45.** Our friend mr jenkins moved to abilene, kansas.
**46.** His sister, miss j l sims, lives on el camino road.
**47.** We saw dr and mrs m b peters in dallas, texas.
**48.** Uncle stu and aunt lila are visiting italy and greece.
**49.** Did you know mr p s lewis moved to 81 nassau street?
**50.** My friend ms ramirez owns the store on lewis avenue.

## Possessive Nouns   pages 48–51

Write a possessive noun for each group of words.

**51.** the house of the family  **52.** the sleds of the boys
**53.** the glasses of the girl  **54.** the hats of the women
**55.** the toy belonging to Ed  **56.** the den of the fox
**57.** the teeth of the puppies  **58.** the prizes of the winners
**59.** the games of the children  **60.** the pencil belonging to Choi

3

# LANGUAGE
Learning About Verbs

# STUDY SKILLS
Using the Dictionary

# COMPOSITION
Writing Letters

# LITERATURE
Reading a Play

**LIGHTS!   CAMERA!   ACTION!**

What do you think of when you hear these words? To an actor, they mean that the stage is lighted, the camera is ready, and the action is about to begin.

Actors use their bodies to show action. Language is also used to show action. You use action words every day. These words tell what you are doing, or what is happening. Words such as *shout, leap,* and *think* are examples of action words. What other words can you think of to tell about action? Look at the pictures on the opposite page for some ideas.

In this unit you will learn to use words to express action. You will learn about using the dictionary to find words for expressing your ideas. You will also learn to write letters. You will read an action-packed play.

# LANGUAGE

## *Lesson 1: Understanding Action Verbs*

Look at the pictures. Then read the sentences. Each sentence tells what is happening in one of the pictures. Which picture goes with which sentence?

1. Jesse throws the basketball.
2. Mira bounces the basketball.

### *Think and Discuss*

Each sentence tells about an action. *Jesse* is the subject of sentence 1. What is the predicate? What is Jesse doing? Which word in the predicate shows the action?

The predicate of a sentence often has an action word. This word is called an **action verb.** *Throws* is the action verb in the predicate of sentence 1. Name the action verb in sentence 2.

> • An **action verb** is a word that shows an action. An action verb is often the key word in the predicate. It tells what the subject does.

## Practice

**A.** Copy each sentence. Draw two lines under the action verbs.

1. Beth runs out of the house.
2. She dashes down the street.
3. She waves to Jamie.
4. Beth and Jamie run to the basketball court.
5. Ten players gather at the court.
6. They split into two teams.
7. Beth's team dribbles the ball down the court.
8. Beth shoots the ball.
9. Beth's team members cheer.
10. Beth just scored the first points.

**B.** Each sentence has more than one action verb. Copy each sentence. Draw two lines under the action verbs.

11. Baseball players throw, catch, and bat the ball.
12. Table tennis players hit or tap the ball.
13. A tennis player serves and volleys the ball.
14. Football players tackle, grab, and fall.
15. A football player passes the ball or runs with the ball.

**C.** Add an action verb and other words. Complete the sentences.

16. People who bowl _____.   **17.** A soccer player _____.
18. Basketball players _____.   **19.** Polo players _____.

## Apply

**D. 20.–25.** Write six sentences about a sport you like. Use six of the action verbs from the list, or use your own action words.

| dive | jump | limp | look | yell |
|------|------|------|------|------|
| roll | hurdle | sprint | dash | vault |

# Lesson 2: Understanding Linking Verbs

Read the sentences. They tell about children dressed up for Halloween. Notice the verb in each sentence.

1. I am a clown.
2. Molly is a hobo.
3. Benjie and Nelson are together in an elephant costume.

## Think and Discuss

What is the subject of sentence 1? What is the predicate? Does the predicate contain an action verb?

The verb in a sentence does not always show an action. Some verbs can link, or join, the subject and words in the predicate. This kind of verb is called a **linking verb.** In sentence 1 the verb *am* links *I* and *a clown. Am* is a linking verb.

What are the linking verbs in sentences 2 and 3? What words do these linking verbs connect?

> ● A **linking verb** connects the subject with other words in the predicate. It tells what the subject is or was.

Forms of the verb *be* are often used as linking verbs. Study the chart. It shows how to use some common linking verbs.

| With Singular Subject | With Plural Subject |
| --- | --- |
| I **am** | We **are** |
| Sam **is** | Sam and May **are** |
| The truck **was** | They **were** |

## Practice

**A.** Copy each sentence. Draw two lines under the linking verbs.

1. My name is Maxine.
2. Halloween is a holiday.
3. My costume is a monster costume.
4. I was a monster last year too.
5. My two brothers are twins.
6. Last year they were twin monkeys.
7. This year they are twin robots.
8. Our block was very dark.
9. There were lighted jack-o'-lanterns in every window.
10. The three of us are friends.

**B.** Write the sentences. Use *am, is, are, was,* or *were*.

11. Now I _____ happy.
12. Today _____ Halloween.
13. Halloween _____ always my favorite holiday.
14. Here _____ my bag full of treats.
15. There _____ three packs of sugarless gum.
16. Those raisins _____ delicious.
17. This Halloween my friend and I _____ ghosts.
18. Last year I _____ a pirate.
19. _____ you ever a pirate on Halloween?
20. What _____ your favorite costume?

## Apply

**C. 21.–25.** What have you worn for Halloween? Tell about your costume or one you would like to wear. Write five sentences. In each use one of the following linking verbs: *is, am, are, was, were*.

# Lesson 3: Understanding Helping Verbs

Read the sentences. Notice the number of words in each verb.

1. Tamara and Carmen <u>paint</u> lovely pictures.
2. Bill <u>will</u> <u>paint</u> a picture.
3. Terry <u>has</u> <u>painted</u> a picture.

## Think and Discuss

The verbs you have studied so far stand alone. What is the verb in sentence 1? The verb *paint* stands alone in that sentence.

Some verbs have more than one word. When they do, the most important word is called the **main verb.** The other words are **helping verbs.** Look at the verb in sentence 2. What word has been added to the main verb? The word *will* is a helping verb. What is the helping verb in sentence 3?

> ● A **helping verb** helps the main verb express an action or make a statement.

These words are often used as helping verbs.

am    is    are    was    were
have    has    had    will

## Practice

**A.** Copy the sentences. Draw two lines under the main verb and its helping verb.

1. My hands are resting on the workbench.
2. They have worked hard.
3. I am looking at them.
4. One finger is covered with paint.
5. One knuckle is coated with clay.
6. I have made a beautiful vase.
7. I will give this wonderful present to my mom.

**B.** Find the main verb and the helping verb in each sentence. Write the words. Write *main verb* next to each main verb. Write *helping verb* next to each helping verb.

8. Jess and Thelma are making an unusual art project.
9. They will paint with their feet.
10. First Jess will mix the paint.
11. Then they will remove their shoes and socks.
12. Now Thelma has started.
13. Thelma is dipping her feet in the red paint.
14. She will step on the paper.
15. Thelma and Jess are stamping the most beautiful footprints.

## Apply

**C.** Use each verb to write a sentence about art.

16. was making    17. have painted    18. are molding
19. am drawing    20. will sell

# Lesson 4: Understanding Verb Tenses

Read the sentences. Find the verb in each sentence. How do the verbs differ?

1. Danny packs his lunch
2. Yesterday Danny packed his lunch.
3. Tomorrow Danny will pack his lunch.

## Think and Discuss

Which sentence tells about an action that happens right now? Which sentence tells about an action that has already happened? Which sentence tells about an action that is going to happen?

Verbs in sentences help tell when the action of the sentence happens. They have different **tenses** to show present, past, or future time. Notice how the verb *pack* changes tense in sentences 1, 2, and 3.

- The time expressed by a verb is called the **tense**. There are three main tenses.
- **Present tense** shows action that is happening now or that happens regularly.
- **Past tense** shows action that happened in the past. Many verbs that tell about past time end in *ed*.
- **Future tense** shows action that will happen in the future. Verbs that tell about the future have the helping verb *will*.

## Practice

**A.** Copy each sentence. Draw two lines under the verb.
Then write *present*, *past*, or *future* to tell the tense of
the verb.

1. My family eats dinner in Chinatown.
2. My grandmother used chopsticks.
3. Now she shows me how.
4. She holds the chopsticks just right.
5. She hands them to me.
6. At the restaurant I followed her plan.
7. I spilled a lot of dinner into my lap.
8. Dessert will arrive soon.
9. I will use my fingers for my fortune cookies.
10. Tomorrow I will practice with chopsticks again.

**B.** Complete each sentence. Use the verb in the given
tense.

11. Every Sunday morning Allison _____
    breakfast for her family.   (make, present)
12. Last Sunday they _____ pancakes.   (cook, past)
13. This Sunday they _____ a surprise.   (create, future)
14. First Allison _____ flour, salt, sugar, and baking
    powder.   (mix, future)
15. She _____ in the eggs and some milk next.
    (beat, future)
16. Allison _____ the blueberries yesterday.   (wash, past)
17. Now she _____ them into the batter.   (drop, present)
18. Her brother _____ the batter into a muffin tin.
    (pour, past)

**19.** Then he _____ the tin into the oven.   (push, past)

**20.** In half an hour, 12 steaming blueberry muffins _____ out.   (come, future)

### Apply

**C. 21.–22.** Write two sentences in the present tense. Tell about something you are doing right now.

**23.–24.** Write two sentences in the past tense. Tell about something you did this morning.

**25.–26.** Write two sentences in the future tense. Tell what you plan to do after school.

# HOW OUR LANGUAGE GROWS

What do you get when you join *school* with *lunch?* You get *scunch* of course! Is it time for *scunch?* What do you get when you join a *hippo* with a *bicycle?* You might get a *hipcycle!* Maybe you get a *bippo!*

What do you get when you join two words together? Do you get a joke? Yes, that can happen. Sometimes you get a new word. This is one way that some of the words in our language are really made. Two words that are joined together are called a *blend.* Here are some words that you may know.

| | |
|---|---|
| smoke + fog = smog | motor + hotel = motel |
| breakfast + lunch = brunch | flame + glare = flare |

What real words are made from joining these words together? Use your dictionary to check.

**1.** growl + rumble = _____     **2.** splash + spatter = _____

**3.** clap + crash = _____     **4.** news + broadcast = _____

**5.** gleam + shimmer = _____     **6.** smack + mash = _____

# Lesson 5: Forming Contractions

Read these sentences.

1. The horses do not kick.
2. The horses don't kick.
3. They are not wild.
4. They aren't wild.

## Think and Discuss

Which two words in sentence 1 were joined to make the word *don't*? What letter is left out of the new word? What takes the place of that letter?

A **contraction** is a short form of two words. Many contractions are formed by joining a verb and the word *not*. Which words in sentence 3 form the contraction *aren't*?

> • A **contraction** is a shortened form of two words.
> • Use an apostrophe to show that one or more letters have been left out in a contraction.

## Practice

**A.** Copy the sentences. Underline the contractions. Then write the two words from which the contraction is made.

1. We aren't going home.
2. We can't leave yet.
3. The horses haven't been fed.
4. My horse won't eat.
5. I hope he isn't sick.
6. He doesn't like this food.
7. He hasn't eaten all day.
8. We don't have any grain.

## Apply

**B.** Write contractions for each word pair. Then use each contraction in a sentence.

9. do not
10. can not
11. are not
12. is not
13. have not
14. was not
15. does not
16. will not

# Lesson 6: Spelling Past Tense Verbs

To form the past tense of many verbs, you simply add *ed.* For some verbs you must do more. Read the sentences. Study the verbs.

dry    1. Dad <u>dried</u> the dishes.
step    2. Then he <u>stepped</u> outside.

## Think and Discuss

Some verbs change their spellings before *ed* is added. The verb in sentence 1 is the past tense of *dry.* How does the spelling change to form *dried?* The verb in sentence 2 is the past tense of *step.* How does the spelling change to form *stepped?*

> - Some verbs end in a consonant and *y.* To form the past tense, change the *y* to *i.* Then add *ed.*
> - Some verbs have one syllable and end with a consonant, vowel, consonant. To form the past tense, double the final consonant. Then add *ed.*

Now read these sentences. Spell the verbs in the past tense.

hurry    3. Dad _____ out the door.
jog    4. He _____ around the block.

## Practice

**A.** Write each sentence. Use the past tense of the verb in parentheses ( ).

**1.** Dad _____ to the fence.   (hurry)
**2.** There he _____ a robin.   (spy)
**3.** Its wings _____ busily.   (flap)
**4.** Dad _____ back to the porch.   (scurry)

5. He _____ his camera.   (grab)
6. He _____ it around his neck.   (strap)
7. Next he _____ the camera back to the fence.   (carry)
8. Dripping, he _____ his brow.   (dry)
9. Finally Dad focused and _____ a picture.   (snap)
10. Hearing the click, the bird _____ away.   (hop)

**B.** Write the past tense of each verb. Then use each one in a sentence.

| | | | |
|---|---|---|---|
| **11.** chop | **12.** trot | **13.** clap | **14.** hum |
| **15.** stop | **16.** bury | **17.** flap | **18.** mop |
| **19.** cry | **20.** empty | **21.** trip | **22.** worry |
| **23.** tip | **24.** trap | **25.** dry | |

## Apply

**C. 26.–30.** Write about taking a picture with a camera. Use these five words in the past tense. Write five sentences or a story.

carry     drop     flap     snap     try

### To Memorize

#### Post Early for Space

Once we were wayfarers, then seafarers, then airfarers;
We shall be spacefarers soon,
Not voyaging from city to city or coast to coast,
But from planet to planet and from moon to moon.

*Peter J. Henniker-Heaton*

How does a wayfarer travel? How would a seafarer or an airfarer travel? How does the poet say travel distance will change?

# Lesson 7: Using Irregular Verbs

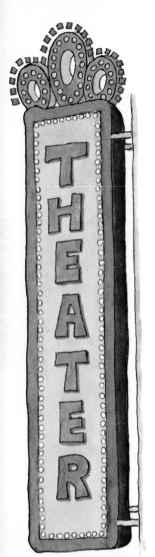

Read the sentences. Each has a verb in the past tense.

1. Carlos <u>came</u> late to the theater.
2. He <u>ran</u> all the way.
3. The play <u>had begun</u>.
4. The chorus <u>had sung</u> its first song.

## Think and Discuss

Other verbs you have studied add *ed* to show the past tense. None of the verbs in sentences 1 through 4 end with *ed*, but they all tell about past time. Verbs that do not add *ed* to show the past tense are called **irregular verbs.**

Study the chart of irregular verbs.

| Verb | Present | Past | Past with *Have, Has,* or *Had* |
|------|---------|------|---------------------------------|
| come | come(s) | came | come |
| run | run(s) | ran | run |
| go | go(es) | went | gone |
| begin | begin(s) | began | begun |
| sing | sing(s) | sang | sung |
| ring | ring(s) | rang | rung |

Look at the irregular verbs *come* and *run*. They have the same form in the present tense and with a helping verb in the past tense. The irregular verb *go* has three different forms. How do *begin, sing,* and *ring* change?

Look for patterns in irregular verbs. This will help you remember them.

## Practice

**A.** Choose the correct word. Write the sentences.

1. Last week my family ———— to a band concert.
   (went, gone)
2. My Aunt Alice ———— with us.   (come, came)
3. Aunt Alice had ———— with us last year too.
   (went, gone)
4. She had ———— with the band many years ago.
   (sang, sung)
5. We ———— from the car and found seats.   (ran, run)
6. Just as we arrived, a bell ————.   (rang, rung)
7. The band ———— to play.   (began, begun)
8. Three women ———— with the band.   (sang, sung)
9. At nine o'clock the last song ————.   (began, begun)
10. Finally the time had ———— to leave.   (came, come)

**B.** Use the correct past form of the verb in parentheses ( ).
   Write the sentences.

11. Last year we ———— to an opera.   (go)
12. The opera ———— like a play.   (begin)
13. People ———— on stage.   (come)
14. Instead of speaking, the people ————.   (sing)
15. A bell had ———— three times.   (ring)
16. The intermission had ————.   (begin)
17. Later the bell ———— again.   (ring)
18. People ———— back to their seats.   (run)
19. After the star had ————, everyone clapped.   (sing)
20. We have ———— to three operas since then.   (go)

## Apply

**C. 21.–25.** Write five sentences. Tell about a musical
   performance you have heard. Use five different verb
   forms from the chart on page 90.

# Lesson 8: Using Other Irregular Verbs

Read the sentences. Do they tell about present or past time?

1. Larry wrote a letter to his grandmother.
2. She has written an answer.

## Think and Discuss

The verbs in sentences 1 and 2 tell about past time. The verb *write* is an irregular verb. Like the verbs in Lesson 7, it does not add *ed* to show past tense. What form of *write* is used without a helping verb? What form is used with a helping verb?

Look at the chart. It lists more irregular verbs.

| Verb | Present | Past | Past with *Have, Has,* or *Had* |
|------|---------|------|--------------------------------|
| do | do(es) | did | done |
| write | write(s) | wrote | written |
| give | give(s) | gave | given |
| take | take(s) | took | taken |
| grow | grow(s) | grew | grown |

Notice that the three forms of all the verbs on the chart are different. All the verbs change in a similar way. To make the verb form with *have* or *has,* the sound of *n* or *en* is added. Say the three forms of *do, write, give, take,* and *grow.*

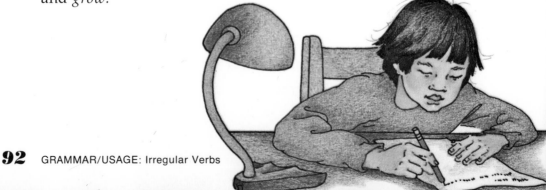

## Practice

**A.** Choose the correct word. Write the sentences.

1. Last week I _____ Sam a plan for making a model dinosaur.   (gave, given)
2. Since then the dinosaur has _____.   (grew, grown)
3. Sam has _____ it out of the house.   (took, taken)
4. He _____ a wonderful job.   (did, done)
5. A reporter _____ an article about it for the newspaper.   (wrote, written)

**B.** Use the correct past form of the verb in parentheses ( ). Write the sentences.

6. I have _____ a story.   (write)
7. I first _____ stories when I was seven years old. (write)
8. Mr. Drake _____ me the idea for my story.   (give)
9. I have _____ it to him to read.   (give)
10. The story _____ longer as I wrote.   (grow)
11. It has _____ to eight pages.   (grow)
12. I _____ the hardest part yesterday.   (do)
13. I had _____ the enjoyable parts first.   (do)
14. It _____ me two weeks to finish my last story.   (take)
15. This one has _____ three weeks.   (take)

## Apply

**C.** Write sentences using each of these verb forms correctly.

16. have done     17. grew        18. took
19. has written     20. has given

# LANGUAGE REVIEW

**Action Verbs**   pages 78–79

Copy the sentences. Draw two lines under the action verbs.

1. Last night the wind howled through the trees.
2. It rattled the doors and windows.
3. Leaves and twigs flew in all directions.
4. My little brother hid under his bed.
5. The thunder and lightning frightened our dog too.

**Linking Verbs**   pages 80–81

Copy the sentences. Draw two lines under the linking verbs.

6. The last few days were wet and chilly.
7. Danny and Ellen are the children in the raincoats.
8. Their favorite puddles are the deepest ones.
9. Our backyard is like a pond.
10. Meredith and Stella are wet and muddy.

**Helping Verbs**   pages 82–83

Write the word in each sentence that is a helping verb.

11. Manuel and Kenneth are building the campfire.
12. Later the campers will sing some folk songs.
13. Richard had chopped plenty of wood.
14. The sun is setting behind the mountains.
15. Some hungry animal has eaten tomorrow's breakfast.

**Verb Tenses**   pages 84–86

Copy the sentences. Use the form of the verb in parentheses ( ).

16. He _____ this horseback ride.   (enjoy, present)
17. Mike and Pedro _____ at this ranch.   (stay, past)
18. We _____ across a wide field.   (gallop, future)
19. Pauline _____ us on the trail.   (join, past)
20. The horse _____ like a circus pony.   (prance, present)

## Contractions   page 87

Make contractions from the pairs of words.

**21.** do not    **22.** have not    **23.** was not
**24.** are not    **25.** can not    **26.** has not
**27.** did not    **28.** were not    **29.** is not
**30.** will not    **31.** had not

## Past Tense Verbs   pages 88–89

Change the verbs to the past tense. Write the sentences.

**32.** Mr. Carne (carry) his son on his back.
**33.** Insects (hum) in the grass along the path.
**34.** He (step) carefully over a little brook.
**35.** His dog Amber (trot) along beside them.
**36.** When Amber fell behind, he (hurry) to catch up.

## Irregular Verbs   pages 90–93

Choose the correct verb. Write the sentences.

**37.** Woodie Guthrie _____ this song.   (wrote, written)
**38.** He _____ many folk songs about America.   (sang, sung)
**39.** My folks have _____ to some of his concerts.   (went, gone)
**40.** Maria has _____ to learn the words to his songs.   (began, begun)
**41.** We have _____ to see a movie about Woodie Guthrie.
(came, come)
**42.** The usher _____ our tickets.   (took, taken)
**43.** The audience has _____ larger.   (grew, grown)
**44.** The actor has _____ a wonderful job.   (did, done)
**45.** He _____ an outstanding performance.   (gave, given)

## Applying Verbs

**46.–50.** Write five sentences that tell about past time. Use the past tense forms of verbs from this list in your sentences.

| hop | grow | run | write |
| --- | --- | --- | --- |
| do | trot | copy | take |

# STUDY SKILLS

## Lesson 9: Finding Words in a Dictionary

Paula's uncle said he was sending her a mauve blouse. Paula wonders what kind of blouse it will be. Where can she look to find what *mauve* means?

### Think and Discuss

Paula will look for the word *mauve* in the **dictionary.** A dictionary is a reference book. It contains many words listed in alphabetical order.

Pretend the dictionary is divided into three sections. This will help you find words quickly. Words beginning with the letters *A* through *F* are in the front of the dictionary. Words beginning with *G* through *P* are in the middle. Words beginning with *Q* through *Z* are at the back. In which section should Paula look to find *mauve*?

At the top of each dictionary page are two **guide words.** They are printed in dark type or in color. The guide word on the left shows the first word listed on that page. The guide word on the right shows the last word. The words *maturity* and *meadowlark* are the guide words for this page. Will Paula find *mauve* on this page?

| **maturity** | 453 | **meadowlark** |
|---|---|---|

**ma·tur·i·ty** [mə·t(y)ŏŏr′ə·tē *or* mə·chŏŏr′ə·tē] *n.* **1** The condition of being mature or fully developed. **2** The time at which a note, bill, etc., becomes due.

**may·flow·er** [mā′flou′ər] *n.* Any of several plants that blossom in the spring, especially the arbutus.
**May·flow·er** [mā′flou′ər] *n.* The ship on

Paula has found the correct dictionary page. She will use alphabetical order to locate the word. Sometimes you can find a word using its first letter. When the first letters are the same, you must look at the second or third letter.

## Practice

**A.** Tell where you would find each word in the dictionary. Write *front, middle,* or *back.*

| | | | |
|---|---|---|---|
| **1.** fountain | **2.** lily | **3.** shelter | **4.** able |
| **5.** hinge | **6.** union | **7.** discuss | **8.** mongrel |
| **9.** plastic | **10.** creek | **11.** triple | **12.** extend |
| **13.** quiz | **14.** igloo | **15.** gumbo | **16.** rooster |

**B.** Write each group of words in alphabetical order.

| | | | |
|---|---|---|---|
| **17.** colt | gosling | lamb | kid |
| **18.** duckling | fawn | pullet | filly |
| **19.** cub | tadpole | heifer | chick |
| **20.** cape | chain | cent | crust |
| **21.** high | haunt | home | huddle |
| **22.** map | many | matter | magazine |
| **23.** pony | poor | poncho | pool |
| **24.** stare | star | stark | start |
| **25.** trim | trio | trifle | trip |

## Apply

**C.** Find each word in the dictionary. Write the guide words that appear on the dictionary page.

**26.** craft    **27.** poem    **28.** tap    **29.** fox    **30.** live

# Lesson 10: Using Entry Words

Sometimes you read words that are new to you. Perhaps you do not know how to say them. Maybe you want to know what they mean. The dictionary can help you learn many new things about words.

## Think and Discuss

Read about some information found in a dictionary.

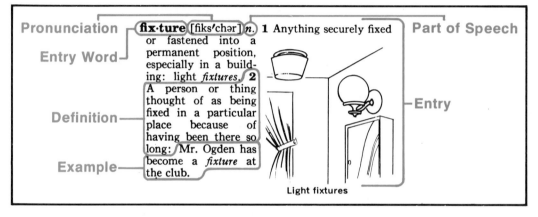

Pronunciation

Entry Word

Definition

Example

**fix·ture** [fiks′chər] *n.* 1 Anything securely fixed or fastened into a permanent position, especially in a building: light *fixtures.* 2 A person or thing thought of as being fixed in a particular place because of having been there so long: Mr. Ogden has become a *fixture* at the club.

Part of Speech

Entry

Light fixtures

The **entry word** is the word to be explained. It is printed in **boldface** type and spelled correctly.

The **pronunciation** shows how to say the word. It also shows the number of syllables.

The **part of speech** tells whether the word is a noun, a verb, or some other part of speech. The names are abbreviated this way: n. for noun, v. for verb, adj. for adjective, adv. for adverb, pron. for pronoun. What part of speech is the word *fixture?*

The **definition** tells what the word means. Sometimes there are several different meanings. The meanings are numbered. How many meanings of *fixture* are listed?

Sometimes an **example** is given. This shows you how to use the word. What is the example sentence for *fixture?*

The entry word and all the information about it is called the **entry.**

P

**per·fo·ra·tion** [pûr′fə·rā′shən] *n.* **1** A hole drilled in or punched through something. **2** The act of perforating. **3** The condition of being perforated.
**per·force** [pər·fôrs′] *adv.* By or of necessity.
**per·form** [pər·fôrm′] *v.* **1** To do; accomplish: to *perform* surgery. **2** To fulfill or discharge, as a duty. **3** To give an exhibition of artistic skill; to act, play an instrument, sing, etc.

Perforations allow the coupon to be torn out neatly.

**pe·rim·e·ter** [pə·rim′ə·tər] *n.* The outer boundary or the length of the outer boundary of any plane figure.
**pe·ri·od** [pir′ē·əd] *n.* **1** A portion of time with a definite beginning and end marked by events that repeat themselves again and again. **2** A time of indefinite length having some specified quality or circumstance. **3** A set portion of time: a lunch *period*. **4** A completion or end. **5** A dot (.) used as a mark of punctuation at the close of a declarative sentence and after abbreviations.

The perimeters of the figures are outlined.

## Practice

**A.** Use the sample dictionary page to answer the questions. Use complete sentences.

1. How many entry words are shown?
2. How many definitions are given for *period?*
3. How do you write the pronunciation for *perform?*
4. How many syllables does *perimeter* have?
5. What part of speech is *period?*
6. Write an example sentence for the last definition of *perform.*
7. Which two words are shown in pictures?
8. Which two words have only one definition?
9. Which words are nouns?
10. Which word is a verb?

## Apply

**B.** Find these words in your dictionary. Write the part of speech and the first definition of each word. Then use each word in a sentence.

**11.** flog    **12.** invent    **13.** shallot    **14.** toxin    **15.** stow

# Lesson 11: Using a Pronunciation Key

Can you read these sentences?

1. Mark rōt a letər to hiz frend Wilma.
2. He sed that he woŏd kum to vizit.

## Think and Discuss

One part of a dictionary helps you say words correctly. It is called the **pronunciation key.**

A pronunciation key is like a code. It uses symbols for sounds. It also lists one or more familiar words that have the sound in them.

Use this pronunciation key. Read sentences 1 and 2.

---

add, āce, câre, pälm; end, ēqual; it, ice; odd, ōpen, ôrder; toŏk, poōl; up, bûrn; ə = a in *above*, e in *sicken*, i in *possible*, o in *melon*, u in *circus*; yoō = u in *fuse*; oil; pout; check; ring; thin; this; zh in *vision*.

---

Can you say these words using the pronunciation key?

3. kwōt　　4. thā　　5. vois　　6. hīd

Remember that the symbols used in the pronunciation key tell you the sounds a word contains. They are not the same as the letters you use to spell the word.

## Practice

**A.** These words are respelled using symbols from the pronunciation key. Say the respelled words aloud.

| | | | |
|---|---|---|---|
| **1.** (h)wen | **2.** fit | **3.** kwēn | **4.** gut·ər |
| **5.** kash | **6.** blak | **7.** nīf | **8.** haf |
| **9.** pāst | **10.** lam | **11.** kwit | **12.** sīz |
| **13.** kāj | **14.** ig·zakt | **15.** kul·er | **16.** prīs |

# Apply

**B.** The first word in each row is respelled using symbols from the pronunciation key. Say the word to yourself. Then write the word that rhymes with it.

| | | |
|---|---|---|
| **17.** klash | **a.** smash | **b.** fish |
| **18.** glōb | **a.** rob | **b.** robe |
| **19.** nēt | **a.** seat | **b.** let |
| **20.** brāk | **a.** lake | **b.** broke |
| **21.** kōm | **a.** come | **b.** home |
| **22.** hŏŏd | **a.** could | **b.** food |
| **23.** īs | **a.** nice | **b.** his |
| **24.** krēp | **a.** crumb | **b.** sleep |
| **25.** chungk | **a.** flunk | **b.** rung |
| **26.** thâr | **a.** or | **b.** care |
| **27.** dok | **a.** lock | **b.** loss |
| **28.** ûrn | **a.** sum | **b.** learn |
| **29.** fāl | **a.** sale | **b.** fan |
| **30.** kēn | **a.** seen | **b.** team |

## A Challenge

Write five sentences. Use the symbols from the pronunciation key to respell the words. Exchange your sentences with a friend. Write each other's sentences, spelled correctly.

# COMPOSITION

## Lesson 12: Writing a Friendly Letter

Everyone likes to receive letters. Letters give news of people far away. They invite you to go places. They may thank you for a present or for something you have done.

### Think and Discuss

Kurt just wrote this letter to his friend Jody.

Heading —————— 5126 El Toledo
Avon, Ohio 44011
October 8, 19--

Greeting —— Dear Jody,
    The boys and girls at my new school are very friendly. Mr. Lopez is our teacher. We are learning about the stars and the planets. What are you studying now? Please write and tell me about it.

Body

Closing ——————— Your friend,
Signature ——————— Kurt

Kurt's letter has five parts. The **heading** contains the letter writer's address and the date. A comma comes between the city and the state. A comma also comes between the day and the year in the date. What words are capitalized in the heading of Kurt's letter?

The **greeting** welcomes the person who receives the letter. What greeting did Kurt use? The greeting begins with a capital letter. A comma follows the greeting.

The **body** of the letter contains the message. Kurt's message was written in a paragraph. What did he tell Jody? What did he ask? The first word of the body is always indented, or moved in.

The **closing** is the end of the letter. The first word of the closing is capitalized. A comma follows the closing. What closing did Kurt use for his letter?

The **signature** is the written name of the person who wrote the letter. Kurt signed his letter.

## Practice

**A.** Copy these parts of a letter correctly in correct letter form. Finish the body of the letter. Remember to put capital letters and commas where they belong.

| | |
|---|---|
| **Heading** | 205 third ave. |
| | new york new york 10003 |
| | april 20 19-- |
| **Greeting** | dear grandma and grandpa |
| **Body** | Our family has been very busy since we visited you last summer. *(Finish the paragraph telling your grandparents what you have been doing.)* |
| **Closing** | your granddaughter |
| **Signature** | jane |

## Apply

**B.** Pretend you are the person who received the letter from Kurt. Write a letter to send back to Kurt. Answer his question about school. Think of something interesting to tell him.

# Lesson 13: Addressing an Envelope

Kathy looked in the mailbox and saw three envelopes. One of them was addressed to her. Kathy knew who had sent her the letter before she opened it. How did she know?

## Think and Discuss

This is what the envelope of Kathy's letter looked like.

Return Address —

Mary Kay Hart
659 West Chestnut St.
Oxford, OH   45056

Receiver's Address —

Kathy Gates
84 Castle Rd.
Salem, OR 97301

Kathy looked in the upper left-hand corner of the envelope for the **return address.** The return address is the name and address of the person who wrote the letter. It should take up a small amount of space. Who wrote the letter to Kathy?

In the middle of the envelope is the **receiver's name and address.** Kathy received the letter, so her name and address are listed.

Look at the last line of Kathy's address. After the name of the city is an abbreviation for the state's name. Postal abbreviations are written with two capital letters and no periods. In what state does Kathy live? Look in the list in this lesson to find out.

After the state abbreviation, you will see five numbers. These numbers are the ZIP code. Every area of the country has a ZIP code. What is Kathy's ZIP code? What is Mary Kay's?

A stamp is placed in the upper right-hand corner of the envelope. A stamp must be on an envelope so that there will be no postage due.

## *Practice*

**A.** Copy these names of states. Next to them write their postal abbreviations. Check the chart on this page.

| | | |
|---|---|---|
| **1.** Pennsylvania | **2.** Arizona | **3.** California |
| **4.** Kansas | **5.** New York | **6.** South Carolina |
| **7.** Ohio | **8.** Vermont | **9.** Utah |

**B.** Write these names and addresses correctly on your paper.

**10.** mr. j. garza
43 sunshine rd.
austin tx 78701

**11.** ms. liza v. macey
2 butler lane
eton ga 30724

## *Apply*

**C. 12.** Fold a piece of paper in half. Make believe it is the outside of an envelope. Address your envelope to the following person.

Joyce Cook
22 Pinebridge Road
Ossining, NY 10562

Use your own name and return address. Draw a stamp on your envelope.

**States:**

|  |  |
|---|---|
| Alabama | AL |
| Alaska | AK |
| Arizona | AZ |
| Arkansas | AR |
| California | CA |
| Colorado | CO |
| Connecticut | CT |
| Delaware | DE |
| District of Columbia | DC |
| Florida | FL |
| Georgia | GA |
| Hawaii | HI |
| Idaho | ID |
| Illinois | IL |
| Indiana | IN |
| Iowa | IA |
| Kansas | KS |
| Kentucky | KY |
| Louisiana | LA |
| Maine | ME |
| Maryland | MD |
| Massachusetts | MA |
| Michigan | MI |
| Minnesota | MN |
| Mississippi | MS |
| Missouri | MO |
| Montana | MT |
| Nebraska | NB |
| Nevada | NV |
| New Hampshire | NH |
| New Jersey | NJ |
| New Mexico | NM |
| New York | NY |
| North Carolina | NC |
| North Dakota | ND |
| Ohio | OH |
| Oklahoma | OK |
| Oregon | OR |
| Pennsylvania | PA |
| Rhode Island | RI |
| South Carolina | SC |
| South Dakota | SD |
| Tennessee | TN |
| Texas | TX |
| Utah | UT |
| Vermont | VT |
| Virginia | VA |
| Washington | WA |
| West Virginia | WV |
| Wisconsin | WI |
| Wyoming | WY |

# Lesson 14: Writing a Thank You Note

Gina received a birthday present from her Aunt Belle. Read the letter she sent her aunt to say thank you.

> 1741 Sage Canyon
> Houston, Texas 77036
> March 22, 19--
>
> Dear Aunt Belle,
>     Thank you for the roller skates you sent me for my birthday. They are much better than my old ones. Every day I practice on the sidewalk in front of my house. I can skate well now.
>
>                     With love,
>                     Gina

## Think and Discuss

A thank you note is a short letter. It has the same five parts as any friendly letter. Name the five parts.

Send a thank you note soon after visiting someone or receiving a gift. This shows that you appreciate what someone has done. The note should tell why you are thanking the person. If you have been a guest at someone's house, tell why you enjoyed yourself. If you received a gift, say how you are using it. Gina's note thanks her aunt for her gift. How does Gina say she is using the gift?

> **How to Write a Thank You Note**
> 1. **Tell what you are thanking the person for.**
> 2. **If you have been a guest at someone's house, tell why you enjoyed yourself.**
> 3. **If you received a gift, say how you are using it.**

## *Practice*

**A.** Study the thank you note on page 106. Then close your book. Write the note as your teacher reads it.

**B.** Copy this thank you note to Aunt Grace. Add a heading, a greeting, a closing, and a signature.

> Thank you for sending me *Key to the Treasure.* It is an unusual adventure story and an exciting mystery. I liked reading the book very much.

**C.** Copy this thank you note to Mr. Dole. Add more sentences to the body of the letter. Add a heading, a closing, and a signature.

> Dear Mr. Dole,
>     Thank you for taking me to the circus yesterday.

## *Apply*

**D.** List three persons to whom you might write a thank you note. Write why you would thank each one. Then write a real thank you note to one of those people.

# Lesson 15: Writing an Invitation

Invitations are letters that ask you to come somewhere. Some invitations ask you to birthday parties or cookouts. Others invite you to visit friends or relatives. Have you ever received an invitation?

## Think and Discuss

Alan wrote this invitation to Martin.

> 5073 Little Spring Road
> Acton, Maine 04001
> May 15, 19--
>
> Dear Martin,
>     Will you come and stay with me at my family's cottage on White Lake? We will leave for the cottage at 10:30 A.M. on July 18. We will return home at about 7:00 P.M. on July 25. You will need to bring your sleeping bag and a pillow. Don't forget some mosquito spray too. Please come.
>
>             Your friend,
>             Alan

Alan's invitation has five parts. What are they?
The body of Alan's invitation answers these questions. Tell the answers.

1. **Who** is to be invited?
2. **What** is the invitation for?
3. **When** is the invitation for?
4. **Where** is it to be held?
5. What **special information** does the guest need?

Notice how Alan wrote the times in his invitation. When you write time, use this mark (:) called a **colon.** Place the colon between the hour and the minutes. Use capital letters and periods for the abbreviations **A.M.** and **P.M.** *A.M.* means morning. *P.M.* means afternoon or evening. What time will Alan's family leave? What time will they return?

---

**How to Write an Invitation**
1. **Tell who is invited.**
2. **Tell what the invitation is for.**
3. **Tell when to come and when the event will end.**
4. **Tell where it is.**
5. **Tell the special information a guest must know.**

---

When you receive an invitation, remember to answer it right away.

## Practice

A. Pretend your class is presenting a play. Write an invitation to your parents. Include this information in your invitation.

**Who:** your parents
**What:** the play, *The Wizard of Oz*
**When:** October 6, 1:00 P.M. until 5:00 P.M.
**Where:** your school
**Special information:** Come early to get a good seat.

## Apply

B. Imagine you are having a party on Halloween night. The date is October 31. The party will be in your basement. You have decided your guests should come in costumes. Make up the time your party will begin and end. Then write an invitation to a friend.

# Lesson 16: Editing an Invitation

Read the invitation Jean wrote to her cousin Ann.

> 4755 Avenue J
> Brooklyn, new york 11230
> november 18, 19--
>
> dear ann
>     Would you like to come with Mother and me
> to new york ? We will see the Thanksgiving
> Day Parade. We'll leave next Thursday. We will
> be home by 5:00 P.M. Please come. *(at 7:30 a.m.)*
>
>                     with love,
>                     Jean

## Editing Marks

| | |
|---|---|
| ☰ | capitalize |
| ⊙ | make a period |
| ∧ | add something |
| ⋏ | add a comma |
| ⌄ | add quotation marks |
| ℘ | take something away |
| ◯ | spell correctly |
| ¶ | indent the paragraph |
| / | make a lowercase letter |
| ∿ tr | transpose |

## Think and Discuss

Jean checked her invitation before she sent it. She found some mistakes in capitalization. Find these mistakes. What editing mark did Jean use to correct the mistakes?

Jean added a comma to the date. She also placed commas after the greeting and after the closing. This editing mark ⋏ shows where the commas belong.

Some important information was missing from Jean's invitation. What information did she add? What editing mark did she use?

## Practice

A. Copy Jean's invitation. Make all the corrections and additions shown.

## *Apply*

**B.** Look at the invitation you wrote in Lesson 15. Your invitation should include all five parts. It should tell all the important information your guest needs. Use the model and the chart in Lesson 15. Edit your invitation. Then copy it again neatly.

# MECHANICS PRACTICE

## Writing Place Names

- Begin each important word in the name of a town, city, state, and country with a capital letter.
- Begin each important word in the names of streets and their abbreviations with capital letters.
- Use a period after an abbreviation of a place name.
- Use a comma in an address to separate the city and state or the city and country.

**A.** Write these place names correctly.

1. 6 winding brook
   carey texas 79222

2. 173 butler pkwy
   eaton georgia 30724

3. 8722 overlook dr
   lima ohio 45806

4. 1192 jerome avenue
   rockford illinois 61120

5. 29 north road
   perry maine 04667

6. 925 adams st
   columbia missouri 65201

**B.** Write the sentences correctly. Use capital letters, periods, and commas where they are needed.

7. Our museum is on front st in ranger city.
8. Drive along red hill road and you will see it.
9. Artists from colorado and wyoming exhibit there.
10. Hugh and Mary Walters are from denver colorado.
11. They will speak at the Town Hall on mission road.
12. They then will come to hartley ave to visit our school.

# LITERATURE

## Lesson 17: Reading a Play

A play is a story that is written to be acted. The story is told in the conversations between the characters.

### Think and Discuss

As you read this play, pretend it is really happening. Imagine what the characters are like. Picture the place where the play is happening.

### The Turtle Who Changed His Tune

*Characters*

**Two Blue Kimonos** ⎫
**Two White Kimonos** ⎬ Narrators
**Musicians,** 2 or more, extras
**Chiba,** a youth
**Taro,** his brother

**Obasan,** their mother
**Three Merchants**
**Three Teahouse Maidens**
**Turtle**
**Stagehands,** 2 or more, extras

*Time: Long ago.*
*Setting: A Japanese village. Obasan's house is at right, represented by two mats, between which are pillows, and a low table holding a plate of rice cakes. A backpack frame holding a bundle of wood is beside one mat. Up center there are three shops, indicated by booths decorated with banners, and a teahouse, indicated by a low table holding tea things and a vase of flowers. Down left, there is a pond in front of short pine trees.*
*At Rise: Blue Kimonos and White Kimonos kneel down right, on stage apron. Musicians are seated on mat beside them. Chiba and Taro are lying on mats, right, sleeping.*

**Obasan** *is kneeling on pillow, asleep, her hands folded against her cheek.* **Musicians** *tap wood blocks three times to signal start of play.*

**Blue Kimonos** and **White Kimonos** *(To audience, together, bowing until heads touch mats):* Welcome.

**White Kimonos:** Please to imagine yourselves in the long-ago past.

**Blue Kimonos:** Please to imagine yourselves in a faraway place. (**Musicians** *strike gong.*)

**Blue Kimonos** and **White Kimonos** *(Together, dramatically):* Japan! *(They bow as before.)*

**First White Kimono** *(Rising, pointing to house, right):* Please to turn your eyes upon the humble house of Obasan, a poor widow. *(Kneels)*

**Second White Kimono** *(Rising, pointing to* **Chiba** *and* **Taro***):* Please to notice Chiba and Taro, her sons. *(Kneels)*

**First Blue Kimono:** Chiba rises early every morning with a smile. (**Chiba** *pantomimes action.*) Meanwhile his lazy brother Taro is still sleeping. (**Taro** *snores.*)

**Second Blue Kimono:** Chiba leaves his mother the money he earns as a woodcutter. (**Chiba** *holds up coin, then puts it on the table, and bows to* **Obasan***.*) Taro never earns any coins.

**First White Kimono:** Chiba takes one small rice cake for his lunch (**Chiba** *takes rice cake from plate on table.*) Taro gobbles the rest later.

**Second White Kimono:** Then Chiba goes off to the town to sell his wood, before the others wake. (**Chiba** *puts on frame of sticks and crosses center.*) He is always trying to help his mother. (**Musicians** *tap wood blocks briskly, in time to* **Chiba's** *steps.*)

**Chiba** *(Calling):* Wood for sale! Dry wood! Good wood! Come, buy my wood! Wood for sale! (**Merchants** *enter, up center, and stand at shops.*)

**Parasol Merchant** *(Shaking head):* Not today. Go away.

**Potter:** Go away. Not today.

**Fan Merchant** *(Waving fan):* Will you trade? Come and see. A fan for you. Wood for me.

**Chiba** *(Sadly):* No, thank you. I need coins, not fans. *(Three **Teahouse Maidens** enter.)* Will you buy my wood?

**Teahouse Maidens** *(Bowing, together):* We are most sincerely and regretfully sorry. *Sayonara. (They kneel at table. **Chiba** bows and crosses down left to pond, as **Musicians** tap wood blocks. He removes frame of sticks and sits, chin in hand.)*

**Chiba** *(Sadly):* Business is bad today. *(Wistfully)* If only something good would happen! *(Shrugs)* Perhaps I should eat my rice cake. *(He nibbles cake, then throws crumbs into pond.)* I will give the crumbs to the fish. *(**Turtle** enters and jumps into pond. **Musicians** play gong. **Turtle** snaps at crumbs, as **Musicians** play rhythm sticks. Then **Turtle** stands on rock and bows to **Chiba**.)*

**Turtle:** Thank you for your crumbs. You are most kind.

**Chiba** *(Surprised):* A turtle who talks!

**Turtle:** There is more I can do. Listen. *(**Musician** plays Japanese song on flute, as **Turtle** puckers lips and pretends to sing.)*

**Chiba** *(At finish of song):* A turtle who talks and sings! I want to show everyone in my village what you can do. *(Bows)* Please, honorable turtle, come with me.

**Turtle:** Why not? You have shared your crumbs with me. I will share my songs with you. *(**Chiba** and **Turtle** cross up center.)*

**Chiba** *(Calling):* Hear me, everybody. Gather round. *(**Merchants** and **Teahouse Maidens** run center and form semicircle around **Chiba** and **Turtle**. At right, **Taro** and **Obasan** rise, and cross to watch, also.)* This turtle can speak, and he sings like a bird, too.

**Merchants** and **Maidens** *(Together):* Show us! Show us!

(**Turtle** *bows, purses lips, and pretends to sing, while*
**Musicians** *play flute melody. At conclusion of song, all sigh,*
*then applaud, and throw coins.* **Chiba** *gathers coins.*)
**Parasol Merchant:** This is a miracle!
**Potter:** Sing again, turtle.
**First Maiden:** Please.
**Second Maiden:** Sing again and again, sweet turtle.
**Turtle:** I cannot sing again today. It will strain my throat. But,
I will be pleased to sing again next week at this time. *(Bows)*
*Sayonara. (Others bow.)*
**Third Maiden:** *Sayonara.*
**Fan Merchant:** Until next week. (**Musicians** *play wood blocks*

as **Merchants** and **Maidens** return to places. **Chiba** and **Turtle** cross to **Obasan**, bow to her, then kneel, holding pose. Meanwhile, **Taro** crosses downstage.)

**Taro** (Aside, nastily): My brother Chiba has found an easy way to make much money. Why should that fool have all the luck? (Greedily) I should be the one to have that turtle. (Slyly) I will have that turtle! Wait and see. (He crosses right and kneels beside **Chiba**.)

**Chiba** (To Obasan, joyfully): Look, Honorable Mother. I have many coins here — more than I could earn in a year by cutting wood. And they are all for you. My good friend the singing turtle has brought us this good fortune. Please, Honorable Mother, may the turtle stay with us?

**Obasan:** Of course, my son. The turtle may stay as long as it pleases him.

**Turtle** (Bowing): Thank you, Honorable Mother.

**Obasan:** Now, go to sleep, my sons. It is late. (**Chiba** and **Turtle** cross to mat, and lie down. **Obasan** kneels on pillow. **Taro** crosses to mat as if sleeping, then half-rises and looks slyly about.)

**Taro** (Aside, in hoarse whisper): I will have that turtle! Wait and see. (He tiptoes to side. **Stagehand** enters and gives him a stick, and bows and exits. **Taro** pokes **Turtle** with stick and pushes him out of house. Others do not wake.)

**Turtle:** Stop! Stop! What do you want?

**Taro:** Sing, turtle! Go into the town and sing, so everyone will give me coins (Pokes **Turtle,** who reluctantly crosses center. **Musicians** tap quick beats on wood block.)

**Merchants** and **Maidens** (Together): What is this noise in the middle of the night?

**Taro:** Gather around and hear the turtle sing. (Waving stick threateningly at **Turtle**) Go ahead — sing!

**Turtle:** Your brother treated me kindly, so I was happy to sing for him. You have been cruel to me. I will sing, but it will not

be the same song that I sang before. (**Turtle** *puckers lips.*
**Musicians** *play sad song on kazoo.*)

**Merchants** *and* **Maidens** (*Grimacing and holding ears*): How
sad! That song makes me want to cry. (*They wipe eyes as if
weeping.*)

**Taro** (*Angrily*): Turtle—you tricked me! No one will pay for
such a sad song. I'll make you sorry for what you did!
(*Threatens* **Turtle** *with stick, as* **Musicians** *play gong.*)

**Merchants:** Stop! Stop! Do not hit that turtle!

**Maidens:** Shame! Shame! Only a bad person would hit a
poor animal!

**Parasol Merchant:** You deserve to be given such treatment
yourself.

**Potter:** That's right. (*Loudly*) Give me a stick!

**Fan Merchant:** Give us sticks! (**Stagehands** *enter and
distribute sticks to* **Merchants** *and* **Maidens.** *All advance on*
**Taro,** *thumping sticks menacingly on stage.* **Taro** *backs down
left, then suddenly turns and runs offstage.* **Merchants** *and
**Maidens** *lift sticks and cheer. Then they return upstage to
places.*)

**Blue Kimonos:** Taro was gone. It was as if a dark cloud had
passed.

**White Kimonos:** Chiba and Obasan took the turtle to their
home again. The sun was smiling! (**Chiba** *and* **Obasan** *cross
to* **Turtle. Chiba** *pats* **Turtle,** *and* **Obasan** *takes his hand.
They smile.*)

**Blue Kimonos:** Good things happened to them from that
day on.

**White Kimonos:** And the turtle sang his sweetest song.
(**Merchants** *and* **Maidens** *surround* **Chiba, Obasan,** *and
**Turtle. Musicians** *play flute, and* **Turtle** *puckers, pretending
to sing. Curtain slowly closes.*)

Japanese Folktale
Adapted by *Claire Boiko*

Most plays begin with a list of **characters.** Who were the characters in this play? What the characters say to each other is the **dialog** of the play. Many characters in the play have dialog to speak. How do you know who is talking? The characters' names or titles are given before their parts of the dialog.

Some plays have **narrators.** Narrators may take part in the play's action. They are storytellers. They tell important facts that the characters cannot say.

The place where the play happens is the **setting.** The setting might be a forest, a palace, or a city neighborhood. What is the setting of the play you read? When a play is acted out, there is **scenery** on the stage. Large pieces of cardboard, wood, or cloth are painted. Buildings, trees, and other parts of the setting are shown.

When you read a play, you will notice words in parentheses ( ). These words are **stage directions.** They are not for the characters to say. They tell the characters how to move, act, or speak. Find some examples of stage directions in the play.

## *Practice*

**A.** Complete the sentences with words from this lesson. Write the sentences.

1. A story meant to be acted out is a _____.
2. People who act in the play are called the _____.
3. People who tell the story and sometimes act are called _____.
4. The place where the play happens is the _____.

**5.** _____ is put on the stage to show the setting.

**6.** Words the characters speak are called the _____.

**7.** Words that tell the characters how to move, act, or speak are called _____.

**B.** Chiba and Taro are two of the characters in this play. Write their names. Under each name write the words that describe that character.

| | | | |
|---|---|---|---|
| **8.** generous | **9.** lazy | **10.** sly | **11.** kind to animals |
| **12.** hard working | **13.** cruel to animals | **14.** greedy | |

## Apply

**C.** Here are some characters who could be in plays. Where could each play happen? Write a setting for each character.

| | | |
|---|---|---|
| **15.** a robot | **16.** a ball player | **17.** a chef |
| **18.** a repair person | **19.** an explorer | **20.** a rabbit |
| **21.** a doctor | **22.** the President | **23.** an elf |

# A BOOK TO READ

Title: **Encyclopedia Brown Carries On**
Author: Donald J. Sobol
Publisher: Four Winds Press

Have you ever wanted to be a super detective? Can you spot the clues to solve a mystery? It's never too soon to start training. Join the action with the great Encyclopedia Brown.

In this book each chapter is a separate mystery story. All the clues to solve the mysteries are there. Of course Encyclopedia Brown solves each case. If you can't think of a solution, don't worry. The answers are right in the back of the book. Now get out your Sherlock Holmes thinking cap. Match wits with Encyclopedia Brown.

# 3 UNIT TEST

● **Action Verbs**   pages 78–79

Write the letter of the word in each sentence that is an action verb.

1. <u>Judy</u> and <u>Linda</u> <u>built</u> a <u>campfire</u>.
   a        b     c       d

2. <u>Judy</u> <u>heated</u> <u>coffee</u> <u>over</u> it.
   a     b     c     d

3. <u>Linda</u> <u>fixed</u> a <u>pot</u> of <u>beans</u>.
   a     b    c     d

4. The <u>girls</u> <u>grilled</u> hot <u>dogs</u> and hamburgers.
    a    b   c     d

5. Later <u>they</u> <u>roasted</u> <u>some</u> <u>marshmallows</u>.
      a     b    c      d

● **Linking Verbs**   pages 80–81

Copy each  sentence. Draw two lines under the linking verbs.

6. My friend and I were apple pickers.
7. Each tree was full of apples.
8. Apples are a delicious treat.
9. I am the best worker.
10. This is the largest apple of all.

● **Helping Verbs**   pages 82–83

Copy each sentence. Draw two lines under the main verb and its helping verb. Then circle the helping verb.

11. We have received our parts for the play.
12. I am studying my lines now.
13. Mark has rehearsed his part.
14. Tara has learned her lines.
15. All week she was building the set.

## Verb Tenses   pages 84–86

Copy each sentence. Draw two lines under the verb. Then write *past, present,* or *future* to tell the tense of the verb.

**16.** I delivered newspapers yesterday.
**17.** Chico will wash the car.
**18.** Ben mows the lawn.
**19.** Martha painted the fence for her dad.
**20.** Sheila runs errands on her bike.

## Contractions   page 87

Write the sentences. Use a contraction for the words in parentheses ( ).

**21.** Ron _____ play hockey this afternoon.   (can not)
**22.** Ron _____ sick, but he sprained his ankle.   (is not)
**23.** Our team _____ played yet.   (has not)
**24.** We _____ want to lose this game.   (do not)
**25.** We _____ going to let the other team win.   (are not)

## Past Tense Verbs   pages 88–89

Use the past tense of the verb in parentheses ( ). Write the sentences.

**26.** After Maria spilled the water, Marty _____ the floor.   (mop)
**27.** Marty _____ his baby sister outside.   (carry)
**28.** Maria _____ as she played in the sandbox.   (hum)
**29.** Marty _____ her wet clothes on the clothesline.   (dry)
**30.** The clothes _____ in the strong wind.   (flap)

## Irregular Verbs   pages 90–93

Use the correct form of the verb in parentheses ( ). Write the sentences.

**31.** Last year we _____ to the mountains.   (went, gone)
**32.** The trip _____ with a long drive.   (began, begun)
**33.** Dad had _____ me a map.   (gave, given)
**34.** He _____ the driving while I gave directions.   (did, done)
**35.** In the car we all _____ songs.   (sang, sung)
**36.** At last we _____ to the ranch.   (came, come)
**37.** I _____ from the car to see my horse.   (ran, run)

## ● Guide Words    pages 96–97

The first two words are guide words. Which word would appear on that dictionary page?

1. float–flour    a. flop    b. forty    c. fled
2. smooth–snap    a. sniff    b. smash    c. smudge
3. balance–ballet    a. baggy    b. ballad    c. bench
4. fount–frame    a. flat    b. four    c. frost
5. plane–plastic    a. plank    b. pity    c. print

## ● Entry Words    pages 98–99

Read the dictionary entry and answer the questions.

> **dan·ger** [dān′jər] *n.* **1** Being exposed to harm, trouble, etc.: A fireman's life is full of *danger*. **2** Something that may cause harm: Smoking is a *danger* to health.

6. What is the entry word in the dictionary sample?
7. What is the respelling of the word?
8. What part of speech is the word?
9. How many definitions does it have?
10. What is the example sentence listed for the first definition?

## ● Pronunciation Key    pages 100–101

Match the respelling with the correct word. Write the word.

11. pēk.    peach    peel    peek
12. grāz    great    graze    gravy
13. fär    for    fair    far
14. grim    grime    grin    grim
15. luk    look    luck    Luke
16. fāth    father    fat    faith
17. lûrn    lurch    learn    loran
18. slō    slow    slue    slot
19. stāt    static    status    state
20. mach    match    mat    make

## Friendly Letters    pages 102–103

Copy each sentence. Write the correct answer in the space.

1. The _____ lists the letter writer's address and the date.
2. The _____ welcomes the person who receives the letter.
3. The _____ is the message of the letter.
4. The _____ is the end of the letter.
5. The _____ is the written name of the letter writer.

## Addressing an Envelope    pages 104–105

Copy these addresses correctly. Write them as you would on an envelope.

6. mr. tom parks
   72 cherry ave
   glendale wi 53209

7. miss ann coreno
   165 peach tree rd
   dayton oh 45419

8. mrs. alice kraus
   220 third st
   new york ny 10003

9. ms. joyce oates
   1949-59th st
   brooklyn ny 11204

## Writing and Editing an Invitation    pages 108–111

10. Write an invitation for a surprise party at your house. Make up the information you need. Then edit the invitation for capitalization and punctuation. Make sure you included all the necessary information.

## Reading a Play    pages 112–119

Copy each sentence. Write the correct answer in the space.

1. A story meant to be acted out is a _____.
2. People who act in a play are _____.
3. Words the characters speak are called the _____.
4. People who tell the story but may not act are _____.
5. The place where the play happens is the _____.
6. Words that tell the characters how to move, act, or speak are called _____.

# LANGUAGE
## Learning About Paragraphs

# COMPOSITION
## Writing Directions

# STUDY SKILLS
## Using Parts of Books

# LITERATURE
## Reading a Story

Have you ever made a collage?

The children in the picture on the opposite page are putting together a collage. They are careful to leave out pictures that do not belong. All the pieces of the collage will make sense together. What subject do all the pictures show? Make up sentences about some of the pictures. Are your sentences all about the same subject?

When you write, you have a subject to tell about. Like the children making the collage, you write only the sentences that are about your subject.

In this unit you will learn how to write sentences that make sense together. You will use this skill to tell about something you know how to do. You will also learn about using parts of books. You will read an exciting adventure story.

# LANGUAGE

## Lesson 1: Understanding Paragraphs

Writers express their ideas in sentences. Sometimes they need more than one sentence to explain an idea. Read this example. How many sentences are there?

Members of the Navajo tribe have varied jobs. Many are farmers or sheep ranchers. Some are engineers, miners, and teachers. Other Navajo workers weave wool blankets and make turquoise jewelry.

### Think and Discuss

A group of sentences that all tell about the same idea is called a **paragraph.** A paragraph can have few sentences or many. To form a good paragraph, the sentences must be related. They must all tell about one main idea. Read the paragraph about Navajo workers again. What is the main idea of the paragraph?

Notice that the first line of the paragraph is indented, or set in. The other lines begin at the left margin.

> ● A **paragraph** is a group of sentences that tell about one main idea.

## Practice

**A.** Decide which groups of sentences would make good paragraphs. Write them using correct paragraph form.

1. The Navajo tribe is the largest tribe of Indians in the United States today. There are 140,000 members of the Navajo tribe. Many of them live on the Navajo reservation in Arizona.

2. The early Navajo people wore clothes made from woven grass. You can weave baskets from grass also. Pictures show styles of Navajo jewelry.

3. The Navajo house is called a hogan. Today the hogan is built on top of the ground. It has six sides. Its flat roof is made of logs. Soil is heaped on top of the logs and shaped into a small hill.

4. The Navajo tribe owns several businesses. There are coal mines on the Navajo reservation. Coal is an important resource. There are coal mines in Ohio. The Navajos also own an electronics business and a lumber mill.

5. Many Navajo women are fine weavers. Some spin their own yarn. They use wool that comes from sheep in tribal herds. They use a loom that is upright. They weave beautiful rugs and blankets.

**B. 6.** Look at the paragraphs you wrote for Practice A. Write the main idea of each one.

## Apply

**C. 7.** Find a good paragraph in your science or social studies book. Copy the paragraph. Then write its main idea.

# Lesson 2: Using Topic Sentences

Read this paragraph. What is the main idea?

Americans eat a lot of popcorn. In fact, one book says they eat 500 million pounds each year! Much of this is popped and eaten at home. Americans also enjoy popcorn at shows, ball games, and fairs. How much popcorn do you think you eat each year?

## Think and Discuss

What is the main idea of the paragraph? Can you find a sentence that states the main idea? Read the first sentence again. That sentence tells what the paragraph is about. It is called the **topic sentence.**

Now read this paragraph. Find the topic sentence.

Native Americans tell a story about popcorn. They say a magic demon lives inside each kernel of popcorn. When the demon's house is heated, the demon gets popping mad. It explodes!

Which sentence tells what the paragraph is about? Where does it come in the paragraph? The topic sentence is usually the first sentence of the paragraph.

> • The **topic sentence** expresses the main idea of the paragraph.

## Practice

**A.** Read each topic sentence. Write the statement that best tells what the paragraph will be about.

1. The people of Milwaukee and Minneapolis eat more popcorn than any other people in the United States.

a. what to see in Milwaukee and Minneapolis
b. how much popcorn people from Milwaukee and Minneapolis eat
c. the places where popcorn comes from

2. There are many ways to eat popcorn.

   a. craft projects to do with popcorn
   b. when Native Americans ate popcorn
   c. ways to fix popcorn for eating

3. Early American colonists ate popcorn for breakfast.

   a. where the colonists came from
   b. what the colonists' houses looked like
   c. when colonists served popcorn

4. Have you ever made a popcorn necklace?

   a. how to make popcorn pictures
   b. directions for making necklaces out of popcorn
   c. diamonds make beautiful necklaces

## *Apply*

B. Read these groups of sentences. Add a good topic sentence for each. Then write the complete paragraph.

5. Pour some oil into a pan. Turn on the stove. When the oil is hot, put some popcorn in the pan. Cover the pan and shake it gently. When the popping stops, enjoy your popcorn treat!

6. Sometimes Barry eats popcorn at home. Sometimes he eats it at the movies. He enjoys it at a fair, and he also eats popcorn at a ball game.

7. The story tells of a hot, dry summer. The corn in the fields got so hot it began to pop. Soon the ground was covered with popcorn. People thought it was snowing. They put on heavy clothes and grabbed their snow shovels.

# Lesson 3: Using Details in Paragraphs

A good topic sentence tells the main idea of a paragraph. A paragraph must have other sentences as well. These other sentences add information. They give details that tell more about the topic sentence.

## Think and Discuss

Read the paragraph. Look for sentences that give details.

It is interesting to watch weavers work. Their hands are quick and sure. They twist wool fiber into yarn. Then they skillfully weave the yarn into cloth.

What is the topic sentence of the paragraph? The sentences that follow the topic sentence give more information about the topic. Read the three detail sentences.

Details explain, expand, or develop the topic sentence of a paragraph. They help the reader understand more about the main idea.

## Practice

**A.** Copy each topic sentence. Under each write the sentences that give details about that topic sentence.

**1.** Jennie Thomas makes patchwork quilts.

   **a.** Jennie stitches for many hours.
   **b.** She cooks dinner.
   **c.** Most of the time Jennie sews her quilts alone.
   **d.** She will sell her quilts at the county fair.

**2.** Mitchell is a woodworker.

    **a.** He makes chairs, cabinets, and toys.
    **b.** His favorite baseball player is Mickey Mantle.
    **c.** He made a wooden cradle for a baby too.
    **d.** Mitchell works in a large studio.

**3.** I'd like to try a craft.

    **a.** Maybe I'll make a bowl out of clay.
    **b.** I think I'll take a walk.
    **c.** Perhaps I will try knitting a sweater.
    **d.** I might even take up wood carving.

## Apply

**B. 4.–8.** Copy the topic sentence. Then write five details that tell more about the topic sentence.

There are many things to see and do at a country fair.

## A Challenge

Write a paragraph about something you have made. It can be a craft, an art project, a special food, or, perhaps, a piece of clothing. Write a topic sentence to tell what the paragraph is about. Then add sentences that give details. Tell about the materials you used, how you made it, and what it looked like when you were finished.

# Lesson 4: Ordering Sentences in Paragraphs

Sentences in a paragraph must be in the right order. If they are not, the paragraph will not make sense. Read this paragraph.

The white-tailed deer change their feeding habits with the seasons. In summer they feed on the new growth of bushes, trees, and forest plants. In autumn the beechnuts and acorns help fatten them for winter. When winter comes food is scarce. Then the deer eat all the twigs of trees and shrubs within their reach. Finally spring comes. Early spring is hardest of all for the hungry deer. Only a few twigs and nuts are left until new growth appears.

## Think and Discuss

What is the topic sentence of the paragraph? In this paragraph the seasons help you know the right order. Can you find other words that show time order? What would be wrong with putting the sixth sentence before the third sentence? Why must the fifth sentence follow right after the fourth?

The words *then* and *finally* show correct order. Other words such as *first, second, third, next,* and *last* can also be used to show correct order.

## Practice

**A.** In each paragraph the topic sentence comes first. One of the other sentences is out of order. Rewrite the paragraphs. Put the sentences in the right order.

1. Some deer grow new antlers each year. In spring the antlers begin to grow. During the winter months the old, hard antlers fall off. By fall the antlers are hardened.

**2.** Raccoons in cold areas prepare for winter. In the fall they eat extra food. The food helps keep them alive through the winter until spring. Then winter comes.

## *Apply*

**B.** Read each group of sentences. Decide what order they should be in. Write a paragraph with the sentences in order. Circle the words that give clues about the correct order of the sentences.

**3.** Finally the beaver bites into the trunk.
Beavers use their front teeth to cut down trees.
First the beaver stands on its hind legs.
Then it turns its head sideways.
Next the beaver puts its front paws on the trunk.

**4.** Then it crawls out of the skin.
This loosens the skin.
Some snakes shed their skins.
First the snake rubs its head on a rough surface.
The empty skin is left inside out.

# HOW OUR LANGUAGE GROWS

Many words in our language used to have different meanings. As years passed, the meanings of some words changed. *Brave* meant "mean." What does it mean today? *Villain* meant "farm worker." What does it mean today?

Read what each word used to mean. Write what it means today.

1. *nice* meant "foolish"
2. *pretty* meant "sly"
3. *stupid* meant "amazed"
4. *silly* meant "blessed"
5. *careful* meant "nervous"
6. *fond* meant "foolish"

# Lesson 5: Keeping to the Topic

Look at the picture. Find the part that does not belong.

One dozen oranges please.

## Think and Discuss

If you think the person buying oranges does not belong, you are right. The picture is about a clothing store. A person buying oranges does not fit.

In the same way, some sentences in a paragraph may not belong. They may not fit the topic of the paragraph.

Read this paragraph. Can you find the sentence that does not belong?

Hats are worn for many reasons. People wear hats for warmth. Wear a costume with a hat to the party. Some hats are worn for protection. Others are worn for decoration.

What is the main idea of the paragraph? What is the topic sentence? Three sentences give details about the topic sentence. Read them. Which sentence does not keep to the topic?

Every sentence in a paragraph should keep to the topic. The topic sentence states the main idea. Every other sentence should give details about it. A single sentence that does not keep to the topic weakens the paragraph.

# Practice

**A.** For each paragraph write the sentence that does not keep to the topic.

1.     Some men wear tall hats for a dress party. They are called stovepipe hats. Some men wear suits called tuxedos. That is because the top of the hat is shaped like a stovepipe.

2.     Americans spend billions of dollars a year on sneakers. In 1975, 100 million pairs were sold. Jacob wears desert boots. That's a lot of sneakers.

3.     Here is an interesting saying about hats. People say, "If it isn't true, I'll eat my hat." I like to eat potato chips. This means the person believes something is true without a doubt.

4.     The pocket has a long history. In the 1700's small bags were attached to a belt. This belt was tied around the waist. I keep gum, paper clips, and change in my pockets. Later, pockets were sewn into clothes.

5.     Shoes are an important part of our clothing. They have been worn for hundreds of years. A hundred years is a century. Long ago, people wore shoes to protect their feet from stones, hot sand, or cold weather. People even told stories about magic shoes.

# Apply

**B. 6.–10.** Pick one of these topic sentences. Write five detail sentences that tell more about it. Be sure all your sentences keep to the topic.

> My sneakers are terrific.
> I have a favorite thing to wear.
> Once I saw a very unusual hat.

# LANGUAGE REVIEW

**Paragraphs**   pages 126–127

Read these paragraphs and the items that follow. Write the item that gives the main idea of each paragraph.

**1.**   A good breakfast is important. It gives you energy all morning long. Your body changes the foods you eat to energy you can use. You need energy all day to run, play, and think.

   a. What to do all morning
   b. What to eat at breakfast
   c. Why a good breakfast is important

**2.**   Different exercises make your muscles strong. Sit-ups help your stomach muscles. Running in place makes your leg muscles stonger. Push-ups are good for the muscles in your back, chest, and arms.

   a. How to run faster
   b. Exercises for strong muscles
   c. The muscles in your legs

**3.**   Your eyes are amazing tools, but you must take care of them properly. Always read in good light. Get plenty of sleep at night. If you have trouble seeing near or far, have your eyes checked.

   a. Amazing tools
   b. Going to the eye doctor
   c. Taking care of your eyes

**Topic Sentences**   pages 128–129

Write the topic sentence of each paragraph.

**4.**   Dogs have been "man's best friend" for thousands of years. Very old cave paintings show men and dogs together. Later dogs guarded homes and herds. Today dogs help people in many ways.

**5.**    Why does a dog have a tail? A tail may help a dog keep its balance. When dogs hunted in packs, they signaled each other with their tails. Today we know why a dog has a tail — to wag it!

## Supporting Details    pages 130–131

Read the topic sentence. Decide which sentences give good supporting details. Rewrite the topic sentence and the detail sentences in paragraph form.

Topic Sentence: Pterodactyls were flying reptiles.

**6.** Some of these reptiles were named "flying dragons."
**7.** Their wings were paper-thin and very light.
**8.** Bats are winged mammals, not reptiles.
**9.** The wings of some pterodactyls were ten feet long.

## Ordering Sentences in Paragraphs    pages 132–133

Put these sentences into a paragraph. Write them in the correct order.

**10.** Second  measure where your eyes, nose, and mouth are.
**11.** Would you like to learn how to make a mask?
**12.** Last decorate your mask with paper, paint, and cloth.
**13.** First get a paper bag that fits over your head.
**14.** Next cut holes so that you can see and talk.

## Keeping to the Topic    pages 134–135

**15.** Copy this paragraph. Underline the topic sentence. Leave out the sentence that does not keep to the topic.

      Last week my father and I went on a fishing trip. We traveled by canoe. We caught trout and bass. I caught more fish than my father! Another hobby of mine is coin collecting.

## Applying Paragraphs

**16.** Write a paragraph about one of these topics. First write a topic sentence. Add other sentences that give details.

      My Favorite Animal    How To Be a Friend    If I Had One Wish

# STUDY SKILLS

## *Lesson 6: Using a Title Page and a Table of Contents*

You use many kinds of books every day. You can use them more easily if you know how they are organized. Most books have several parts. Each part contains special information.

### *Think and Discuss*

Two important parts are found at the front of most books.

The **title page** is usually the first printed page of a book. It tells the title of the book. It gives the name of the author. The title page also tells the name of the publishing company and where the publisher is located.

The **table of contents** comes after the title page. It lists the titles of the chapters or units in the book. It tells the page numbers on which they begin. Everything is listed in the order in which it appears.

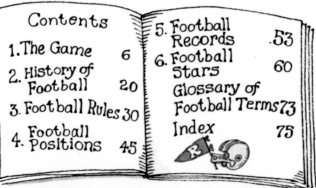

Contents

1. The Game — 6
2. History of Football — 20
3. Football Rules — 30
4. Football Positions — 45
5. Football Records — 53
6. Football Stars — 60
Glossary of Football Terms — 73
Index — 75

Look again at the title page and table of contents on the opposite page. What is the title of the book? What is the name of the publisher? How many chapters does the book contain? What are some subjects you can learn about by reading this book?

## Practice

A. Tell where the information would be found. Write *title page* or *table of contents.*

1. the author's name
2. the number of chapters in the book
3. the title of the book
4. what company publishes the book
5. on what page a certain chapter begins
6. the titles of each chapter or unit

B. Use the title page and table of contents on page 138 to answer these questions. Use complete sentences.

7. Who is the author of the book?
8. What is the title of the book?
9. On what page does Chapter 4 begin?
10. What is the title of the chapter that begins on page 53?
11. What would be the best chapter to read to find out how football began?

## Apply

C. Use the title page and the table of contents from this textbook. Answer the questions in complete sentences.

12. What is the title of this book?
13. Who is the publisher?
14. How many units are in this book?
15. On what page does Unit Five begin?

# Lesson 7: Using a Glossary and an Index

Every book has a title page. Most books have a table of contents. Where are these found? Textbooks, biographies, and other nonfiction books often have two other important parts. They are found in the back of the book.

## Think and Discuss

A **glossary** is like a small dictionary. It gives definitions of special words used in a book. Words are listed in alphabetical order. Look at the words from a glossary.

> **amphibian**—a class of cold-blooded animals that can live on land or in water.
>
> **extinct**—something that is no longer in existence, like a dinosaur.
>
> **lizard**—a kind of reptile, usually with a small body, four legs, and a long tail.
>
> **reptile**—any one of a group of cold-blooded animals that crawl.
>
> **scorpion**—a small animal, related to the spider, having a long curved tail with a poisonous sting.

What is the definition of *amphibian?* In what kind of book might this glossary be found?

Age of Fishes, 15, 82–86
Algae, 17, 19
Allosaurus, 55
Amphibian, prehistoric, 92
Armored animal,
    amphibian, 94, 200
    dinosaur, 59
    mammal, 50–68, 210, 225

An **index** is a list of all the topics in a book. It is arranged in alphabetical order. The index lists the page numbers on which each topic appears. Part of an index is shown on this page. If you want to find facts about amphibians, you would look under the main topic *Amphibian* in the index. What kinds of amphibians can you read about in this book?

## Practice

**A.** Use the glossary and index on page 140 to answer these questions.

1. What does a lizard look like?
2. What is the definition of *extinct*?
3. What is a small animal related to the spider?
4. What is the first main topic in the index?
5. On what page is information about allosaurus found?
6. On what page is information about prehistoric amphibians found?
7. What are the kinds of animals listed under armored animal?
8. On how many pages will you find information about algae?

## Apply

**B.** Find these topics in the index of this textbook. Write the topic and the page numbers on which the topic can be found.

9. atlas
10. card catalog
11. synonyms
12. nouns
13. thesaurus
14. telephone directory

# Lesson 8: Using an Encyclopedia

Where could you look to find information about these subjects?

- the science of astronomy
- the country of Ireland
- the life of Joe Lewis

## Think and Discuss

A good place to look for information on these and many other subjects is an **encyclopedia.** An encyclopedia is usually a set of books. Each book is called a volume. The volumes are arranged in alphabetical order.

The narrow back, or spine, of each book has a letter or letters. These show the beginning letter of subjects included in that volume. In which volume would you find subjects beginning with *N* and *O*? In which volume would you find the subject *Kenya*? In which volume would the subject *snakes* be listed?

Suppose you are looking for the name of a famous person. You must look under the first letter of the person's last name. Where would you find information on the life of Wilma Rudolph? Look in the volume that has subjects beginning with the letter *R*. What volume number is that?

Look back at the three subjects listed at the beginning of the lesson. In which volume would you look to find each one?

## Practice

A. Look at the encyclopedia on the opposite page. Write the number of the volume in which you would look for each subject.

1. armadillo
2. Molly Pitcher
3. whale
4. kindergarten
5. Paul Revere
6. United States
7. climate
8. Frankenstein
9. Harriet Tubman
10. Roanoke Island

B. Write the one word you would use to look up the following information in an encyclopedia.

11. playing baseball
12. growing corn
13. the size of the moon
14. fishing for trout
15. different kinds of boats
16. where Iowa is located
17. the life of Laura Ingalls Wilder
18. the food a caribou eats
19. the inventions of Benjamin Franklin
20. the climate of Spain

## Apply

C. Look at an encyclopedia in your school or public library. Answer these questions.

21. What is the title of the encyclopedia?
22. How many volumes does it have?
23. Does it have an index?
24. What is the name of the publisher?
25. What is the number of the volume in which you would find the subject *transportation?*

# COMPOSITION

## *Lesson 9: Giving Directions*

What would happen if you followed these directions to make an ice cream cone?

1. Scoop the cone.
2. Put the ice cream in the freezer.
3. Get a scoop and cone.

### *Think and Discuss*

The steps in the directions you read are not in order. They are not clear or complete. It would be difficult to follow such directions.

Now read these steps for making an ice cream cone.

1. Take ice cream out of the freezer.
2. Get a scoop and a cone.
3. Open the carton of ice cream.
4. Scoop a ball of ice cream from the carton.
5. Gently but firmly place the ball on the cone.
6. Put the ice cream back in the freezer.

What information is given first? Are the steps in order? Does each sentence tell one step of the directions?

---

**How to Give Directions**
1. **State information simply and clearly.**
2. **Give each step in the right order. Numbering each step will help.**
3. **Mention needed materials, tools, and actions in each step.**

---

## Practice

**A.** Add the missing steps to the directions. Write all the directions in the correct order.

**1.** Pour water into a pan until the pan is half full.

**2.**

**3.** Place the egg gently in the pan of water.

**4.** Put the pan on a burner and turn the burner on.

**5.**

**6.**

- *Missing Steps:*  Boil the egg for five minutes.
  Take out an egg.
  Use a large spoon to take the egg out of the water.

**B.** Rewrite the directions in the correct order.

**7.** Open a box of strawberry pudding mix and pour it into a pan.

**8.** Use an eggbeater to beat the pudding mix and milk for two minutes.

**9.** Measure 2 cups of milk.

**10.** Add the milk to the strawberry pudding mix in the pan.

**11.** Pour the pudding into small serving dishes.

## Apply

**C. 12.** Write directions for making a favorite sandwich, scrambled eggs, cereal, or another kind of food. Remember to follow the suggestions on page 144.

# Lesson 10: Writing a Direction Paragraph

Chen wanted to tell his class how to make a special kind of book called a "zigzag" book. Read his directions.

It is fun to make a zigzag book. First get a piece of white construction paper. Use scissors to cut a long strip 4 inches high from the paper. Next fold the strip back and forth like a fan. Finally draw a picture or write words on each section or page.

How are these directions different from the directions you read in Lesson 9?

## Think and Discuss

Chen wrote his directions in a paragraph. The first sentence is the topic sentence. It tells what the directions are for. The other sentences give details about how to complete the book.

The steps in a direction paragraph are not numbered. Instead, words are used to show correct order. What words did Chen use to show order?

---

**How to Write a Direction Paragraph**

1. **Write a topic sentence. This tells what the directions are for.**
2. **Add detail sentences to tell the steps in the directions. Use words such as *first, second, third, next,* and *last* or *finally* to show the correct order.**
3. **Mention needed materials, tools, and actions in each step.**
4. **State information simply and clearly.**
5. **Keep to the topic. Do not include unnecessary information.**

---

## Practice

**A.** Put the sentences in the correct order. Write the paragraph. Then underline the words that show order.

Second get a long piece of paper a bit narrower than the rods. A scroll is a kind of old-fashioned book that is easy to make. Last tie the scroll with a ribbon or a piece of string. First find two rods of wood like round rhythm sticks. Third glue the top of the paper to one rod and the bottom to the other rod and let the glue dry. Then draw pictures or write a message on the scroll and roll it up.

## Apply

**B.** Choose one of these topics, or think of one of your own. Write a direction paragraph.

How to Sharpen a Pencil
How to Make a Mud Pie
How to Make a Fried Egg
How to Blow Up a Balloon
How to Make a Paper Airplane
How to Make an Ice Cream Sundae

### To Memorize

Behold, nothing surpasses books.

*Unknown Egyptian author,*
*written about 2150* B.C.

The word *surpass* means to go beyond or be better than. What did the author think about books? Do you agree?

# Lesson 11: Editing a Direction Paragraph

Read the directions Sara wrote for making a feeder for winter birds.

> Make a peanut feeder so that birds can eat all winter. ~~They will find their own food in the spring.~~ Get a piece of thin wire about 20 inches long. You will also need unshelled peanuts. ^First^ Bend the bottom end of the wire so that the peanuts won't fall off. ^Then^ Poke the wire through each peanut to string them on the wire. Bend the top end of the wire into a small loop. ^Finally^ Hang the finished peanut feeder on a nail or tree branch.

When Sara checked her direction paragraph, what mistakes did she find?

## Think and Discuss

What words did Sara add to show the order of the steps? Notice what happens when words are added at the beginning of a sentence. The words *bend, poke,* and *hang* are no longer the first words of sentences. Sara uses this editing mark / to show they should now be small, or lowercase, letters. Why did Sara take away the second sentence?

## Practice

**A.** Copy Sara's direction paragraph. Make all the additions and corrections shown.

## Apply

**B.** Read the direction paragraph you wrote in Lesson 10. Edit your direction paragraph. Then copy it neatly.

# MECHANICS PRACTICE

## Writing Days, Months, and Holidays

- Begin the name of a day of the week with a capital letter.
- Begin the name of a month with a capital letter.
- Begin each important word in the name of a holiday or special day with a capital letter.
- Use a period after an abbreviation of a day or month.

**A.** Write these days, months, and holidays correctly.

| | | | |
|---|---|---|---|
| **1.** tuesday | **2.** nov | **3.** oct | **4.** memorial day |
| **5.** april | **6.** may | **7.** sun | **8.** halloween |
| **9.** friday | **10.** aug | **11.** father's day | **12.** new year's day |
| **13.** thurs | **14.** jan | **15.** labor day | |

**B.** Write these sentences correctly.

**16.** My birthday is in june.

**17.** People celebrate flag day right after my birthday.

**18.** My sister's birthday is thursday, nov 27.

**19.** That is the same day as thanksgiving this year.

**20.** Send these cards on monday, april 1.

**C.** **21.–25.** Listen while your teacher reads some sentences. Write the sentences using capital letters correctly.

# LITERATURE

## Lesson 12: Reading an Adventure Story

In newspapers and magazines you often read about people who have exciting adventures. They may climb mountains. They may sail across the sea in small sailboats. They may win marathon races.

### Think and Discuss

Here is part of an adventure story about Wesley Paul. The author has written the story to make it seem as if Wesley Paul is telling it. As you read, find out about the main character and the setting.

### Wesley Paul, Marathon Runner
*by Julianna A. Fogel*

My name is Wesley Paul. I'm nine years old. When I was three, my dad started jogging to lose weight, and he took me along. I've been running ever since.

One of my most exciting races was the New York City Marathon the year I was eight. I ran that marathon in 3 hours, 31 seconds. That meant I broke the national record for eight-year-olds by 15 whole minutes.

Before long, I began thinking about running a marathon even faster. During the whole next year I worked to build up my speed and strength. I ran in a lot of shorter races and trained hard. All my training was aimed at a new goal: to finish a marathon in under 3 hours.

When September finally came, I had been looking forward

to the New York City Marathon for weeks. I guess that's why I was so nervous. The race wasn't supposed to begin until 10:30 in the morning, but I made sure we were there by 7:00.

Big city . . . big race . . . big butterflies! The worst part of a marathon is standing around waiting. It seemed like forever before the starting cannon went off.

BOOM! I heard something else that sounded like a huge roar, but it was just the crowd cheering. We started up slowly. There were so many runners I could hardly move. After about 2 miles, the runners finally began to spread out. I didn't feel so crowded, and running was easier.

The next 10 miles clicked off fast. I had lots of time to think. I thought about music and made up tunes and hummed them. I worked math problems in my head; I took the number of miles I had run and multiplied it by $6\frac{1}{2}$, to keep track of how much time should have passed.

By the 15-mile mark, I was hot and thirsty. My legs had begun to feel sore, as if some invisible hammer were hitting them. I couldn't imagine running 11 more miles.

Some boy yelled, "Hey, kid! What are you doing in this race? You'll never make it. Why don't you just quit now?"

He did me a real favor. He made me more determined than ever to break 3 hours.

At the 25-mile mark, I heard the crowd yelling. This time it was encouragement: "C'mon! You can do it! Go!"

I told myself, "Wesley, you're almost finished. Run!"

Soon I could see the big clock at the finish line. When I got close enough to read what it said, I almost couldn't believe it. Two hours, 59 minutes.

As I crossed the finish line, somebody rushed up to me, handed me a medal, and said, "Good job!"

All the months of training had paid off. In spite of the heat, I had broken 3 hours. It felt wonderful to have reached that goal.

In an adventure story the author writes about people who do unusual or exciting things. What was Wesley Paul's adventure? An adventure story has a lot of action. The **plot** of the story is the development of the action. Usually the plot begins with a problem or challenge. What was the challenge Wesley Paul faced? During the story the main character tries to solve the problem or meet the challenge. The plot ends with a conclusion. Usually the problem is solved or the challenge is met. Did Wesley Paul meet his challenge?

## *Practice*

**A.** Complete each statement about the story.

**1.** The main character of the story is _____.
**2.** A word you could use to describe the main character is

_____.

**3.** The setting of the story is _____.

**4.** The problem or challenge that the main character faces
is _____.

**5.** At the conclusion of the story, the main character _____.

## *Apply*

**B.** Think of an adventure story you read recently or
a television adventure show you saw. Use that story
or show to answer these questions in full sentences.

**6.** Who was the main character in the adventure?

**7.** What was the setting of the story or show?

**8.** How would you describe the main character?

**9.** What was the challenge the character faced?

**10.** How did he or she solve the problem?

## A BOOK TO READ

Title: **Ed Emberley's Great Thumbprint Drawing Book**
Author: Ed Emberley
Publisher: Little, Brown

One important time to follow directions is when you are making
something. Here is a book that gives directions for making hundreds
of drawings—all beginning with a thumbprint. Remember, there
are more than 4 billion thumbs in the world. No two thumbprints
are exactly alike. You can make lots of things very personally yours
with your thumbprint. Greeting cards, stationery, bulletin boards,
masks, dolls, even covers and pages of reports can be illustrated
with some of the many pictures shown in this book.

*Ed Emberley's Great Thumbprint Drawing Book* is part of a
series of drawing books by Ed Emberley. Look for others in your
library.

# 4 UNIT TEST

● **Paragraphs**   pages 126–127

Read each passage. Write the letter of the sentence that best states the main idea.

**1.**    The first underground train in the United States opened in 1904. It was in New York City. The train system was called the subway.

   **a.** New York had the first underground train in the United States.
   **b.** The subway is an underground train.
   **c.** New York City has a train.
   **d.** In 1904 something opened in New York City.

**2.**    A male cardinal is a beautiful red bird. I like the color green. John wears black boots to school.

   **a.** A male cardinal is red.
   **b.** Green is a nice color.
   **c.** John wears black boots.
   **d.** There is no main idea because the group of sentences is not a paragraph.

● **Topic Sentences**   pages 128–129

Copy the paragraphs. Underline the topic sentences.

**3.**    George Washington liked to count things. He counted how many bushels of wheat and corn he raised in one year. He counted how many seeds were in a pound of grass. He counted other things too.

**4.**    There are many kinds of tropical fish in this fish tank. The ones with the glowing stripes are called neon tetras. The little ones with the big colorful tails are male guppies. The black ones are mollies.

● **Supporting Details**   pages 130–131

Copy the topic sentence and the detail sentences that tell about it.

   **5.** On August 17, 1974, a young girl from Egypt swam the English Channel.

   It took her 12 hours and 30 minutes.
   The girl was just under 14 years old.
   Egypt is in Africa.
   She became the youngest person to swim the Channel.

● **Ordering Sentences in Paragraphs**   pages 132–133

Write the paragraph in the correct order. Circle the words that give clues about the correct order of the sentences.

   **6.** Carl made fingerprints. Last he looked at his fingerprint through a magnifying glass. First he got some paper and an ink pad. Then he stamped his finger on the paper. Second he pressed his finger on the pad.

● **Keeping to the Topic**   pages 134–135

Copy the paragraph. Leave out the sentence that does not belong. Draw one line under the topic sentence. Draw two lines under each detail sentence.

   **7.** Helicopters can fly in many different ways. They can move straight up or down. They can fly sideways and backwards. I would like to fly in a helicopter. Helicopters are even able to hover in one place.

● **Title Page and Table of Contents**   pages 138–139

Read the title page of the book. Answer the questions.

**1.** What is the title of the book?
**2.** Who is the author?
**3.** Who is the publisher?
**4.** Where is the publisher located?

```
COOKIES FOR KIDS

by Lena May

The Cookie Press
New York City
```

Read the table of contents. Answer the questions.

CONTENTS

5. What is the title of Chapter 3?
6. On what page does Chapter 2 begin?
7. What is Chapter 4 about?
8. On what page does it begin?
9. Might a recipe for crispy oatmeal cookies appear in this book?

**Glossary and Index**   pages 140–141

Read each statement. Write whether the statement is *true* or *false.*

10. A glossary is like a small dictionary.
11. An index lists the page numbers of topics found in the book.
12. An index lists topics in alphabetical order.
13. A glossary gives the definitions of special words used in the book.
14. An index is found in the front of a book.

**The Encyclopedia**   pages 142–143

Write the volume number of the encyclopedia where each subject can be found.

15. infantry
18. metal
21. dinosaur
16. Uruguay
19. education
22. zebra
17. beetle
20. Betsy Ross
23. George Catlin

**24.** Burma    **25.** careers    **26.** newspaper

**27.** Saturn    **28.** Asia    **29.** Woodrow Wilson

● **Giving Directions**   pages 144–145

**1.** Write these directions in order.

It's fun to write letters.
Fold it neatly and stuff it in an envelope.
Collect some writing paper, an envelope, a pen, and a stamp.
Write a long, interesting letter.
Mail the letter.
Address the envelope and stick a stamp on it.

● **Writing and Editing a Direction Paragraph**   pages 146–149

**2.** Write a paragraph giving directions for making one of these things: a paper airplane; a snow angel; a bookmark; a valentine; a face on a pumpkin.

Write your sentences in correct order. Use words to show correct order. Then edit your paragraph.

● **Reading an Adventure Story**   pages 150–153

Read this story and answer the questions that follow it.

One cold, winter morning Maria Hilton discovered a small package on the sidewalk near her house. She picked up the package and looked inside. It contained six thousand dollars.

Maria thought about what to do with the money. She decided to take it to the police. That afternoon she walked to the police station and turned in the money.

A week later, Maria received a letter from the Biggs Products Company. In it was two hundred dollars in reward money for returning the lost package.

**1.** Who is the main character in the story?
**2.** What is the setting?
**3.** What is the problem faced by the main character?
**4.** Does the main character solve the problem?
**5.** Who might be another character in this story?

# MAINTENANCE and REVIEW

## Complete Subject and Predicate    pages 10–11

Copy each sentence. Draw one line under the complete subject.
Draw two lines under the complete predicate.

1. Tara wrote a letter.
2. Her mother helped her.
3. They drove downtown.
4. Tara mailed the letter.
5. A machine sorted mail.
6. A postal worker bagged it.
7. The carrier delivered it.
8. Tara's friend wrote back.

## Proper Nouns and Abbreviations    pages 42–47

Write the sentences correctly.

9. My doctor, dr suarez, works on east allen road.
10. She came here from miami, florida.
11. She will travel from the united states to japan.
12. Her brother, mr. suarez, teaches on bates street.
13. Have you met sen d v tarkington?
14. He is moving to washington from kansas.

## Possessive Nouns    pages 48–51

Write a possessive noun for each group of words.

15. the shoes of the dancer
16. the paints of the artist
17. the picks of the workers
18. the drill of the dentist
19. the plants of the florist
20. the files of the clerk

## Verbs    pages 78–81

Write each sentence. Draw two lines under the verb. Then write
*action* or *linking* to tell the kind of verb.

21. Yesterday I received a new puppy.
22. My puppy's name is Chester.

**23.** Chester chased the kitten into the house.

**24.** Now Chester and the kitten are friends.

## Helping Verbs    pages 82–83

Write each sentence. Draw two lines under the main verb and its helping verb. Then circle the helping verb.

**25.** Michelle has beaten Gretchen in the relay race.

**26.** Louisa is passing the baton to Theresa.

**27.** The sixth grade team was racing against us.

**28.** I am jumping in fifteen minutes.

## Verb Tenses    pages 84–86

Write each sentence. Draw two lines under the verb. Then write *past, present,* or *future* to tell the tense of the verbs.

**29.** Anthony studies dolphins and whales.

**30.** Last night he painted an underwater picture.

**31.** He enjoys the exhibits at the city aquarium.

**32.** He will go there again early next week.

## Irregular Verbs    pages 90–93

Choose the correct verb. Write the sentences.

**33.** She has (went, gone).          **34.** Al (give, gave) it to me.

**35.** Pam has (did, done) it.        **36.** The telephone (rang, rung).

**37.** Ben (went, gone) inside.       **38.** They have (come, came) here.

**39.** Ann (sang, sung) happily.      **40.** Rover has (ran, run) away.

## Paragraphs    pages 126–127

Write this group of sentences in correct paragraph form. Begin with the topic sentence. Leave out the sentence which does not keep to the topic.

**41.** They used the stars to find their way. The Vikings were fine sailors. My family has a sailboat. Viking ships were well built. With them, the Vikings sailed the North Atlantic.

# LANGUAGE
## Learning About Adjectives and Adverbs

# COMPOSITION
## Writing Descriptive Paragraphs

# STUDY SKILLS
## Building Vocabulary

# LITERATURE
## Reading Poetry and Tall Tales

Artists make pictures. They use chalk or pencil, oil paint, or water colors. They show you the world as they see it.

Writers make pictures also. They do it in a different way. What do writers use to describe their world?

Think about a flower. The picture on page 160 shows a flower. It shows its color and size.

How would a writer describe the flower with words? The writer might talk about one flower or a large, pink flower or a sweet flower bowing gracefully in the breeze. Words such as *one, large, pink, sweet,* and *gracefully* help make word pictures about flowers. What words can you use to tell about flowers?

Talk about the other pictures on page 160. Think of words that will help someone else see, hear, feel, smell, or taste what you are describing.

In this unit you will learn how to make pictures with words. You will study words with similar and opposite meanings. You will write descriptions and read descriptions in poetry and a tall tale.

# LANGUAGE

## Lesson 1: Understanding Adjectives

You know that nouns name people, places, or things. The word *dog* is a noun. When you say or write the noun *dog*, it brings a picture to your mind. Perhaps you see a dog like one of these.

1. huge dog    2. fuzzy dog    3. brown dog

### Think and Discuss

Examples 1, 2, and 3 tell about different *kinds* of dogs. The words that tell *what kind* give a more exact picture of the dogs. Name the words that tell what kind.

*Huge, fuzzy,* and *brown* describe the noun *dog.* They describe by telling what kind. These describing words are called **adjectives.**

Now read these sentences.

4. This big collie walked the beach.
5. A noisy puppy barked at me.
6. Trixie has a cold nose.

What are the adjectives? Which nouns do the adjectives describe?

> ● An **adjective** is a word that describes a noun.

## Practice

**A.** The underlined words in these sentences are nouns. Copy the sentences. Circle the adjectives that describe the nouns.

1. Dogs are helpful <u>animals</u>.
2. Loyal <u>dogs</u> are friends to people.
3. In ancient <u>times</u>, dogs were hunters.
4. Dogs pull heavy <u>sleds</u> for the Eskimos.
5. The St. Bernard helps lost <u>travelers</u>.
6. Clever <u>collies</u> herd sheep.
7. The trusty <u>shepherds</u> lead blind <u>people</u>.

**B.** Copy the sentences. Circle the adjectives.

8. Dogs are popular pets.
9. A golden retriever will hunt or play.
10. A beagle is a good tracker.
11. The Airedale is a powerful swimmer.
12. The red setter has a pretty coat.
13. A spotted dalmatian helps firefighters.
14. The poodle has curly hair.
15. An intelligent dog can be trained.

**C.** Use an adjective in each blank. Write the sentences.

16. Lisa took her _____ poodle for a walk.
17. The _____ sun was shining.
18. Lisa and her dog walked along a _____ path.
19. Some _____ birds watched them.
20. Lisa had a _____ time.

## Apply

**D.** Think of an adjective to describe each noun. Use the words to write five sentences about an imaginary animal.

21. pet  **22.** house  **23.** food  **24.** water  **25.** environment

# Lesson 2: Understanding Adjectives That Compare

Look at the pictures. Then read the sentences. Notice the underlined adjectives.

1. Ted is <u>tall</u>.

2. Frank is <u>taller</u> than Ted.

3. Mike is <u>tallest</u> of all.

Which adjective describes Ted?

## Think and Discuss

You know that adjectives describe nouns. The adjective in sentence 1 describes the noun *Ted*. Adjectives can also describe by comparing two or more nouns. The adjective in sentence 2 compares two nouns—*Frank* and *Ted*. What is the adjective? What two letters end it? The adjective in sentence 3 compares more than two nouns. It compares *Mike* to both *Frank* and *Ted*. What three letters end the adjective *tallest*? One-syllable adjectives that compare often end in *er* or *est*.

Adjectives of two or more syllables usually make comparisons in a different way. Read these sentences.

4. Ted is *helpful.*
5. Frank is *more helpful* than Ted.
6. Mike is the *most helpful* of all.

Notice how the adjective *helpful* changes in sentences 5 and 6. *More* is added to compare two nouns—*Frank* and *Ted.* What word is added to compare more than two nouns?

> - One-syllable adjectives use *er* or *est* to make comparisons.
> - Adjectives of two or more syllables usually use *more* or *most* to make comparisons.

## *Practice*

**A.** Copy this chart. Write the missing adjectives.

| 1. | small | _____ | smallest |
|---|---|---|---|
| 2. | soft | softer | _____ |
| 3. | dangerous | more dangerous | _____ |
| 4. | playful | more playful | _____ |
| 5. | clean | _____ | cleanest |
| 6. | difficult | _____ | most difficult |
| 7. | bright | _____ | brightest |
| 8. | long | _____ | longest |

**B.** Choose the correct adjective. Write the sentences.

9. The temperature is _____ today than yesterday.
   (lower, lowest)
10. Today is the _____ day of the year.
    (colder, coldest)
11. Miguel is _____ inside than outside.
    (more comfortable, most comfortable)

**12.** The snow is _____ in our town than in your town.
(deeper, deepest)

**13.** Mary's snowman is _____ than mine.
(smaller, smallest)

**14.** These icicles are the _____ I've ever seen.
(longer, longest)

**15.** This is the _____ winter ever!
(more exciting, most exciting)

## Apply

**C. 16.–40.** Add *er* or *more* to each adjective. Then add
*est* or *most*. Write 20 new adjectives. Use 5 of your new
adjectives in sentences.

| | | | |
|---|---|---|---|
| **16.** warm | **17.** beautiful | **18.** deep | **19.** thoughtful |
| **20.** peaceful | **21.** interesting | **22.** slow | **23.** thick |
| **24.** hard | **25.** careful | | |

# HOW OUR LANGUAGE GROWS

When it *rains cats and dogs,* do animals really fall from the sky?
If a joke *cracks you up,* do you really break into pieces?

Words such as these are called **figures of speech.** We use
figures of speech to describe things in unusual and interesting ways.
Figures of speech paint pictures in your mind. They say a lot in a
few words.

Here are some more figures of speech to think about—*blow
your top; talk a blue streak; sweet as sugar; cool as a cucumber;
barrel of laughs.*

**1.** Look back at the figures of speech. What does each one mean?
**2.** Share some figures of speech that you know.

# Lesson 3: Using Articles

There are three adjectives that you use many times each day. Read these sentences. Notice the underlined words. These words are adjectives too.

1. <u>The</u> fox ate <u>an</u> egg.
2. <u>The</u> kangaroo gobbles <u>a</u> grape.
3. Can <u>an</u> elephant have <u>a</u> snack too?

## Think and Discuss

*A, an,* and *the* are special adjectives called **articles.** In a sentence, articles often come before nouns. Which article comes before each noun in sentences 1, 2, and 3?

> - *A, an,* and *the* are adjectives called **articles.**
> - When a singular noun begins with a consonant sound, use *a.*
> - When a singular noun begins with a vowel sound, use *an.*
> - *The* is used with singular and plural nouns.

## Practice

**A.** Choose the correct article. Write the sentences.

1. Did you ever visit (a, an) zoo?
2. (The, A) children in Mr. Park's class did.
3. They saw (the, an) lions and tigers first.
4. They saw (a, an) ostrich and (a, an) flamingo.
5. (A, An) elephant ate (a, an) peanut.

## Apply

**B.** Copy each word and write *a* or *an* before it. Then use each group of words in a sentence.

6. camel   7. eagle   8. alligator   9. walrus   10. panther

# Lesson 4: Understanding Adverbs

Compare these pairs of sentences. Notice the underlined action verbs.

1. Hungry gulls <u>hunt</u> for food.
2. Hungry gulls <u>hunt</u> eagerly for food.

3. Artie and Dawn <u>watch</u> them.
4. Now Artie and Dawn <u>watch</u> them.

5. The gulls swoop and <u>fly</u>.
6. The gulls swoop and <u>fly</u> away.

Which words have been added to sentences 2, 4, and 6?

## Think and Discuss

The added words tell more about the action verbs in sentences 2, 4, and 6. *Eagerly* tells about the verb *hunt.* It tells **how** the gulls hunt. *Now* tells about the action verb *watch.* What does it tell? *Away* tells **where** the gulls fly. The words *eagerly, now,* and *away* are **adverbs.**

Adverbs can appear in different places within a sentence. *Eagerly* is in the middle of sentence 2. Where are the adverbs *now* and *away?*

> ● An **adverb** is a word that tells more about a verb.

## Practice

**A.** Copy each sentence. Circle the adverbs. The underlined action verbs will help you.

1. At sea storms <u>strike</u> suddenly.
2. Gulls <u>fly</u> easily through the wind and rain.
3. People <u>travel</u> carefully in a storm.
4. Sailors often <u>look</u> for shelter.

5. They <u>seek</u> a safe harbor nearby.
6. The winds <u>blow</u> fiercely from the north.
7. The sailors <u>steer</u> slowly out of the storm.
8. The big ship <u>moves</u> safely into the harbor.
9. In quiet waters it <u>floats</u> peacefully.
10. Now the sailors <u>will rest</u>.

**B.** Copy each sentence. Circle the adverbs. Draw two lines under each verb.

11. The howling wind blew hard.
12. Torrents of rain fell heavily.
13. People held umbrellas tightly.
14. All the cars, trucks, and buses moved slowly.
15. Now the rain has stopped.
16. The sun will shine tomorrow.
17. Colorful flowers will bloom brightly.
18. Many birds will sing cheerfully.
19. We will play then.
20. My friends and I will go outside.

## *Apply*

**C.** Write each adverb in a sentence of your own.

21. easily  22. never  23. inside  24. playfully  25. suddenly

# Lesson 5: Understanding Adverbs That Tell _How_, _When_, and _Where_

Read this paragraph. Each sentence has an adverb. Find the adverbs.

Yesterday Felicia shopped. She had carefully made a list. She looked everywhere for the best camping equipment. Felicia went quickly from place to place. Soon she finished her shopping.

## Think and Discuss

Adverbs add interesting details to sentences. Some adverbs tell _how_ an action happens. Others tell _when_ or _where_ an action happens.

Look back at the paragraph that begins the lesson. Find the adverbs that answer these questions: **When** did Felicia shop? **How** did she make a list? **Where** did she look for equipment? **How** did she go from place to place? **When** did she finish shopping?

Here are more adverbs that tell _how_, _when_, or _where_.

| How | When | Where |
|---|---|---|
| slowly | then | here |
| neatly | always | there |
| smoothly | never | down |
| bravely | often | around |

How do the adverbs in the first column end? Most adverbs that tell _how_ end in _ly_.

## Practice

**A.** Copy the sentences. Underline the adverbs. After each sentence write whether the adverb tells *how, when,* or *where.*

1. Yesterday we went camping.
2. We looked carefully for a good campsite.
3. Martin easily found a large tree.
4. He and Lisa pitched our tent nearby.
5. Today we found a stream.
6. Lara quickly decided to go fishing.
7. She came back with fish for dinner.
8. Soon we ate a delicious meal.
9. Later we roasted marshmallows.
10. Then we told ghost stories.
11. Lara always tells good ones.
12. Martin smiled bravely as he listened.

**B.** Complete the sentences with adverbs that tell *how, when,* or *where.* Write the sentences.

13. Our group will camp _____.   (where)
14. _____ we planned our route.   (when)
15. We arrived _____.   (when)
16. _____ we have to work.   (when)
17. We look _____ for wood.   (where)
18. We _____ collect only the driest pieces.   (how)
19. The cooks work _____ preparing a good meal.   (how)
20. _____ we tell stories around the campfire.   (when)

## Apply

**C.** Add *ly* to these words to form adverbs. Then write the adverbs in sentences of your own.

**21.** slow   **22.** soft   **23.** safe   **24.** quick   **25.** loud

# Lesson 6: Using Adjectives and Adverbs

Look at the underlined words in these sentences. Which are adjectives? Which are adverbs?

1. <u>Yesterday</u> Sarah bought <u>new</u> gloves.
2. Sarah is a <u>good</u> catcher.
3. She plays baseball <u>well</u>.

## Think and Discuss

You know that adjectives describe nouns. You also know that adverbs tell more about verbs.

In sentence 1 the word *new* is an adjective. It describes the noun *gloves. Yesterday* is an adverb. It tells more about the verb *bought.* It tells *when.*

Look at sentence 2. The word *good* is an adjective because it describes a noun. What noun does it describe? Now look at sentence 3. *Well* tells more about the verb *plays.* What does *well* tell about Sarah's playing? The word *well* is an adverb.

Remember to use adjectives to describe nouns. Use adverbs to tell more about verbs. You can use adverbs to tell *when* and *how* about verbs.

## Practice

**A.** Tell whether the underlined word is an adjective or an adverb.

1. cheered <u>wildly</u>
2. a <u>good</u> pitcher
3. a <u>fair</u> umpire
4. an <u>easy</u> win
5. <u>suddenly</u> threw
6. <u>loudly</u> yelled
7. hit <u>hard</u>
8. a <u>wild</u> pitch
9. the <u>strongest</u> hitter
10. played <u>well</u>

**B.** Choose the correct adjective or adverb for each sentence. Write the sentences.

11. Our softball team played (good, well) today.
12. Danielle (quick, quickly) made the first hit.
13. She ran (swift, swiftly) to second base.
14. Charlie is a (slow, slowly) runner.
15. He is a (good, well) hitter.
16. He (easy, easily) hit a line drive.
17. Rosa got a (solid, solidly) hit.
18. She (proud, proudly) drove in two runs.
19. We had practiced (eager, eagerly) for the game.
20. We didn't win, but we had a (good, well) time.
21. The people watching cheered (loud, loudly).
22. The other team waved (cheerful, cheerfully).
23. Then the (happy, happily) team members invited us to lunch.
24. We (grateful, gratefully) accepted.
25. We made some (good, well) friends that day.

## Apply

**C. 26.–30.** Write two sentences of your own that use adjectives. Write three sentences that use adverbs. You may use any of the adjectives or adverbs in Practice A or B.

### To Memorize

Icicles are the walking sticks of the winter winds.

*Bella Coola Indian proverb*

What are icicles? Why would the Native Americans describe them this way? How would you describe icicles?

# LANGUAGE REVIEW

## Adjectives   pages 162–163

Copy the sentences. Underline the adjectives.

1. Peter rowed out onto the clear lake.
2. The blue water sparkled in the sunshine.
3. Peter dipped the wooden oars into the water.
4. He cast his strong line into the lake.
5. Peter caught a huge fish and cooked it for dinner.
6. He slept under the twinkling stars at night.

## Adjectives That Compare   pages 164–166

Choose the correct adjective. Write the sentences.

7. Which package is the (lighter, lightest) of the three?
8. Brad's painting is (more colorful, most colorful) than Kim's painting.
9. The chair by the window is the (more comfortable, most comfortable) in the house.
10. The sun is (brighter, brightest) today than yesterday.
11. The red dress is (plainer, plainest) than the green dress.
12. This teddy bear is the (softer, softest) of all the stuffed animals.

## Articles   page 167

Choose the correct article. Write the sentences.

13. Lee saw (a, an) big icicle one morning.
14. The icicle hung outside (a, an) igloo.
15. The icicle was as long as (a, an) spear.
16. Lee threw snowballs at (a, the) icicle.
17. (An, The) snowballs hit the icicle and broke it.
18. It crashed into (a, an) thousand pieces.

## Adverbs    pages 168–169

Copy the sentences. Underline the adverbs.

19. He usually drives a bus.
20. We often see him.
21. Today he took his car.
22. He drove here.
23. He drove slowly in town.
24. He waved quickly.
25. He arrived early.
26. He parked carefully.
27. Look around to find him.
28. He stands outside.
29. We honked loudly.
30. He never saw us.

## Adverbs That Tell <u>How</u>, <u>When</u>, and <u>Where</u>    pages 170–171

Copy the sentences. Underline the adverbs. After each sentence write whether the adverb tells *how, when,* or *where.*

31. Sometimes I take walks by myself.
32. As I walk along, I think about the day.
33. I usually go to MacArthur Park.
34. Many children play there.
35. The children laugh loudly.
36. They play happily in the park.

## Adjectives and Adverbs    pages 172–173

Choose the correct answer. Write the sentences.

37. Leona is a (careful, carefully) bird-watcher.
38. She watches (quiet, quietly) in the woods.
39. She takes (good, well) pictures of the birds.
40. She saw a (cheerful, cheerfully) robin.
41. The birds are (good, well) parents to their young.
42. Leona takes notes (good, well) too.

## Applying Adjectives and Adverbs

Add an adjective and an adverb to each sentence. Write the new sentences.

43. Rabbits hopped
44. Hens squawked.
45. Hawks soared.
46. Dogs bayed.
47. Sparrows chirped.
48. Ducks swam.
49. Owls hooted.
50. Turkeys gobbled.

# STUDY SKILLS

## Lesson 7: Understanding Homographs

When you are looking for a word in the dictionary, you may see something strange. You may find two or more entry words spelled exactly the same way.

### Think and Discuss

Words that have the same spelling but different meanings are called **homographs.** Homographs are listed one after the other in the dictionary. Each entry has a numeral printed after it. The numerals show they are different entry words.

Look at these homographs. Then read the sentences next to them.

| |
|---|
| **friz·zle¹** [friz′(ə)l] *v.* **friz·zled, friz·zling** To fry or cook with a sizzling noise.<br>**friz·zle²** [friz′(ə)l] *v.* **friz·zled, friz·zling,** *n.* **1** *v.* To curl tightly; kink, as the hair. **2** *n.* A crisp curl. — **friz′zly** *adj.* |

1. The rain will *frizzle* my hair.
2. The bacon will *frizzle* as it fries.

Which entry goes with sentence 1? What does *frizzle* mean in sentence 2?

Some homographs have different pronunciations. Look at these homographs. Then read the sentences.

| |
|---|
| **dove¹** [duv] *n.* A pigeon, especially any of a number of small, usually wild pigeons.<br>**dove²** [dōv] A past tense of DIVE. |

3. I hear the coo of the *dove.*
4. Melissa *dove* into the water.

How do you pronounce *dove* in sentence 3? Which pronunciation and meaning fit *dove* in sentence 4?

> • **Homographs** are words that have the same spelling. They have different meanings. Sometimes homographs have different pronunciations.

## *Practice*

**A.** Copy the sentences. Underline the homographs.

1. It wasn't fair that Ted couldn't attend the fair.
2. The dove dove through the air.
3. She wound a bandage around her wound.
4. The wind caused the flag to wind around the pole.
5. Will you let a live snake live in the house?

**B. 6.–9.** Write the definitions for the homographs in Practice A that have different pronunciations.

## *Apply*

**C.** Write the meanings of the underlined homographs.

10. Do you know the answer to the riddle?
11. Punch a hole in this paper.
12. What kind of cereal is that?
13. The young boy fell off the dock.
14. The fine for littering was fifty dollars.
15. Susan pressed the shirt in a mangle
16. Les walked toward the bow of the ship.
17. The camels walked in a desert caravan.
18. Katy will punt the football.
19. The minute bacteria can be seen with a microscope.
20. Don't tire yourself by working too hard.

### *A Challenge*

Think of a homograph for each underlined word in Apply. Write each homograph in a sentence.

# Lesson 8: Understanding Synonyms and Antonyms

Some words mean almost the same thing. Other words have very opposite meanings. Read the pairs of sentences. Notice the underlined words. Which words mean the same thing? Which words are opposites?

Roberta is happy.           Tim is unhappy.
Roberta is cheerful.        Tim is sad.

## Think and Discuss

In the first picture the words *happy* and *cheerful* describe Roberta. These words mean almost the same thing. They are **synonyms.** Find another pair of words that are synonyms.

The words *happy* and *unhappy* are opposite in meaning. They are **antonyms.** Find another pair of words that are antonyms.

Writers use synonyms and antonyms to make more exact word pictures.

> - A **synonym** is a word that has almost the same meaning as another word.
> - An **antonym** is a word that means the opposite of another word.

## Practice

**A.** Copy the sentences. Underline the two words in each sentence that are synonyms.

1. Tim raced on the smooth, slick ice.
2. He could see water under the ice, below the surface.
3. As he slid and slipped over the ice, Tim fell.
4. He ripped his jacket and tore his pants.
5. Tim's arm was painful and sore.
6. A woman noticed Tim limping and saw that he was hurt.
7. She bundled Tim in blankets and wrapped his arm with a bandage.

**B.** Copy the sentences. Underline the two words in each sentence that are antonyms.

8. Roberta walked away from her house, toward the pond.
9. The ice was thick in some places and thin in others.
10. Roberta could do easy turns or difficult turns.
11. She could skate quickly or slowly.
12. Roberta started late, but she came home early.
13. She loved the pond, and she hated having to go home.
14. After her exciting day, television seemed dull to her.
15. As it grew colder outside, Roberta was glad to be indoors.

## Apply

**C.** Write a synonym for each word. Then write an antonym.

| 16. shut | 17. difficult | 18. incorrect | 19. giggle |
| 20. gloomy | 21. quick | 22. above | 23. coarse |
| 24. happy | 25. silent | | |

VOCABULARY: Synonyms and Antonyms   **179**

# Lesson 9: Using Synonyms and Antonyms

Mike wrote this paragraph for a story.

Anne's room is very neat. The posters are hung on the wall in a neat way. The bookcase is neat. The rug and bedspread are neat. Everything looks nice, except for Anne's desk. It is not neat.

What word has Mike used too often? To make the paragraph more interesting, he can use synonyms for the word *neat*. Synonyms are words that have the same or nearly the same meaning.

## Think and Discuss

To find synonyms Mike can look in a **thesaurus.** A thesaurus is a reference book. It lists entry words and their synonyms. A thesaurus often lists antonyms as well. The words in a thesaurus are usually arranged in alphabetical order.

Mike found the entry for *neat* in a thesaurus. The entry word *neat* is printed in dark, or **boldface,** type. After the entry word, an abbreviation tells the word's part of speech. What part of speech is *neat?* The synonyms come next, followed by a list of antonyms.

Mike discovered several words to use in place of the word *neat*. Which synonym for *neat* would you choose to use in the first sentence of his paragraph? Name the antonyms for *neat*.

> **neat,** adj., tidy, orderly, uncluttered, trim, spic-and-span, well-kept, immaculate. *Antonyms,* disorderly, unclean, untidy, messy, slovenly.

## Practice

**A.** Use these thesaurus entries to answer the questions.

> **lovely**, adj., charming, delightful, beautiful, attractive,
>     graceful, adorable, pleasing, enchanting.
>     *Antonyms*, ugly, hateful, horrible, unpleasant,
>     unattractive, hideous, unlovely, unlovable.
> **noise**, n., disquiet, din, clamor, uproar, hubbub, bang,
>     thunder, crash, peal, slam.
>     *Antonyms*, quiet, hush, still, peace, silence.

1. Which of these entries would you find listed first in a thesaurus?
2. What part of speech is the word *lovely?*
3. Write two synonyms for *lovely.*
4. Write two antonyms for *noise.*
5. Does a thesaurus give the pronunciation of the word?

**B.** Use the thesaurus entries. Rewrite these sentences using synonyms for the underlined words.

6. The barking dog made a lot of noise.
7. Next door the noise from the party could be heard.
8. The lovely girl had sparkling brown eyes.
9. The noise from the rainstorm frightened me.
10. Our class saw a lovely ballet.
11. As they hit the floor, the falling dishes made a loud noise.
12. The lovely baby was laughing.
13. My grandmother is a lovely lady.
14. The lovely story was enjoyable.
15. The hiker's loud noise startled the deer.

## Apply

**C. 16.–20.** Write five sentences about the noise of a drum. Use synonyms for *noise.*

# COMPOSITION

## Lesson 10: Combining Sentences with Adjectives

Mara is writing about plants. Read her sentences.

1. The red flowers are roses.
2. The pink flowers are roses.

### Think and Discuss

What is the subject of each of Mara's sentences? The words *pink* and *red* are adjectives. Here they describe flowers. The adjectives in sentences 1 and 2 describe the same subject. Mara combines the sentences this way.

3. The red and pink flowers are roses.

What word was used to combine the adjectives?
Now read these sentences.

4. Buttercups are tiny.
5. Buttercups are glossy.
6. Buttercups are yellow.
7. Buttercups are tiny, glossy, and yellow.

Sentence 7 uses three adjectives. When three adjectives follow each other in this way, commas are needed. Which sentence below needs commas?

8. The orange and yellow marigolds are pretty.
9. Marigolds are orange yellow and white.

> ● Commas are used to separate three or more adjectives in a row.

## Practice

**A.** Copy each sentence. Underline the adjectives. Put commas where they are needed.

**1.** The soft and fluffy seeds of a dandelion blow in the breeze.
**2.** The leaves of lilies are smooth shiny and green.
**3.** Wintergreen is glossy and green.
**4.** A violet's petals are tiny fragrant and delicate.

**B.** Combine each set of sentences into one sentence. Do not forget to add commas where they are needed.

**5.** Queen Anne's lace is lacy.
Queen Anne's lace is white.
**6.** Strawberries are sweet.
Strawberries are red.
Strawberries are juicy.
**7.** The thorns on a rose are sharp.
The thorns on a rose are prickly.
The thorns on a rose are pointed.
**8.** The rough leaves of the mayflower scratched me.
The hairy leaves of the mayflower scratched me.

**C. 9.–13.** Listen while your teacher reads some sentences. Write the sentences correctly.

## Apply

**D. 14.–15.** Describe the flower in each picture. One description should use two adjectives. One description should use three adjectives.

tulip                              carnation

# Lesson 11: Writing a Descriptive Paragraph

Suzanne wrote this paragraph about camping with her family. Notice the descriptive words.

> Many wild animals visit our campground. Striped chipmunks search busily for uncracked nuts. A fat, frisky raccoon walks nearby. Two squirrels race playfully between the trees. Screeching bluejays nest in rustling branches. They chatter noisily at us when we come near.

What adjective describes the chipmunks? What adverb tells how the squirrels race?

## Think and Discuss

Some paragraphs tell about a person or an animal. They may describe a place or a happening. Colorful adjectives and adverbs tell about the topic. Lively verbs explain the action. This kind of paragraph is called a **descriptive** paragraph.

A descriptive paragraph is like any good paragraph. It contains a topic sentence and detail sentences. The detail sentences use words to give an exact picture of a person, animal, place, or happening. What is the topic sentence of Suzanne's paragraph? Do the sentences that follow it give an exact picture of the wild animals?

> **How to Write a Descriptive Paragraph**
> 1. **Indent the first sentence.**
> 2. **Begin with a topic sentence telling what the paragraph is about.**
> 3. **Add detail sentences. In them use colorful and lively words to describe the topic. Make an exact picture with the words you choose.**
> 4. **Keep to the topic.**
> 5. **Use good sentence order.**

## Practice

**A.** Add adjectives, adverbs, or both to these sentences. Write the sentences.

1. One _____ place to camp is along the _____ shore.
2. The _____ waves crash _____.
3. We stay _____ in our _____ tent.
4. Then the _____ sun shines _____.
5. We _____ collect _____ shells.
6. _____ we return to our _____ camp.
7. In the _____ evening we rest _____.

**B.** Write one or more sentences about each object. Use colorful and exact words. Help someone else see, hear, taste, smell, or feel what you are describing.

8. a house     9. a storm     10. a wheat field
11. a road     12. a hamburger     13. a shadow

## Apply

**C.** **14.** Write a descriptive paragraph about one of these topics. Follow the directions on this page.

A Wonderful Pet     The Haunted House
The View from My Window     A Train Ride

# Lesson 12: Editing a Descriptive Paragraph

Frankie edited a descriptive paragraph about camping that he had written. Notice the changes he made.

Each june we go camping. The best thing about camping is the ~~scenry~~ *beautiful scenery*. We camp near *a clear stream* water. In the sunlight the water sparkles *brightly*. The wind *gently* blows the branches of the *tall pine* trees in the *thick* forest. The air is clear *clean and cold*. ~~The air is clean. The air is cold.~~

**Editing Marks**

≡ **capitalize**

⊙ **make a period**

∧ **add something**

⋏ **add a comma**

⌄⋰ **add quotation marks**

ℯ **take something away**

◯ **spell correctly**

¶ **indent the paragraph**

/ **make a lowercase letter**

∼ tr **transpose**

## Think and Discuss

Frankie added adjectives and adverbs to his descriptive paragraph. What editing mark shows that words are added?

The adjectives *clear, clean,* and *cold* all described the same noun. Which noun did they describe? Frankie combined these three sentences. He used this mark ⋏ to add commas between the adjectives. Words are taken out with this editing mark ℯ.

Frankie circled the word *scenry* because it was not spelled correctly. Why did he use this mark ≡ ?

## Practice

**A.** Copy Frankie's edited paragraph correctly. Make all the changes shown.

## *Apply*

**B.** Look back at the descriptive paragraph that you wrote in Lesson 11. Did you use interesting adjectives and lively verbs? Did you use adverbs to tell more about verbs? Are all the words spelled correctly? Edit your paragraph. Then copy it again neatly.

# MECHANICS PRACTICE

### Writing Dates and Times of Day
- Begin the name of a month with a capital letter.
- Use a comma between the day and the year in a date.
- Use a colon between the hour and the minute in the time of day.
- Use a period after the abbreviations A.M. and P.M.

**A.** Write these dates correctly.

**1.** january 27 1983　　　**2.** july 4 1776
**3.** april 1 1902　　　　**4.** march 16 1943

**B.** Write these times correctly.

**5.** 7 15 am　　**6.** 10 30 pm　　**7.** 12 45 pm
**8.** 3 20 pm　　**9.** 9 00 am　　**10.** 11 25 am

**C.** Write the sentences correctly. Use capital letters, periods, and commas where they are needed.

**11.** I was invited to a party on august 4.
**12.** From 7 00 pm until 9 00 pm we danced and played games.
**13.** The letter was dated february 14 1802.
**14.** The auction lasted from 9 00 am until 4 30 pm
**15.** I will go to day camp the last week in july.

# LITERATURE

## Lesson 13: Understanding Description in Poetry

Like all good writers, poets try to describe objects and feelings. They try to use just the right words to paint a picture for you. Then when you read their poems, you see the picture too. Read Aileen Fisher's poem "Skins."

### Skins

Skins of lemons are waterproof slickers.
Pineapple skins are stuck full of stickers.
Skins of apples are skinny and shiny
and strawberry skins (if any) are tiny.

Grapes have skins that are juicy and squishy.
Gooseberry skins are vinegar-ishy.
Skins of peaches are fuzzy and hairy.
Oranges' skins are more peely than pare-y.

Skins of plums are squirty and squeezy.
Bananas have skins you can pull-off-easy.
I like skins that are thin as sheeting
so what-is-under is bigger for eating.

*Aileen Fisher*

### Think and Discuss

Poets often tell us about ordinary things in a new or different way. Descriptive words help the poet do this. Look back at the poem "Skins." How is the skin of a lemon like a waterproof slicker? Why are skins of plums squirty and squeezy?

Now read this poem. Look for descriptive words.

### Apple Song

The apples are seasoned
And ripe and sound.
Gently they fall
On the yellow ground.

The apples are stored
In the dusky bin
Where hardly a glimmer
Of light creeps in.

In the firelit, winter
Nights, they'll be
The clear sweet taste
Of a summer tree!

*Frances Frost*

## Practice

**A.** How does the poet Aileen Fisher describe each fruit skin? Write the words.

**1.** skins of apples     **2.** grape skins
**3.** peach skins     **4.** strawberry skins

**B.** How does Frances Frost describe each object? Write the words.

**5.** apples     **6.** the apples' taste
**7.** the apple bin     **8.** the nights

## Apply

**C. 9.** Think of a food that you would like to write about. Make a list of all the adjectives you can think of that describe that food. Then write a poem.

# Lesson 14: Understanding Comparison in Poetry

Poetry is filled with description. Poets often describe by comparing things. Read these examples. What things are compared?

1. Trees are like brooms sweeping the sky.
2. Falling leaves are like pennies for the sidewalk to catch.

## Think and Discuss

Poets often use the words *like* or *as* to compare two things you might not think were alike. Read this poem.

### The Hills

Sometimes I think the hills
That loom across the harbor
Lie there like sleeping dragons,
Crouched one above another,
With trees for tufts of fur
Growing all up and down
The ridges and humps of their backs,
And orange cliffs for claws
Dipped in the sea below.
Sometimes a wisp of smoke
Rises out of the hollows,
As if in their dragon sleep
They dreamed of strange old battles.

What if the hills should stir
Some day and stretch themselves,
Shake off the clinging trees
And all the clustered houses?

*Rachel Field*

What are like sleeping dragons in the poem? Two
things can be compared if they are alike in some way.
How are hills and sleeping dragons alike? Think about
their color, size, and shape. Find other things the poet has
compared.

A poet may compare two things without using the
words *like* or *as*. Read this poem. Notice the words that are
used to form pictures.

The dark gray clouds,
the great gray clouds,
the black rolling clouds are elephants
going down to the sea for water.
They draw up the water in their trunks.
They march back again across the sky.
They spray the earth again with the water,
and men say it is raining.

*Natalia M. Belting*

## Practice

**A.** Look back at the poem on this page to answer these
questions.

1. Write two comparisons that you find in the poem.
2. For each comparison tell at least one way the two
things are alike.

## Apply

**B.** Copy these word groups. Fill in the blanks with nouns
that fit the comparison.

3. as furry as a _____
4. as loud as a _____
5. as tiny as a _____
6. as bright as a _____
7. as peaceful as a _____
8. as exciting as a _____
9. as fast as a _____
10. as thin as a _____

# Lesson 15: Understanding Description in a Tall Tale

You have probably read stories about unbelievable characters who had perfectly amazing adventures. Perhaps some adventures were so amazing that you knew the truth had been stretched a bit. Stories that stretch the truth are called **tall tales.** Why do you think they are called tall tales?

## Think and Discuss

Many tall tales were first told by American settlers. These people were proud of their own hard work. They made up boastful tales. The characters were loggers, cowpunchers, or farmers like themselves. The men and women in the tales were smarter, bigger, and braver than real people.

Read this tall tale about Paul Bunyan. Paul was a logger. Tales about Paul were told by loggers from Maine to Wisconsin.

### Split Pea Soup

*retold by Wallace Wadsworth*

Wonderful stories are told of the food served in Paul Bunyan's logging camps. Never were there such cooks as Hot Biscuit Slim and Sourdough Sam. They ruled over a mess hall that was so big there were lunch counters along the sides. This was so the loggers could stop and get something to eat while finding their places at the tables. The cooks always had to use field glasses when they wanted to see if people liked a new dish. Doggone if the mice didn't grow so big just from eating the crumbs in the mess hall they ran all the wolves out of the country.

No doubt about it, Paul's crews ate a tremendous amount of food. Paul's beautiful blue ox, Babe, had to carry all the supplies to camp. On one of these supply trips the Great Blue Ox was carrying a load of split peas (this being shortly after Paul had invented the split pea so that the cooks could make twice as much soup out of a load of peas). Paul got careless and led Babe across a lake where the ice was only six feet thick. Babe, of course, broke through the thin ice and spilled the entire load of peas into the lake.

Paul worried because he knew how much the loggers loved their pea soup, but he didn't stay worried long. He just called out some of the men and had them pry up the lake enough so that they could build a big fire under it. Hot Biscuit Slim made the peas into soup then and there. Everyone liked that soup the best of all because the fish from the lake were cooked in it.

The whole thing gave Paul a new idea which saved a lot of trouble. He had heard of a place where there were a lot of boiling hot springs. From that time on, Paul would start off the season by dumping in three or four loads of split peas. Then he would throw in the meat from a few big herds of steers which were driven up from Texas for the purpose, and he would have pea soup. He piped this soup to all the camps.

In the first paragraph of the tall tale, the author states that the mess hall was big. Then the author begins to stretch the truth. Stretching the truth is called **exaggeration.**

How does the author exaggerate the amount of food eaten at the logging camp?

Look at the second paragraph of the story. Is it true that Paul Bunyan invented the split pea? Why is this a funny idea?

Remember that tall tales are filled with exaggeration. Exaggeration makes the tales humorous and fun to tell.

## Practice

**A.** Here are some details from the tall tale about Paul Bunyan. Write an exaggeration about each.

**1.** Paul's mess hall was big.
**2.** The mice in the hall were big.
**3.** The ice on the lake was thin.
**4.** Hot Biscuit Slim did not use an ordinary pot to cook pea soup.

**B.** Answer these questions. Write your answers in complete sentences.

**5.** What is a tall tale?
**6.** Why did people tell tall tales?
**7.** About whom were tall tales told?
**8.** What is exaggeration?
**9.** Why did the tellers of tall tales exaggerate?

**C.** **10.–14.** Find five places where facts are exaggerated in this paragraph. Copy the sentences that show exaggeration.

It was a hot day. It was so warm that the dogs had shed their fur. I placed an egg on the sidewalk, and it fried up in a minute. Even my parakeet was sweating. I turned the fan on. It spun so fast that it blew the roof off. Then the fan gave up and keeled over in a dead faint.

## Apply

**D.** Finish each sentence. Exaggerate the facts. Make sure your sentences stretch the truth.

15. Paul Bunyan was so big that _____.
16. Sam was such a good cook that _____.
17. Babe the Blue Ox was so strong that _____.
18. Paul's men were so hungry that _____.
19. The springs were so hot that _____.
20. The lake water was so cold that _____.

# A BOOK TO READ

Title: **American Tall Tales**
Author: Adrien Stoutenberg
Publisher: The Viking Press

"The winter started out cold and grew colder. By January, it was so cold that smoke froze in fireplace chimneys. One morning, daybreak froze solid."

It took Davy Crockett some time to discover why everything was so cold. How he got the earth moving again with the help of "an exceptionally fat bear" is an even "taller" tale than most.

Many oversized American heroes and adventures are here in this book of tall tales. There's Stormalong, the sea captain who kicked sharks away from his ship when they swam too close. There's John Henry, who could whirl his big hammer "so lightning-fast you could hear thunder behind it."

Humorous language and spirited pictures tell the stories of these tall tale characters. Whether they tell of riding a cyclone or digging the Grand Canyon with a stick, these tales are exciting reading!

● **Adjectives**    pages 162–163

Write the letter of the word in each sentence that is an adjective.

1. Mark saw four animals.
   a    b    c    d

2. Blanco and Greco were white puppies.
   a              b    c    d

3. Dandelion and Sunrise were furry kittens.
   a          b    c    d

4. Tiny Blanco barked at Mark.
   a    b    c         d

5. Sunrise purred happily over warm milk.
   a       b      c         d

● **Adjectives That Compare**    pages 164–166

Copy this chart. Fill in each missing adjective.

6. cool          _____          _____

7. _____    more difficult        _____

8. _____    _____       greatest

9. _____    rounder               _____

10. enormous       _____        _____

● **Articles**    page 167

Choose the correct answer. Write the sentences.

11. Juanita read (a/an) interesting book.

12. The book was about (a/an) stunt actor.

**13.** The actor ran into (a/an) wall of fire.

**14.** (A/The) flames covered the actor.

**15.** Luckily, the actor wore (a/an) overcoat of safety cloth.

● **Adverbs**   pages 168–169

Use an adverb to complete each sentence. Write the sentences.

**16.** _____ Alex visited the zoo.

**17.** He saw many animals _____.

**18.** The seals barked _____.

**19.** _____ a tall zoo keeper threw some fish to the seals.

**20.** Each seal _____ ate its lunch.

● **Adjectives and Adverbs**   pages 172–173

Choose the correct answer. Write the sentences.

**21.** The runners passed by (slow, slowly).

**22.** They had finished a (hard, hardly) race.

**23.** Linda ran (good, well) in the race.

**24.** She won the (second, secondly) prize.

**25.** A very (good, well) runner beat Linda by a meter.

● **Homographs**   pages 176–177

Read each sentence. Copy the letter of the correct definition for the underlined word in the sentence.

**1.** A <u>live</u> toad is in my pocket.
   **a.** to make one's home       **b.** alive

**2.** Will you <u>record</u> the president's speech?
   **a.** to write down       **b.** the best achievement

**3.** Is Adam <u>present</u> in school today?
   **a.** to give as a gift       **b.** not absent

**4.** The <u>dove</u> flew through the open window.
   **a.** a pigeon       **b.** past tense of *dive*

**5.** The <u>wind</u> blew the balloon away.
   **a.** air movement       **b.** to coil around something

## Synonyms and Antonyms    pages 178–179

Write a synonym (S) or an antonym (A) for each word.

**6.** lovely (S)      **7.** empty (A)      **8.** little (S)
**9.** difficult (A)   **10.** awful (S)     **11.** sparkling (A)
**12.** neat (S)       **13.** early (A)     **14.** nibble (S)
**15.** future (A)     **16.** large (S)     **17.** first (A)
**18.** narrow (S)     **19.** night (A)     **20.** giggle (S)

## Using Synonyms and Antonyms    pages 180–181

Use this thesaurus entry to answer these questions.

---

**huge,** adj., large, immense, enormous, great,
mammoth, gigantic, tremendous
*Antonyms,* undersized, puny, petty

---

**21.** What is the entry word in this thesaurus sample?
**22.** How many antonyms does the word have?
**23.** Is *mammoth* a synonym or an antonym for the word *huge*?
**24.** What part of speech is *huge*?
**25.** What synonym could you use in place of *huge* in this sentence?
The new skyscraper was *huge*.

## Combining Sentences with Adjectives    pages 182–183

Combine the adjectives from the sentences in each set into one
sentence, using the word *and*. Write the sentences. Remember to use
commas where they are needed.

**1.** The man's beard was long.
The man's beard was black.
The man's beard was curly.

**2.** The porcupine's quills are sharp.
The porcupine's quills are long.
The porcupine's quills are hollow.

**3.** The kitten's fur is silky.
The kitten's fur is soft.

**4.** The bird's cry is shrill.
The bird's cry is piercing.

**5.** The clouds are big.
The clouds are white.
The clouds are fluffy.

## Writing and Editing a Descriptive Paragraph   pages 184–187

**6.** Write a paragraph describing your favorite food. It might be a favorite meat dish, or a favorite vegetable dish, or a favorite dessert. Then edit it for descriptive adjectives and adverbs.

## Description in Poetry   pages 188–189

**1.** Read the poem. List the eight words in the poem that describe the dog.

> I'm a lean dog, a keen dog, a wild dog, and lone;
> I'm a rough dog, a tough dog, hunting on my own;
> I'm a bad dog, a mad dog, teasing silly sheep;
> I love to sit and bay the moon, to keep fat souls from sleep.
>
> "Lone Dog" by *Irene Rutherford McLeod*

## Comparison in Poetry   pages 190–191

**2.** Read this part of a poem. What two things are compared in the first line of the poem? Write a sentence to tell how these two things may be alike.

> A road like brown ribbon,
> A sky that is blue,
> A forest of green
> With that sky peeping through.
>
> "September" *by Edwina Fallis*

## Description in a Tall Tale   pages 192–195

**3.** Read this part of a tall tale about Joe Magarac, a steelworker. Then list three examples of exaggeration from the tale.

Joe Magarac worked with his hands. He stirred the cooking steel with his hands and scooped it up by the handful and poured it into the ingot molds. He often made horseshoes and cannonballs with his bare hands. He'd grab the hot steel and squeeze out eight fine steel railroad rails at once from between his fingers, four to each hand.

# LANGUAGE
Learning About Pronouns

# COMPOSITION
Writing a Report

# STUDY SKILLS
Organizing Information

# LITERATURE
Reading an Article

Have you ever written a report? What was it about? Why did you write it? Writing a report is one way of finding out more about something that interests you. It is also a way of telling facts about a topic in an orderly way to someone else.

Look at the pictures on the opposite page. They show several different subjects. What do you know about these subjects? Which ones could you tell about in a report?

In this unit you will learn how to organize information to write a report. You will find tips on how to give an oral report in front of your class. You will also read an interesting magazine article.

# LANGUAGE

## Lesson 1: Understanding Pronouns

Read these two paragraphs. Both tell what is happening in the picture. How are the paragraphs different?

1.     Francine took the bicycle out of the garage. Francine noticed a flat tire, so Francine fixed the flat tire. Marcy helped Francine.

2.     Francine took the bicycle out of the garage. She noticed a flat tire, so she fixed it. Marcy helped her.

### Think and Discuss

In paragraph 1 the same nouns are repeated over and over. In paragraph 2 **pronouns** are used in place of the nouns. The word *she* is a pronoun. It replaces the noun *Francine.* In paragraph 2 what other pronoun means *Francine?* The word *it* is also a pronoun. Find the pronoun *it* in paragraph 2. What words in paragraph 1 have this pronoun replaced?

Study this list of pronouns.

| I | me | we | us | he | him |
|---|----|----|----|----|----|
| she | her | it | they | them | you |

Now read these sentences. Find the pronouns. Tell which nouns the pronouns replace.

3. Sue rode the bicycle.     4. She rode away.

5. Jed pedaled hard.     6. He followed Sue.

> • A **pronoun** is a word used in place of a noun or nouns.

## Practice

**A.** Write the sentences. Underline the pronouns.

1. Bicycles are fun, but they can be dangerous.
2. Jan always wears light colors when she rides at night.
3. Signal to drivers when you plan to make a turn.
4. We are careful to ride with the traffic.
5. Jan checks the bike often and keeps it clean.
6. We try to carry water with us on long bike trips.
7. I will follow you on this busy street.
8. She showed them how to pump up a tire correctly.

**B.** Find the pronoun in the second sentence of each pair. Write the pronoun and the noun or nouns it replaces.

9. Fran talked to the class. She explained bicycle safety.
10. Jody and Sue made a safety poster. They wanted to tell rules for riding at night.
11. Beth listened carefully. A police officer showed her ways to protect a bicycle from thieves.
12. A bell on the handlebars is important. It warns people a bike rider is coming.
13. Reflectors help drivers see a rider. Put them on the back and front of a bike.
14. Paul let Marcy ride the bike. He said Marcy rode well.
15. The police officer praised Marcy and Paul. The officer gave them an award.

## Apply

**C. 16.–20.** Write a paragraph about bicycles. Use at least five different pronouns from the list on page 202. Write five sentences.

# Lesson 2: Using Subject Pronouns

Remember that a pronoun takes the place of a noun or nouns. Read these pairs of sentences. Look at the underlined pronouns. Name the noun or nouns each pronoun replaces.

1. Jeff rides a new skateboard.
2. He rides down the sidewalk.
3. Janice and Miriam are bringing skateboards.
4. They want to ride with Jeff.

## Think and Discuss

*Jeff* is the subject of sentence 1. What pronoun takes the place of *Jeff* in sentence 2? The subject of sentence 3 is *Janice and Miriam*. What pronoun takes the place of these words in sentence 4? The words *he* and *they* are **subject pronouns.** They take the place of a noun or nouns in the subject of a sentence.

> ● The words *I, you, he, she, we, they,* and *it* are **subject pronouns.**

## Practice

**A.** Rewrite each sentence. Use a subject pronoun to replace the underlined noun or nouns.

1. Lou and his sister Maria check their skateboards.
2. Lou spins the wheels of his board.
3. A screw needs to be tightened.
4. Maria checks the deck of the board for cracks.
5. Lou and Maria use wrenches for their work.

**B.** Write the second sentence of each pair. Use a subject pronoun to replace the underlined word or words in the first sentence.

Michelle and Richie go skateboarding often.

6. _____ will take a long ride on this hot day.

Michelle places her feet on the board.

7. _____ gets her balance.

Richie does the same thing.

8. Then _____ pushes off.

The skateboard makes a roaring sound.

9. _____ rolls down the street.

Michelle and Richie keep their arms out.

10. _____ glide smoothly.

Then Michelle makes a turn.

11. _____ turns to the right.

Richie follows her.

12. _____ is getting worried.

A hill is in front of them.

13. _____ is very steep and long.

Michelle and Richie talk for a moment.

14. "_____ should turn around," they say.

The two skateboarders head for town.

15. _____ stop for some juice.

## *Apply*

**C. 16.–20.** Use five different subject pronouns. Write five sentences about your favorite pastime on wheels. Your sentences might be about riding a bicycle, taking a car ride, skateboarding, or roller-skating.

# Lesson 3: Using Pronouns After Action Verbs

Look at the pictures and read the sentences. Notice the underlined words.

1. Lila helps Ralph.
2. Ralph thanks Lila.
3. Lila helps <u>him</u>.
4. Ralph thanks <u>her</u>.

The words *him* and *her* are pronouns. Name the noun each pronoun replaces.

## Think and Discuss

In sentences 1–4 the subjects are nouns. Pronouns replace nouns in the predicates of sentences 3 and 4. The pronouns follow action verbs. What action verb does *him* follow? What action verb does *her* follow?

Read the paragraph. The underlined words are all pronouns. Some of the pronouns follow action verbs.

Lila and <u>I</u> are making sandwiches. <u>We</u> make <u>them</u> today. Barry is here too. <u>He</u> doesn't know what to do, so <u>I</u> teach <u>him</u>. Then <u>he</u> helps <u>us</u>.

Find the verbs *make, teach,* and *helps.* What are the pronouns that follow these action verbs?

> • The words *me, you, him, her, it, us,* and *them* are pronouns that follow action verbs.

## Practice

**A.** Write the sentences. Underline the pronoun that follows each action verb.

1. Heidi invited us to a surprise party.
2. The class is planning it.
3. Barry told her about the party.
4. Lila told me.
5. Sue gave them a birthday cake.

**B.** Use pronouns to replace the underlined words. Write the new sentences.

6. Barry, Lila, and I invited <u>Ramon</u> to a party.
7. We asked <u>Kelly and Ned</u> too.
8. Lisa brought <u>the present</u>.
9. We surprised <u>Loretta</u>.
10. Everyone thanked <u>Barry, Lila, and me</u>.

## Apply

**C.** Use these pronouns in sentences. Be sure each one follows an action verb.

**11.** you  **12.** them  **13.** me  **14.** us  **15.** him

### A Challenge

Think of ten action verbs. Write ten sentences, using one action verb in each. Use pronouns from this lesson to follow the action verb. You might want to write all of your sentences about a party you attended.

# Lesson 4: Understanding Possessive Pronouns

Read these sentences.

1. Marty's suitcase is packed for camp.
2. His suitcase is packed for camp.

The underlined word in sentence 1 is a possessive noun. It tells that Marty owns the suitcase. Which word in sentence 2 takes the place of the possessive noun?

## Think and Discuss

The word *his* is a **possessive pronoun.** Possessive pronouns are used in place of possessive nouns. A possessive pronoun shows who or what owns or has something.

Read these sentences. Find the possessive nouns. Then find the possessive pronouns.

3. Penny's suitcase dropped open.
4. Her suitcase dropped open.
5. The camp's lunch bell rang.
6. Its lunch bell rang.

Whose suitcase dropped open? Which word is used in place of the word *Penny's* in sentence 4? *Camp's* is a possessive noun. Which pronoun has been used in place of *camp's*? The words *her* and *its* are possessive pronouns.

> ● The words *my, your, his, her, our, their,* and *its* are **possessive pronouns.**

## Practice

**A.** Write the sentences. Underline the possessive pronouns.

1. My camp is terrific.
2. Our cabin is like an old log cabin.
3. Its walls are built out of real logs.
4. Katie Gold is my bunk mate.
5. Her family is from Vermont.
6. Their house is not far from Burlington.
7. Muriel Steele is my counselor.
8. Her favorite sport is canoeing.
9. Say hello to your brother.
10. His letter came in the mail today.

**B.** Use possessive pronouns to replace the underlined words. Write the new sentences.

11. The parents' visting day is next Saturday.
12. Ramona's parents are coming.
13. John's team is getting ready for the canoe races.
14. Do you think the canoe's paint is dry yet?
15. Pedro and Carmen's canoe is the red one.

## Apply

**C.** **16.–20.** Pretend you are at camp. Write a letter to a friend. Use five possessive pronouns in your letter. Remember to include all the parts of a letter. Sign your name at the end.

# Lesson 5: Using the Pronouns I and Me

When you speak of yourself, you use the pronouns *I* and *me*. Read the sentences that Neka wrote. Notice how *I* and *me* are used.

1. My brother and I play stoopball.
2. Dad gave Fran and me some tadpoles.

## Think and Discuss

You have used the pronouns *I* and *me* before. Remember that *I* is a subject pronoun. Use it in the subject of a sentence. The pronoun *me* follows an action verb. Use it in the predicate of a sentence. Look at these examples. Should you use *I* or *me*? Why?

3. Aunt Alice brought Ginny and (I, me) a present.
4. Ginny and (I, me) thanked her.

When you speak of yourself and someone else, always name yourself last. Read sentences 1 and 2 again. Why did Neka use *I* in sentence 1? Why did she use *me* in sentence 2? Did she name herself last?

## Practice

**A.** Use *I* or *me*. Write the sentences.

1. My family and _____ do things together.
2. Last year my sister Nan and _____ went on a bike trip together.
3. The trip tired Nan and _____.
4. Yesterday Mom and _____ built a doghouse.
5. Nan told Mom and _____ that we did a good job.

**B.** Complete each sentence. Use the correct phrase—*Sally and I* or *Sally and me.* Write the sentences.

6. _____ also do things together.
7. _____ went to see the whales at the aquarium.
8. Paul helped _____ build a treehouse.
9. Tomorrow _____ will plant a flower garden.
10. Mom bought _____ a book about flower gardens.

## Apply

**C. 11.–15.** Write five sentences about yourself and your friends. Use these words.

      my friends and I         my friends and me

# HOW OUR LANGUAGE GROWS

Do you ever wear borrowed clothes? Perhaps not, but the names for many of the clothes you wear are borrowed. The words *dress, boot,* and *scarf* come from an older form of French. The word *belt* comes from a word in Old German.

1. For each of the clothing words, write the language and word from which it comes.

   **a.** moccasin     Italian, *pantalone*
   **b.** poncho       Sanskrit, *sati*
   **c.** pants         Spanish, *pontho*
   **d.** skirt          Native American, *mokkussin*
   **e.** sari          Old Norse, *skyrta*

2. Tell the language from which each word comes. Then tell what kind of clothing it is. Use your dictionary for help.

   a. sombrero    b. kimono    c. beret

# Lesson 6: Using Pronouns That End with <u>self</u> or <u>selves</u>

Read the sentences. How do the underlined words end?

1. Mike bought <u>himself</u> a book to read on the trip.
2. Tina packed a lunch for Mike and <u>herself</u>.
3. The children went on a bus by <u>themselves</u>.

## Think and Discuss

Some pronouns end in *self* or *selves*. They are formed by adding *self* or *selves* to other pronouns.

In sentences 1, 2, and 3, which words end in *self* or *selves*? These words refer to nouns in the sentences. What are those nouns? The word *himself* stands for Mike. The word *herself* refers to Tina. *Themselves* refers to the children.

Look at the chart of pronouns that end in *self* and *selves*.

| Singular Pronouns | Plural Pronouns |
|---|---|
| myself | ourselves |
| yourself | yourselves |
| himself | themselves |
| herself | |
| itself | |

Which pronouns end in *self?* Use these singular pronouns to talk about one person.

4. Dad saw *himself* in the mirror.

Which pronouns end in *selves?* Use these plural pronouns to talk about more than one.

5. Mom and Dad saw *themselves*.

## Practice

**A.** Use pronouns ending in *self* and *selves.* Write the sentences.

1. My sister taught _____ to play the drums.
2. Grandpa and Grandma take long trips by _____.
3. We want to watch TV by _____.
4. Ron told _____ not to be scared.
5. My ski slid down the hill by _____.
6. I was happy with _____ for running so fast.
7. Lois is going to fix the squeaky door _____.
8. Paula, you made _____ late by not setting the clock.
9. Mom and I painted the basement _____.
10. You boys should have seen _____.

## Apply

**B. 11.–18.** Use each of the eight pronouns from the chart on page 212. Write a sentence for each word.

### To Memorize

**Night**

Stars over snow,
 And in the west a planet
Swinging below a star —
 Look for a lovely thing and you will find it.
It is not far —
 It never will be far.

*Sara Teasdale*

Where does the poet suggest you will find something lovely? Name some things that you think are lovely. Can ordinary things be lovely?

# LANGUAGE REVIEW

**Pronouns**    pages 202–203

Copy the pairs of sentences. Underline the pronoun in the second sentence. Circle the word or words it refers to in the first sentence.

1. Bill caught the baseball. Bill threw it to Vicky.
2. Bill and Vicky are here. They live nearby.
3. Vicky is in the fifth grade. She is 10 years old.
4. Vicky and I were roller-skating. We went fast.
5. Vicky got new skates. Vicky uses them often.
6. Aren't Bill and I good skaters? May taught us.

**Subject Pronouns**    pages 204–205

Copy the sentences. Underline the subject pronouns.

7. She rides and jumps in horse shows all summer.
8. Every morning before school they feed the horses.
9. I love to watch horses playing in the field.
10. Last Wednesday we had a riding lesson in the ring.
11. He is the biggest horse in the stable.
12. It is a huge stable, with stalls for 30 horses.

**Pronouns After Action Verbs**    pages 206–207

Copy the sentences. Underline the pronouns that follow action verbs.

13. The teacher chose me.
14. Will Ralph answer it?
15. Ben gave her a pen.
16. Jo read him the story.
17. The children heard him.
18. Heidi brought them.
19. Is Bob chasing us?
20. The play made me laugh.
21. Guy and Amy know you.
22. Did Julie find it?
23. Rosie sent us a note.
24. The boy is watching you.

## Possessive Pronouns    pages 208–209

Copy the sentences. Underline the possessive pronouns.

**25.** Gary helped his mother make a salad for lunch.
**26.** Their tunafish sandwiches are on the table.
**27.** Sue brought her homemade bread to the meeting.
**28.** The fruit in my lunchbox is not ripe enough.
**29.** Will Peggy and Bob bring their friend to dinner?
**30.** Ann's recipe book has lost half its pages.

## Using I and Me    pages 210–211

Complete each sentence with *I* or *me*. Write the sentences.

**31.** Sally and (I, me) write letters to each other since she moved away.
**32.** Sally sends (I, me) pictures of her family.
**33.** Grandfather gave Sally and (I, me) special stamps.
**34.** Grandfather and (I, me) live on the same block.
**35.** Yesterday he helped my brother and (I, me) with our homework.
**36.** He showed him and (I, me) some tricks with numbers.

## Pronouns That End with self or selves    pages 212–213

Write the sentences. Use the correct pronoun that ends with *self* or *selves*.

**37.** I mowed the backyard lawn _____.
**38.** We treated _____ to some fresh fruit.
**39.** Melissa taught _____ a forward roll.
**40.** The ball rolled by _____.
**41.** Did you two girls build this by _____?
**42.** The boy earned the money _____.

## Applying Pronouns

**43.–50.** Write eight sentences. Use at least three subject pronouns. Use at least three pronouns after action verbs. Include some possessive pronouns and pronouns that end in *self* or *selves*.

# STUDY SKILLS

## Lesson 7: Choosing and Limiting a Topic

Ella had to write a report for her social studies class. The class was studying America between the years 1900 and 1940. Ella had to write about something that happened during this period.

Ella was interested in airplanes. She thought she would write about this part of America's history. However, when she went to the library she found a whole shelf of books on aviation. What do you think Ella should do?

### Think and Discuss

Ella decided that her report topic was too big. She thought pilots might make an interesting subject. However, she realized that this might be too big a topic also. After all, she was told to write a few paragraphs. What should Ella do now?

Ella narrowed her topic further. She decided to write about only one woman who was a famous pilot—Amelia Earhart.

---

**How to Choose a Report Topic**

1. **Choose a topic that interests you.**
2. **Limit your topic so that it is not too big or too small. The whole report should be about the topic.**
3. **Be sure you can tell about your topic in a short report. Ask yourself this question: Can I tell about this topic in two or three paragraphs?**

---

## Practice

**A.** For each group choose the topic that would make the best short report.

1. A History of Dancing
   Modern Dancers
   Martha Graham's Dance Company
2. George Washington's Boyhood
   The Life of George Washington
   American Presidents
3. The History of Quilting
   How to Make a Quilt
   Ten Famous Quilt Makers
4. The Knights of Europe
   The Jobs of a Knight
   The Armor of a Knight
5. The Blue Whale
   Mammals
   Whales
6. All About Insects
   How Bees Communicate
   Insect Homes

**B.** For each subject, write a smaller topic that you could use for a report.

7. Planets    **8.** Foods    **9.** Animals
10. Presidents    **11.** Sports    **12.** Holidays
13. School    **14.** Hobbies    **15.** Travel

## Apply

**C. 16.** Pick one of these subjects or a subject from Practice B. Limit the topic for a report you will write.

| Cars | States of the United States | Books |
| Science | Famous People | Countries |

In her report about Amelia Earhart, Ella wants to answer two questions. What records did Amelia Earhart set? What happened on her flight across the Atlantic Ocean?

## Think and Discuss

Here is some information Ella read about Amelia Earhart.

Once Amelia Earhart became a trained pilot she began setting one record after another. She became the first woman to fly alone across the United States and back again. Then she flew across the Atlantic Ocean with a friend. She became the first woman to fly across the Atlantic Ocean.

After setting this record, Earhart decided to fly across the Atlantic alone. On May 20, 1932, she took off from Harbor Grace, Newfoundland. It was 7:12 P.M. Soon after takeoff, she flew through a heavy ice storm that rocked and jolted the plane. Then suddenly part of her plane's engine cracked. Earhart flew on for many fearful hours. Exactly 13 hours and 30 minutes after takeoff, she landed safely in Ireland.

Now read what Ella wrote about her first question.

---

*Amelia Earhart*, by John Parlin, pages 58-60
What records did Amelia Earhart set ?
first woman to fly by herself across the
U.S. and back
first woman to fly across Atlantic
first woman to fly alone across Atlantic

---

For her report, Ella must remember important ideas that she read. To do this she took the notes shown on page 218. Notice that Ella does not copy the information exactly. She does not write complete sentences. She leaves out information that does not apply to her questions.

**How to Take Notes**
1. **List the title of the book, the author, and the page numbers on which you find information.**
2. **Write only facts you want to include in your report.**
3. **Write the information in your own words.**
4. **Write sentences or write short groups of words.**

## Practice

A. Pretend you are writing a report about the Wright brothers' airplane. Write the notes you would use.

1. Wright brothers' plane was a biplane
2. wings were wooden frames covered with cloth
3. British inventor George Cayley built first glider
4. plane had wooden runners instead of wheels
5. Wright brothers manufactured bicycles
6. lightweight gasoline engine propelled the plane

B. Use the article about Amelia Earhart on page 218. Take notes to answer Ella's second question:

7. What happened on Earhart's famous flight across the Atlantic Ocean?

## Apply

C. 8.–9. Use the topic you chose in Lesson 7. Write two questions about it. Visit your school or public library to find information about your topic. Take notes to answer your questions.

# Lesson 9: Making an Outline

Ella wrote the notes for her report. Next she will put her notes in an order that makes sense.

## Think and Discuss

Ella will make an **outline**. An outline is a way to organize information. Read Ella's outline.

Amelia Earhart's Flight Records

I. Records Amelia Earhart set
  A. First woman to fly by herself across the U.S. and back
  B. First woman to fly across the Atlantic
  C. First woman to fly alone across the Atlantic
  D. First woman to fly alone across the Pacific

II. Earhart's record flight across the Atlantic
  A. Left on May 20, 1932
  B. Took off at 7:12 P.M.
  C. Flew through ice storm
  D. Plane's engine cracked
  E. Landed in Ireland 13 hours and 30 minutes after takeoff

Notice that Ella used her two questions to make the two **main topics** for her outline. Main topics are shown by Roman numerals. What are the main topics?

Facts are written as **subtopics** under main topics.
Each one is set off with a capital letter. Read the subtopics.

> **How to Make an Outline**
> 1. **Write a title that tells the subject of your report.**
> 2. **Begin each main topic at the margin. Use a Roman numeral and a period. Begin each main topic with a capital letter.**
> 3. **Indent subtopics under each main topic. Use a capital letter and a period. Begin each subtopic with a capital letter.**

## Practice

**A.** Study the outline on page 220. Then close your book. Write the outline as your teacher reads it.

**B.** Write each main topic. Put subtopics under the correct main topic. Make an outline.

Main Topics
    What Charles Lindbergh's plane was like
    Lindbergh's flight across the Atlantic

Subtopics
    Took off May 19, 1927
    Flew through ice storm and heavy fog
    Weighed two and a half tons
    Had five gas tanks
    Knew land was near when he saw fishing fleet
    Was first person to fly alone across Atlantic

## Apply

**C.** Use your notes from Lesson 8. Write an outline. Write your two questions as the two main topics. List subtopics under each main topic.

# COMPOSITION

## Lesson 10: Writing a Research Report

Ella has followed these three steps to prepare a report.

1. Choose a topic.
2. Decide on some questions about the topic. Take notes.
3. Write an outline from the notes.

Now Ella will use her outline to write a report. Read her report.

### Think and Discuss

---

*Amelia Earhart's Flight Records*

Amelia Earhart set many flying records for women pilots. She was the first woman to fly by herself across the United States and back. Another first was when she flew with a friend across the Atlantic. She also flew alone across the Atlantic Ocean and the Pacific Ocean.

One of Amelia Earhart's most important records was her flight across the Atlantic. She left Newfoundland at 7:12 P.M. on May 20, 1932. She flew through a dangerous ice storm. The engine of her plane cracked, but she made it to Ireland in 13 hours and 30 minutes.

---

What is the title of Ella's report? Notice that Ella has underlined the title of her report. What is the topic sentence of each paragraph? The topic sentence gives the main idea. The topic sentences are written from the main topics of Ella's outline. Notice that Ella wrote complete sentences from all her outline notes. Look back at the outline in Lesson 9. Does each paragraph of Ella's report follow her outline?

**How to Write a Report**

1. **Use the title and notes from your outline. Underline the title of your report.**
2. **Write a paragraph for each main topic in your outline.**
3. **Write a topic sentence from each main topic. Write detail sentences from the subtopics.**
4. **Indent the first word of each paragraph.**

## *Practice*

**A.** Use this outline. Write the first paragraph of a report about Jackie Cochran.

  I. Why Jackie Cochran was famous
    A. One of the first female pilots
    B. Entered a flying race in 1938
    C. Only woman in race
    D. Won first place

## *Apply*

**B.** Use your outline from Lesson 9. Write a two-paragraph report.

# Lesson 11: Editing a Report

Ron is writing a report. Read the outline he wrote for the first part of the report.

*Even Elephants Go to School*
I. Facts about the school
  A. Is called Young Elephants' Training Center
  B. In northern Thailand
  C. Teachers are called mahouts

## Think and Discuss

Now read the first paragraph of Ron's report. Notice the corrections he has marked.

*Even Elephants Go to School*

Did you know that elephants go to school? Their school is called the Young Elephants' Training Center School. It is in northern southern Thailand. Teachers in the school are called mahouts.

**Editing Marks**

≡ capitalize

⊙ make a period

∧ add something

∧̦ add a comma

ᵛ add quotation marks

ˏ take something away

○ spell correctly

¶ indent the paragraph

/ make a lowercase letter

∿ tr transpose

Which words did Ron change? Why? What marks did he use to show this? Why is one word circled? Ron forgot to indent the first line of his paragraph. He used this editing mark ¶ to show that the paragraph should be indented.

## Practice

**A.** Copy Ron's report. Make all the corrections shown.

## Apply

**B.** Look back at the report you wrote in Lesson 10. Then check your outline. See that all the facts are correct. Be sure you started a new paragraph for each main topic. Edit your report, and recopy it neatly.

# MECHANICS PRACTICE

### Writing Titles

- Use a capital letter to begin the first, last, and all important words in the title of a book, report, story, poem, song, or television show.
- Underline the title of a book or report.
- Use quotation marks before and after the title of a story, poem, song, or television show.

   *Examples:* ''Cinderella'' (story)    ''Yankee Doodle'' (song)

**A.** Write these titles correctly.

1. the planet venus (report)
2. nova (TV show)
3. shark lady (book)
4. oklahoma (song)
5. the park (poem)
6. black beauty (book)
7. happy days (TV show)
8. three ring circus (story)
9. yellow submarine (song)
10. dolphins (report)

**B.** Write the sentences correctly. Use capital letters, underlines, and quotation marks where they are needed.

11. We read the book inn of the four seasons in class.
12. During assembly we sang the star-spangled banner.
13. For my class show I memorized a poem called bees.
14. The story the princess and the admiral is in my reading book.
15. Do you like to watch i love lucy on television?

# Lesson 12: Presenting and Listening to an Oral Report

Every student in Carla's class will give an oral report this week. Carla wants her report on macrame to be interesting to her classmates. What has she brought to class?

## Think and Discuss

Carla planned her report carefully. She gave it a good title. She knows all the facts that belong in each paragraph. There are other important things that can help when Carla talks to her classmates. Read the suggestions.

---

**How to Give an Oral Report**

1. **Stand straight.**
2. **Look at your audience.**
3. **Speak clearly.**
4. **Have your material organized, complete, and ready to give.**
5. **Have examples, drawings, or other materials for listeners to look at.**
6. **Review the report and practice it in advance.**

---

The speaking rules will help you give a better report, but do not forget that quiet and interested listeners will help you too. Read the rules for good listeners.

**How to Listen to a Report**

1. **Listen for main ideas.**
2. **Listen for details.**
3. **Try to form pictures in your mind.**
4. **Write down questions you have about the report.**

How can mental pictures help you as you listen? Why is it important to write down questions?

## Practice

**A.** Carla's classmates gave their reports. The sentences below describe what some of them did. Write down the speaking rules from page 226 that each student broke.

1. Felipe chewed gum, which made him mumble his words.
2. Laurie kept her eyes on her saddle shoes.
3. Pete left out a paragraph of his report.
4. Anna's report was ten pages of straight reading.
5. David sat in a chair with his head resting on his hand.

**B.** **6.** Find a paragraph in this book to read aloud. You might use the story on page 264. Prepare to read it to a classmate. Ask the classmate to tell you the rules of good speaking that you follow correctly. Your classmate should follow the rules for good listening.

## Apply

**C.** **7.** Find a poem or a favorite short story that you like. Practice reading it at home in front of a mirror. Bring it to school to read aloud to your classmates.

# LITERATURE

## Lesson 13: Reading a Magazine Article

There are many places to look for information if you are going to write a report. Books, encyclopedias, filmstrips, and newspapers are good sources of information. Where else can you look for information?

### Think and Discuss

If you need information for a research report, a magazine can also help. Magazines have a variety of features. They have stories, poems, even puzzles and games. They also have **articles.** An article is a nonfiction feature. Articles give interesting information about many different topics.

Here is an article about dew from *Ranger Rick's Nature Magazine.*

### Dew

by Mark Warner

Where does dew come from and what is it made of?

In ancient times Greeks and Romans thought that dew came from goddesses. They thought that if they washed their faces with dew their skins would be clearer and better.

Until recently people thought that dew fell from the sky during the night. That was easy to believe because dew can be seen only in the morning. Since it wasn't there the evening before, people thought it must have fallen like rain. But now we know that dew does not fall from the sky; it comes out of the air around us.

Even though we can't see it, there is moisture called WATER VAPOR in the air. Warm air can hold more water vapor than cool air can. On certain hot summer days you can feel how humid it is.

When warm air cools, it gives up some of its water vapor. It CONDENSES. That is, it forms droplets of water that you can see.

Sometimes you see condensation as clouds and rain. In cold weather you see it as snow or frost! When a lot of it hangs near the ground, you see it as fog. And on a clear morning you see it clinging to grass and leaves. That's dew.

Here is an experiment. Put a glass of water and ice cubes in the refrigerator. After the glass is fairly cold, remove it. Place it on a table for a few minutes. Soon water droplets will form all over the outside of the glass. What happens is that the warm air next to the cold glass cools. This cooling makes the water vapor condense and form droplets, which cling to the glass.

Nature makes dew in the same way. During a warm sunny day the air is heated. The hot air contains a lot of water vapor. At night when the sun goes down, thin things like grass and leaves cool off very quickly. The air close to them cools off too. The water vapor in the cooled air condenses to make dew. The dew stays on the grass and leaves until the warmth of the sun makes it EVAPORATE—go back into the air as vapor.

Dew is very pure water, even purer than rain. If you

want to collect dew, you'll need to put a clean towel on the ground on a clear, cool evening following a warm sunny day. A towel is not as thin as a leaf, so it will take longer to cool and to collect drops of dew. Leave the towel outside overnight and wring it out in the morning. If the weather is right, you'll have dew water. Then you too can wash your face with some of the purest water nature can make.

As for those ancient Greeks and Romans, even if dew didn't make their skin more beautiful, it probably made it very clean.

## Practice

**A.** Write the words that answer each question.

1. If you were writing a report about how dew is formed, which fact would you use?

   **a.** Greeks and Romans washed their faces with dew.
   **b.** People thought dew fell like rain.
   **c.** Water vapor forms as cooled air condenses.
   **d.** Dew can be seen only in the morning.

2. If you were writing a report about an experiment to show condensation, which paragraph would you use?

   **a.** paragraph 3          **b.** paragraph 6
   **c.** paragraph 7          **d.** paragraph 9

3. If you were writing a report about how to collect dew, which paragraph would you use?

   **a.** paragraph 3          **b.** paragraph 6
   **c.** paragraph 7          **d.** paragraph 9

4. Which three topics could you write about using facts from this article?

   **a.** Greeks and Romans      **b.** Collecting Dew
   **c.** Formation of Dew       **d.** Old Beliefs About Dew

## Apply

**B. 5.** Use information from the article. Complete the outline.

   I. Old beliefs about dew

     A.

     B.

  II. Steps in an experiment to show condensation

     A.

     B.

     C.

# A BOOK TO READ

Title: **All About Mud**
Author: Oliver R. Selfridge
Publisher: Addison-Wesley Publishing Company

Did you ever think of writing a report about mud? Here is a whole book about it! Included is information about how mud acts, where to find mud, and animals that like mud. Amusing stories about the discovery of mud, and about a boy who filled a mud hole with chocolate pudding and fooled his dad, are just part of the fun. You're even invited to send in your ideas about how mud was discovered. The author gives you the address.

Oliver R. Selfridge is a computer scientist and mathematician. He still found mud an interesting subject. You will too when you read this book!

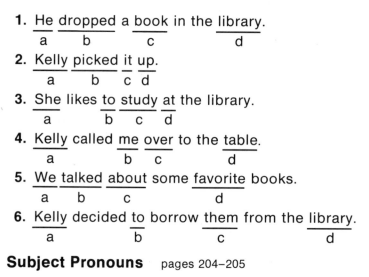

# 6 UNIT TEST

● **Pronouns**     pages 202–203

Write the letter of the word in each sentence that is a pronoun.

1. He dropped a book in the library.
   a    b        c              d
2. Kelly picked it up.
   a      b      c d
3. She likes to study at the library.
   a     b   c   d
4. Kelly called me over to the table.
   a            b   c          d
5. We talked about some favorite books.
   a    b      c              d
6. Kelly decided to borrow them from the library.
   a            b          c              d

● **Subject Pronouns**     pages 204–205

Copy each sentence. Underline the subject pronouns.

7. We love the snow.
8. Most of all I like to make snow angels.
9. Sometimes we meet at the hill for sledding.
10. They always build a snow fort.
11. Yesterday she made a beautiful snow sculpture.

● **Pronouns After Action Verbs**     pages 206–207

Copy the sentences. Underline the pronouns that follow action verbs.

12. Please take us to the beach.
13. You can also drive them in the car.
14. Call us when it is time to leave.
15. His mother wants him home by four o'clock.
16. I told her not to worry.

## Possessive Pronouns    pages 208–209

Copy each sentence. Underline the possessive pronouns.

17. At last the day came to sail in our boat.
18. The breeze blew his hair.
19. Cally had a great smile on her face.
20. The sailboat found its course.
21. I lay on my back all day in the sun.
22. When the rain started, he dashed to his car.
23. They left their books out in the rain.
24. I hear the rain pounding on our car roof.
25. She put on her raincoat.
26. I saw your mother waiting for us under an umbrella.

## Using I and Me    pages 210–211

Write each sentence. Use the correct pronoun.

27. Dad took Brad and _____ on a train.   (I, me)
28. Brad and _____ had a snack in the snack car.   (I, me)
29. Then Brad and _____ took our seats.   (I, me)
30. Dad called to Brad and _____ to look out of the window.
    (I, me)
31. Brad and _____ saw some beautiful mountains.   (I, me)

## Pronouns That End with self or selves    pages 212–213

Write each sentence. Use the correct word.

32. We paid the conductor _____.   (ourselves, myself)
33. I explored the long train _____.   (themselves, myself)
34. We left Dad to read his book by _____.   (himself, herself)
35. Mrs. David left the train by _____.   (ourselves, herself)
36. Do you want to leave by _____? (yourselves, themselves)
37. The people on the train departed by _____.   (ourselves, themselves)
38. Dad and I toured the city by _____.   (ourselves, yourselves)
39. Dave explored the museums by _____.   (himself, themselves)
40. Let's stay in the city a few more days by _____.   (themselves, ourselves)

## Choosing a Topic    pages 216–217

For each group choose the topic that would make the best short report.

1. **a.** Rain
   **b.** All About Storms
   **c.** Why Rain Falls
2. **a.** Giraffes
   **b.** A Giraffe's Appearance
   **c.** Zoo Animals
3. **a.** My Favorite Book
   **b.** Books
   **c.** Children's Books
4. **a.** Astronauts
   **b.** Space Travel
   **c.** The First Astronaut

## Taking Notes    pages 218–219

Read this article.

An avocado is a fruit that is round, egg-shaped, or bottle-shaped. It is sometimes called an *"alligator pear."* That's because its green outer skin is so leathery and tough. Inside the skin is yellow-green pulp. It is soft as butter and has a nutty flavor. In the center of an avocado is a large, hard seed.

5. Write the notes that answer the question, What are the parts of an avocado?

   **a.** has outer green skin
   **c.** has yellow-green pulp
   **b.** sometimes called alligator pear
   **d.** has large, hard seed in center

## Outlining    pages 220–221

6. Read the notes about bats. Write the main topics and subtopics in outline form.

   | Main topics | Subtopics |
   | --- | --- |
   | How bats navigate | Flying foxes |
   | Kinds of bats | Brown bats |
   | | By using sense of smell |
   | | Vampire bats |
   | | By means of echoes |
   | | By vision |

## ● Writing and Editing a Research Report   pages 222–225

**1.** Choose a topic and write a research report about it. Take notes and prepare an outline. Then edit your report. Be sure all the details are correct.

## ● Giving a Report in Class   pages 226–227

Is each sentence a rule for good public speaking? Write *true* or *false* to answer.

**2.** Stand up straight and look at your audience.
**3.** Speak quickly.
**4.** Organize your material and have it ready to deliver.
**5.** Display examples, drawings, or other materials to support your research.
**6.** Never practice a report before giving it.
**7.** Do not look at your audience.
**8.** Speak clearly.

## ● Reading a Magazine Article   pages 228–231

Read this part from an article to find information on the food of salamanders.

Salamanders are timid, harmless animals that look like lizards but are related to frogs and toads. They are cold-blooded animals with moist, slimy skins, four legs, and a long tail.

Most salamanders are night hunters that eat insects, worms, slugs, snails, and other small creatures. One kind eats water plants called algae, and a few kinds may even eat smaller salamanders.

Write the facts that you would use to write a report about the food of salamanders.

**1.** They eat insects and worms.
**2.** One kind eats water plants called algae.
**3.** A few eat smaller salamanders.
**4.** Salamanders live under rocks.

# MAINTENANCE and REVIEW

**Complete Subject and Predicate**   pages 10–11

Copy each sentence. Draw one line under the complete subject.
Draw two lines under the complete predicate.

1. Pablo lives in the country of Mexico.
2. He owns a burro named Angelito.
3. They carry vegetables to a little town.
4. His three friends walk with him.

**Common and Proper Nouns**   pages 42–43

**5.–12.** Look back at sentences 1.–4. Write eight nouns from the
sentences. Then write *common noun* or *proper noun* to tell the kind
of noun.

**Verbs**   pages 78–81

Copy each sentence. Draw two lines under the verb. Then write
*action* or *linking* to tell the kind of verb.

13. My family bought a new blue chair.
14. It is pretty.
15. Our dog chewed the cover of the old chair.

**Paragraphs**   pages 126–135

16. Write this group of sentences in correct paragraph form. Begin
    with the topic sentence. Leave out the sentence which does not
    keep to the topic.

    We even stayed up late to see the Northern Lights. We also saw
    herds of reindeer. I saw reindeer in the zoo at home. My family
    traveled to Scandinavia last summer. We saw an old Viking
    ship there.

## Adjectives and Articles    pages 162–163, 167

Write the sentences. Underline the adjectives and articles.

17. The roaring fire warms our hands and faces.
18. Freddie brings in two logs from the porch.
19. Bright sparks fly from an ember in the fireplace.

## Adverbs    pages 168–169

Write the sentences. Underline the adverbs.

20. Sing the lullabye softly.
21. Did your music teacher already teach the song?
22. Yesterday we marched to some fast music.

## Using Adjectives and Adverbs    pages 172–173

Choose the correct word. Write the sentences.

23. Juanita is a (good, well) scuba diver.
24. Underwater, she breathes (slow, slowly).
25. The oxygen tank is (safe, safely) to use.
26. You will learn (good, well) if you listen to Juanita.

## Pronouns    pages 202–203

Write the sentences. Underline the pronouns.

27. She surprised mother with it.
28. Maria and I gave them two crayons.
29. Why don't you go ahead and find her for us?

## Possessive Pronouns    pages 208–209

Use a possessive pronoun for the underlined word or words. Then use each new word group in a sentence.

30. Bob's horse
31. John and Leroy's notes
32. Marcy's house
33. Carol's smile
34. Bob's and Marcy's report
35. Leroy's laugh

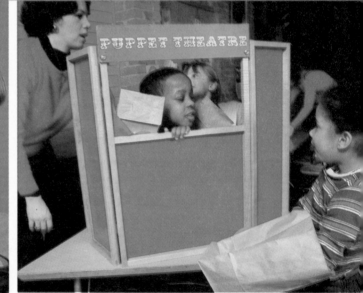

# LANGUAGE
Building Sentences
# COMPOSITION
Writing Varied Sentences

# STUDY SKILLS
Building Vocabulary
# LITERATURE
Reading a Story

Since early times people have loved to build. They have put pieces of wood or stone together to make boats, houses—even pyramids.

Look at the picture on the opposite page. What are the children doing? They are using paints and other materials to make puppets. Later they will build a puppet theater. How do you think they might use their puppet theater?

In this unit you will learn how to build new words. You will also build more interesting sentences. You will read some special stories with interesting and unusual characters. So clear your desk top, turn the page in your textbook, and begin!

# LANGUAGE

## Lesson 1: Understanding Simple Subjects

Read these sentences.

1. Five beautiful shells lay on the beach.
2. One small sand crab scurried across the sand.

Find the complete subject in sentence 1. Remember that the complete subject is all the words that make up the subject. What is the complete subject of sentence 2?

### Think and Discuss

One word in the complete subject of sentence 1 is the key or main word. That word—*shells*—is the **simple subject.** What is the simple subject of sentence 2?

The simple subject is the key word or group of words in the subject. Other words in the subject may tell more about the simple subject. The simple subject and these other words make up the complete subject.

What is the simple subject of each sentence below?

3. A large sailboat floated by.
4. Five young people dove off the boat.

> • The **simple subject** is the key word or group of words in the subject.

## Practice

**A.** Copy each sentence. Draw one line under the *complete subject* in each sentence. Circle the *simple subject* in each sentence. Sometimes the complete subject and the simple subject will be the same.

1. Three good friends went to the beach.
2. The sun baked the sand.
3. Many people crowded the beach.
4. Some families sat under umbrellas.
5. Four boys dug a hole in the sand.
6. A woman collected shells and flat stones.
7. Happy swimmers splashed in the water.
8. The lifeguard suddenly spotted the three friends.
9. He chased them off the beach.
10. No dogs are allowed at this beach.

**B.** Copy each sentence. Circle the simple subject in each sentence.

11. My birthday party took place at the beach.
12. My friends came in swimsuits.
13. Everybody buried gifts in the sand.
14. I dug up each gift and opened it.
15. Then we made a sand table.
16. My father carried a cake to the table.
17. The baker had decorated the cake with frosting.
18. Jessica asked for a big piece.
19. The best birthday gift was in my piece of cake.
20. I found a sparkling silver dollar there.

## Apply

**C.** Use each word as the simple subject of a sentence.

21. ant
22. wing
23. grasshopper
24. leaf
25. seed

# Lesson 2: Understanding Simple Predicates

Read these sentences.

1. I work hard on the weekend.
2. My whole family is busy on Saturday.
3. My sister goes to the store.

What is the complete subject of each sentence? What is the simple subject of each sentence?

## Think and Discuss

The simple subject is the key word or group of words in a complete subject. The **simple predicate** is the key word or words in a complete predicate. It tells what the subject is or does. What are the simple predicates in sentences 1, 2 and 3?

Now read these sentences. Each one contains a helping verb as well as an action verb. Helping verbs can be part of the simple predicate.

4. My brother will paint his room.
5. He has cleaned it already.

What are the simple predicates of sentences 4 and 5?

- The **simple predicate** is the key word or words in the predicate. The simple predicate is an action verb or a linking verb with any helping verbs.

## Practice

**A.** Copy each sentence. The complete predicates are underlined. Circle the simple predicates.

1. Tuesday is Rose's favorite day.
2. She stays in bed until ten in the morning.

3. She <u>smells the odors of breakfast</u>.
4. She <u>imagines stacks of waffles on the kitchen table</u>.
5. Rose <u>climbs out of bed</u>.

**B.** Copy each sentence. Draw two lines under the complete predicate. Circle the simple predicate.

6. She dresses quickly.
7. Everyone is waiting for her at the table.
8. Rose was right.
9. Stacks of waffles are piled high.
10. Rose feels happy.

## Apply

**C.** Read these sentence starters. Finish each with a complete predicate. Then circle the simple predicate.

11. Last week I
12. My school
13. In class I
14. Those three books
15. The weather on Saturday
16. Every Saturday I

## HOW OUR LANGUAGE GROWS

Would you like to have something named after you? When someone invents or discovers something, it is often named after that person.

In 1945 doctors discovered an antibody in the blood of Margaret Tracy. The antibody would fight surface infections. The ointment *bacitracin,* used on cuts and wounds, is named for her.

1. Draw a picture of a make-believe invention that you would like to have named after you.
2. Look in a dictionary or encyclopedia to find out what these people invented: Robert Bunsen, Samuel Morse, and Sylvester Graham.

# Lesson 3: Making Subjects and Verbs Agree

Read these sentences.

1. John arrives at the library.
2. The students arrive at the library.

The simple subject in sentence 1 is *John. John* is a singular noun. The simple predicate in this sentence is *arrives.* What is the simple subject in sentence 2? Is it singular or plural? What is the simple predicate?

## Think and Discuss

Simple subjects and simple predicates work together in a sentence. We say that they *agree.* In sentence 1 the verb agrees with the singular subject. The verb ends in *s.* In sentence 2 the verb agrees with the plural subject. It has no *s* ending. Now read this sentence.

3. John searches for some books.

The verb in sentence 3 agrees with the singular subject *John.* How does this verb end? When a verb ends with *s, ch, x,* or *sh,* it agrees with a singular subject by adding *es.* Now read this sentence.

4. John and Judy search for new books.

The simple subject in sentences 4 is *John and Judy.* It is plural. The verb *search* agrees with the plural subject.

> - Most verbs have one form that agrees with singular subjects. Another form agrees with plural subjects.
> - Most present tense verbs agree with singular subjects by adding *s.*
> - Present tense verbs that end in *s, ch, x,* or *sh* agree with singular subjects by adding *es.*

## Practice

**A.** Complete each sentence with the form of the verb that agrees with each subject. Choose from the words in parentheses ( ).

1. Bookshelves (stand, stands) along each wall.
2. A bookshelf (stand, stands) near the door.
3. The librarian (push, pushes) a cart.
4. The librarians (push, pushes) the carts.
5. The bookmobile (pass, passes) here on Tuesday.
6. The bookmobiles (pass, passes) here on Tuesday.
7. Students (check, checks) out their books.
8. One student (check, checks) out her books.
9. Carla (relax, relaxes) with some books.
10. The girls (relax, relaxes) with some books.

**B.** Change the verbs to agree with each subject. Rewrite each sentence with the correct verb.

11. A message need to reach the library.
12. The library close at 4:00 P.M.
13. Jeff and Sara leaves the apartment at 3:45 P.M.
14. Jeff rush down the stairs.
15. Suddenly the children hears a noise.
16. Jeff search under the stairs.
17. Sara rescue a kitten.
18. The frightened kitten hiss.
19. Jeff and Sara reaches the library.
20. Jeff turn the knob of the library door.

## Apply

**C. 21.–25.** Did the children arrive at the library in time? What was the important message they were supposed to deliver? You decide the answers. Write five sentences that tell what happens next. Be sure your subjects and verbs agree.

# Lesson 4: Changing Word Order in Sentences

Compare these sentences.

1. Is Sarah going to the fair?
2. Sarah is going to the fair.

Which sentence is a question? Which sentence is a statement?

## Think and Discuss

The words in sentences 1 and 2 are exactly the same. The words are not arranged in the same order though. In sentence 1 the helping verb comes before the subject. What is the helping verb? What is the subject?

Now look at this question.

3. Will Sarah buy a hero?

Suppose you change the word order to make this question a statement. If you change the word order you will answer the question.

4. Sarah will buy a hero.

The words *yes* or *no* are sometimes included in answers to questions. Compare these statements.

5. Yes, the fair will end by noon.
6. No, the fair will not end by noon.

Notice that a comma follows the words *yes* and *no*. Notice also that the word *not* appears in statement 6. What question do both statements 5 and 6 answer?

You can change yes/no questions to statements by changing the word order.

 • Use a comma after the words *yes* and *no* when they begin a statement.

## Practice

**A.** Write an answer to each question by changing the word order.

1. Is a fable a very short story?
2. Are the heroes in fables usually animals?
3. Are heroes also sandwiches?
4. Am I hungry enough to eat a hero now?
5. Was I hungry enough to eat one yesterday too?

**B.** Change these statements to yes/no questions. Write the questions.

6. Sue has read a fable.
7. It was about a fox.
8. The fable was very interesting.
9. The fox will learn a lesson.
10. The crow is in the fable too.

**C.** **11.–15.** Rewrite the sentences in Practice B. Begin each one with *yes* or *no*. Be sure to use correct punctuation.

## Apply

**D.** **16.–25.** Write five yes/no questions. Then write five statements that answer the questions. Begin your statements with the words *yes* and *no*.

# LANGUAGE REVIEW

**Simple Subjects**    pages 240–241

Copy the sentences. Underline the simple subject.

1. A single bird softly sang near our cabin window.
2. We hurried out to the swimming pool after breakfast.
3. A brown lizard quickly ran across the path.
4. Seth was changing into his suit.
5. The weather was dry and hot in the Arizona desert.
6. The children were diving into the swimming pool searching for pennies.
7. Four families hiked up into the mountains behind the ranch last weekend.
8. They were tired and thirsty after the hike.
9. The shadows in the desert are becoming longer as night falls.
10. Soon the tourists will pack to leave for their home in Ann Arbor, Michigan.

**Simple Predicates**    pages 242–243

Copy the sentences. Draw two lines under the simple predicate of each sentence.

11. Randy and Jeff are building a clubhouse here.
12. Inside they will have room for six people.
13. Pam and Josh went to the store for nails.
14. It is down the block, next to a grocery store.
15. The storekeeper carries all kinds of tools.
16. Amanda is painting the door of the clubhouse.
17. An hour or two from now, she will finish.
18. I am thinking of a name for our club.
19. My younger sisters are hiding behind the tree.
20. They ran quickly into the house.

## Subject-Verb Agreement    pages 244–245

Choose the correct answer. Write the sentences.

21. Grandmother and I (plan, plans) a trip.
22. We (visit, visits) the museum today.
23. Grandmother (wear, wears) comfortable shoes.
24. She (enjoy, enjoys) vacations.
25. Kevin and Janice (come, comes) with us.
26. They (enter, enters) the room where the Egyptian mummies are kept.
27. Our guide (teach, teaches) us about the ancient history and culture of Egypt.
28. Barbara (watch, watches) a slide show.
29. I (walk, walks) to the bookstore in the museum.
30. Grandmother and I (buy, buys) an art book.

## Word Order in Sentences    pages 246–247

Change these statements into questions that can be answered by *yes* or *no*.

31. The Pony Express was an early postal service.
32. One of the Pony Express riders was Buffalo Bill.
33. These mail carriers were brave.
34. We will read about them in social studies.
35. The students will write reports in class.

## Applying Sentence Building

Use these simple subjects and simple predicates in sentences of your own. Make sure your subjects and verbs agree. Write some questions too.

36. are playing      37. does know
38. people           39. friends
40. buildings        41. he
42. has begun        43. houses
44. ran              45. will go

# STUDY SKILLS

## Lesson 5: Building Words with Prefixes

Read these sentences.

1. The *happy* children found a pot of gold.
2. The *unhappy* elf forgot where he had put it.

How do the children feel? How does the elf feel?

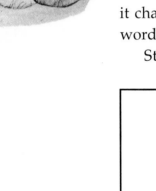

### Think and Discuss

You can change the meaning of a word by adding letters to it. The word *happy* is a base word. What letters have been added to *happy* in sentence 2? *Un* is a prefix. It means "not." Added to the beginning of a base word, it changes the meaning of the word. What does the new word mean?

Study this chart of prefixes and their meanings.

| Prefix | Meaning | Example |
|--------|-------------|-----------|
| dis | not | dislike |
| im | not | impossible |
| in | not | inactive |
| mis | incorrectly | mislabel |
| non | not | nonstop |
| pre | before | prepay |
| re | again | reread |
| re | back | repay |
| un | not | unkind |
| un | opposite of | unbutton |

> • A **prefix** is a letter or group of letters added
>   to the beginning of a base word. A prefix changes
>   the meaning of a word.

## Practice

**A.** Copy the word in each sentence that has a prefix.

**1.** I disagree with that idea.
**2.** This is a nonprofit organization.
**3.** The answer he gave is incorrect.
**4.** When we play *Statues,* I am immobile.
**5.** There is a misprint in that newspaper story.
**6.** The hiker will retrace his steps.
**7.** We saw the preview of that movie.
**8.** Taking that book was dishonest.
**9.** I have to rewrite my story.
**10.** My little brother is unable to ride a bike.

**B.** Rewrite these sentences. Add a prefix from the list
on page 250 to the word in parentheses ( ).

**11.** Susan (tied) the knot.
**12.** I read a (fiction) book.
**13.** The author (wrote) the chapter.
**14.** The student took the (test).
**15.** Stan (understood) the message.
**16.** The tailor (pinned) the cloth.
**17.** I (paid) the loan.
**18.** The tourist took an (direct) route.
**19.** The trainer grew (patient) with the puppy.
**20.** Do not be (loyal) to your friends.

## Apply

**C. 21.–25.** Choose five prefixes from the chart. Think of a word
that uses each prefix. Then write a sentence using each word.

# Lesson 6: Building Words with Suffixes

Read these sentences. Notice the underlined words.

1. The sleepy hiker rested quietly.
2. She dozed by herself under a tree.

The underlined words have endings added to base words. What are the base words?

## Think and Discuss

You know that you can build new words by adding prefixes to the beginning of base words. You can also build new words by adding letters to the end of a base word. Such endings are called **suffixes.**

You can add *y* to some base words to get a new word that tells *what kind*. What kind of hiker is described in sentence 1? You can add *ly* to some base words too. Words that end in *ly* tell *how*. How did the hiker rest?

Look back at sentence 2. What suffix has been added to *her?*

Now look at this chart. It shows some suffixes and what they mean. Notice the examples.

| Suffix | Meaning | Example |
|--------|---------|---------|
| able | able to be | breakable |
| er | one who | singer |
| ful | full of | helpful |
| less | without | homeless |
| or | one who | sailor |

> ● A **suffix** is a letter or group of letters added to the end of a base word.

## Practice

**A.** Write the sentences. Underline the words that have a suffix.

1. My uncle is a successful builder.
2. He makes comfortable new houses from old ones.
3. Sometimes the old houses are rickety.
4. The rooms are drafty.
5. I am hopeful that he can fix the walls.
6. The roofs are leaky.
7. My uncle is the director of the workers.
8. He himself checks to be sure they are not careless.
9. He sees that nothing is poorly done.
10. When he is done, the old house is more valuable.

**B.** Rewrite these sentences. Choose a suffix from the list at the right. Add it to the word in parentheses ( ).

| | |
|---|---|
| 11. The (visit) saw the new home. | **a.** ly |
| 12. Everyone thought it was (love). | **b.** or |
| 13. The (design) had done a good job. | **c.** er |
| 14. She had drawn the plans (her). | **d.** ful |
| 15. The home was in a (peace) setting. | **e.** less |
| 16. It was not at all (wind). | **f.** able |
| 17. The house looks (comfort). | **g.** self |
| 18. We will not be (home) any more. | **h.** y |

## Apply

**C.** Add a suffix to each of these words. Use each new word in a sentence of your own.

| | | |
|---|---|---|
| 19. teach | 20. slow | 21. luck |
| 22. truth | 23. care | 24. my |
| 25. govern | 26. it | 27. your |
| 28. edit | 29. truck | 30. safe |

# Lesson 7: Building Compound Words

Each of the underlined words in these sentences is made of two smaller words. Name the words.

1. A <u>cloudburst</u> is a heavy <u>rainfall</u>.
2. <u>Raindrops</u> fell on my <u>overcoat</u>.

## Think and Discuss

Some words are made by putting two smaller words together. The new word is a **compound word.**

You can often guess the meaning of a compound word if you know the short words in it. What do the words *cloudburst* and *rainfall* mean?

Read these sentences. Find the compound words. What does each compound word mean?

3. Overnight, the rain stopped.
4. Slowly, snowflakes began to fall.
5. Snow covered the rooftops of the town.

## Practice

**A.** Find the word of each pair that is a compound word. Write the two words that form the compound.

1. silky, silkworm
2. highway, highest
3. snowing, snowball
4. sailor, sailboat
5. goldfish, golden
6. playing, playground

**B.** Copy each sentence. Complete the sentence with a compound word. Put two words together from the box to make each compound word.

7. Kate played in the _____.
8. She spread an old _____ on the table.

| | |
|---|---|
| club | cloth |
| water | corn |
| story | book |
| pop | house |
| table | melon |
| red | bug |
| base | light |
| flash | ball |
| lady | bird |

9. She sliced a juicy _____.
10. Kate popped _____ too.
11. Then she read a _____.
12. Kate heard a _____ singing in the tree.
13. She saw a _____ crawl up the wall.
14. She played with a _____.
15. When it got dark, Kate turned on the _____.

## Apply

**C.** Make a list of two compound words beginning with each of these words. Then use each word in a sentence of your own. Use a dictionary if you need help.

**16.** any      **17.** out      **18.** rain      **19.** some      **20.** blue

### To Memorize

#### April Rain Song

Let the rain kiss you.
Let the rain beat upon your head with
    silver liquid drops.
Let the rain sing you a lullaby.
The rain makes still pools on the sidewalk.
The rain makes running pools in the gutter.
The rain plays a little sleep-song on our
    roof at night.
And I love the rain.

*Langston Hughes*

How does the poet describe rain? Do you love the rain?
Tell why or why not.

# Lesson 8: Using Homophones

Emily found these riddles in a book.

1. These creatures with wings *to* fly have *two* legs on which they waddle *too*. What are they?
2. *They're* creatures that scurry here and *there* on *their* eight legs. What are they?

Emily knew that the answers to the riddles were ducks and spiders. Emily also noticed that there were three words in each riddle that sounded the same. What are the words?

## Think and Discuss

The words *to, two,* and *too* appear in the first riddle. *They're, there,* and *their* are found in the second riddle. These words are **homophones.**

Study the meanings of some common homophones.

*two*—a number

*too*—also

*to*—toward something; for what purpose

*your*—belonging to you

*you're*—a contraction for *you are*

*there*—at that place

*their*—belonging to them

*they're*—a contraction for *they are*

*its*—belonging to it

*it's*—a contraction for *it is*

Now read these sentences. Decide which homophone you should use.

3. (Your, You're) watch shows (its, it's) time to go.
4. (Your, You're) going to miss the riddle contest.
5. (Its, It's) winner gets a prize.

> • **Homophones** are words that sound alike. They are spelled differently and have different meanings.

## Practice

**A.** Choose the correct homophone. Write the sentences.

1. These _____ children are my friends.   (to, two)
2. _____ names are Beth and Nathan.   (They're, Their)
3. They are sitting over _____.   (there, their)
4. _____ catching a bus soon.   (They're, There)
5. _____ arrival time is 2:00 P.M.   (It's, Its)
6. Oh, _____ coming now.   (it's, its)
7. Bring _____ lunches.   (you're, your)
8. Hurry, or _____ going to miss the bus.   (you're, your)
9. My friends are hurrying _____ the bus stop.   (to, too)
10. They are going _____ a ball game.   (to, two)
11. _____ a play-off game.   (It's, Its)

**B. 12.–15.** Listen while your teacher reads some sentences. Use the correct homophone in each sentence.

## Apply

**C.** Here are some other homophones. Read each riddle. Find the answer to it in the pair of homophones at the end of each sentence. Write the correct homophone on your paper.

16. I can sting you.   (be, bee)
17. I am found on the bottom of your shoe.   (heal, heel)
18. I am worth one penny.   (cent, scent)
19. I am a large, furry animal.   (bear, bare)
20. I can be climbed.   (stares, stairs)

### A Challenge

Write a riddle for one of the homophones in each pair. Write the answer next to your riddle.

1. sail, sale          2. sun, son          3. flour, flower
4. Sunday, sundae      5. night, knight     6. weak, week

# COMPOSITION

## Lesson 9: Combining Subjects and Predicates

Tanya wrote two sentences about the fish in her new fish tank. Then Tanya thought of another way to write the sentences. Read the sentences she wrote.

1. An angelfish swims in my fish tank.
2. A hatchetfish swims in my fish tank.
3. An angelfish and a hatchetfish swim in my fish tank.

### Think and Discuss

Read sentences 1 and 2. What is the subject and predicate of each sentence? What do the two sentences have in common? When the predicates of two sentences are the same, the subjects can often be combined. The word *and* may be used between the subjects.

Remember that the verb must agree with the complete subject of the new sentence. There are two simple subjects in sentence 3. How does the verb change?

Now read more sentences Tanya wrote.

4. My fish are beautiful.
5. My fish are healthy.
6. My fish are beautiful and healthy.

In sentences 4 and 5 the subjects are the same. When the subjects of two sentences are the same, the predicates can often be combined. What word did Tanya use to combine the predicates of sentences 4 and 5?

## Practice

**A.** Combine the subjects of each pair of sentences with the word *and*. Remember to make the verb agree with the new subject. Write the new sentence.

1. Goldfish like cool water.
   Minnows like cool water.
2. Guppies like warmer water.
   Other tropical fish like warmer water.
3. Fish live at different levels in a fish tank.
   Other creatures live at different levels in a fish tank.
4. A catfish stays near the bottom of the tank.
   A snail stays near the bottom of the tank.
5. A pearl danio swims near the top of the water.
   A hatchetfish swims near the top of the water.

**B.** Combine the predicates of each pair of sentences with the word *and*. Write the new sentences.

6. The King family chose a fish tank.
   The King family bought it.
7. Mr. King scrubbed it clean.
   Mr. King rinsed it out well.
8. He placed marbles on the bottom.
   He filled it half full of water.
9. Lou King set some plants in the bottom.
   Lou King filled the fish tank completely.
10. Sally King bought some fish.
    Sally King placed them in the fish tank.

## Apply

**C. 11.–20.** Write five short pairs of sentences. Make the subjects or predicates of each pair the same. Then combine the sentences.

# Lesson 10: Varying Sentences

Read these sentences.

1. Gloria works.
2. Gloria works at the hospital every morning.

How do the sentences differ? Which is more interesting to read?

## Think and Discuss

One way to make sentences more interesting is to add details. What details were added to sentence 2? The words *at the hospital* tell *where* Gloria works. The words *every morning* tell *when*.

Here are more sentences. What details have been added?

3. Gloria works hard.
4. Gloria works because she enjoys her job.

In sentences 3 and 4 details tell *how* and *why*.

Notice that sentences 1–4 all begin with the same words. Another way to vary your sentences is to begin them in different ways. Do not always begin with the subject. Sometimes you should add words to tell *when, where, how,* or *why* at the beginning of your sentences. Change the word order of sentence 2. Say the sentence in three different ways.

## Practice

**A.** Change the way each sentence begins by moving the words that tell *when* or *where*. Write the new sentences.

1. I dive into the pool sometimes.
2. Work is being done in the tunnel.
3. Tad and Manny took a long hike this morning.
4. We will go to the block party tomorrow.
5. We paid for our groceries at the store.

6. Fans shout at the baseball game.
7. We moved to this town two years ago.
8. Fred delivers newspapers every morning.
9. The group hung a poster on the fence.
10. The tumbleweed blew through the street.

B. Add words to the beginning or end of each sentence.
Tell *when, where, why,* or *how.* Write the new sentences.

11. There are seesaws.   (where)
12. My best friend visited.   (when)
13. The child cried.   (why)
14. Clara played golf.   (where)
15. The tubas and trumpets played.   (how)
16. These clothes fit.   (how)
17. A show about snakes is on TV.   (when)
18. Carl will come back.   (why)
19. Mr. Samuels hears a motorcycle.   (where)
20. The boys clapped.   (where)

## Apply

C. 21. Think of something you saw in a movie or on TV
that made you laugh. Write a paragraph about it.
Use words to tell *when, where, how,* and *why* at the
beginning or end of your sentences.

# Lesson 11: Editing for Sentence Variety

Read the paragraph Liz wrote about the darkling beetle. Notice the changes she has marked.

> *A darkling beetle is a common kind of beetle. It makes a good pet. ^Every morning It likes to be fed dry dog food or pieces of potato. It likes a wet sponge ^in its bowl. It will live in good health/for many years.*

**Editing Marks**

= capitalize

⊙ make a period

∧ add something

⋏ add a comma

⌄ add quotation marks

⌇ take something away

◯ spell correctly

¶ indent the paragraph

/ make a lowercase letter

∿ tr transpose

## Think and Discuss

Each sentence of the paragraph begins with the subject. To make her paragraph more interesting, Liz decided to begin some sentences in different ways. She added words that tell *when* or *where*. What editing mark shows added words? Why did Liz use this mark / ? She used this editing mark ∿ to begin a sentence with words from the end of that sentence. It tells her to change the word order, or to **transpose.** How did her changes make Liz's paragraph more interesting?

## Practice

**A.** Copy Liz's paragraph. Make all the changes shown.

## Apply

**B.** Read the paragraph you wrote in Lesson 10. Do many of your sentences begin in the same way? Change the way some sentences begin. Move words or add words that tell *when, where, why,* and *how.* Then recopy your paragraph neatly.

# MECHANICS PRACTICE

## Using Commas

- Use a comma to separate three or more words in a series.
- Use a comma after the words *yes* and *no* when they begin a statement.

Write the sentences correctly. Use commas where they are needed.

1. No we did not go to the movies this weekend.
2. No we did not work in the yard.
3. Yes we did go to the beach.
4. The cold clear and refreshing water is nice.
5. Yes we brought our new family boat.
6. Shells rocks and seaweed cover the beach.
7. The sun sand and surf are wonderful.
8. Yes we fished for mullet and bluefish.
9. The warm calm and pleasant breezes blow.
10. No we do not have a motorboat.
11. Our sailboat is red white and blue.
12. My friends Jim Samira and Liz sailed with us.
13. Yes we had a picnic at the beach.
14. We brought salad sandwiches fruit and pretzels.
15. We played tag volleyball and dodgeball.
16. At night the beautiful dark and starry sky is peaceful.
17. Yes I was tired by the time we went home.
18. My friends and I were wet tanned and happy.
19. No we will not sail next weekend.
20. Yes we can come to visit you then.

# LITERATURE

## Lesson 12: Reading Fables

For thousands of years people have been telling and listening to stories. One of the most famous storytellers was a Greek slave named Aesop. More than 2,000 years ago he told a special kind of story called a **fable.**

Fables are very short stories that are fun to read and to tell. The characters in a fable are usually animals that often act like people. Each fable teaches a lesson about these characters. Although the story is about animals, the lesson is for people. Through an interesting story, you can learn how people act. Have you ever heard any of Aesop's fables?

### Think and Discuss

Read these fables by Aesop. As you read, think about what lesson each fable teaches.

### The Fox and the Goat

A Fox fell into a deep well and could not find a way to get out. A thirsty Goat, coming to drink at the same well, saw the Fox. "Friend Fox," the Goat said in surprise, "what are you doing down there?"

The Fox thought it best to conceal his unhappy plight. "Ah," he replied, "I could not resist this excellent water. You have never tasted such fresh, clear water in all your life. I had intended to drink it up myself, but since you are a friend I will save some for you."

The Goat was so thirsty that he jumped into the well without a second thought. Then the Fox, just as quickly, leaped upon the Goat's back. Holding onto his long horns. he was able to reach the top of the well safely.

"Wait!" cried the Goat. "Help me out too."

The Fox called down, "If you had as many brains in your head as you have hairs in your beard, you would never have gone down before you had inspected the way up. I'll help you this time, but in the future *look before you leap.*"

## The Boastful Bullfrog and the Bull

A Bullfrog lived in a little bog. He thought himself not only the biggest thing in the pond but the biggest thing in the world.

"I am not like other frogs," he told anyone who would listen. "I am the biggest thing of its kind. That's why they call me a Bullfrog. I am to other frogs what a Bull is to little calves."

He had heard about Bulls, but he had really never seen one. Then one day an enormous Bull came down to the pond for a drink. For a moment the Bullfrog was startled, but it did not take long before he was as conceited as ever.

"You think you're big, don't you?" he said to the Bull. "Well, I can make myself just as big as you."

The Bull said nothing. He barely looked at the croaking creature.

"You don't believe it?" said the Bullfrog. "Just you watch!"

He blew himself up to twice his size. The Bull still ignored him.

"Not big enough?" croaked the Bullfrog. "I can make myself still bigger. See!"

This time the Bull made a scornful sound and turned his head away.

This was too much for the Bullfrog. He took a huge breath and blew, and blew, and blew himself up — until he burst.

*Don't try to seem bigger than you really are.*

The lesson at the end of the fable is called a **moral.** What is the moral of each of the fables? Sometimes the moral is not stated in the fable. Readers are left to figure out the lesson for themselves.

## *Practice*

**A.** Answer these questions. Write your answers in complete sentences.

1. In "The Fox and the Goat," the Fox teaches the Goat to "Look before you leap." In your own words, what does that mean?
2. Why do you think the Fox's advice might be good advice for people?
3. Sometimes we all brag a little or try to impress other people. What happens to the Bullfrog when he tries to impress the Bull?
4. What does Aesop mean when he says, "Don't try to seem bigger than you really are"?
5. Why is Aesop's advice good advice?

**B.** Write the names of these three animal characters from the fables you read. Next to each write a word that best describes that animal.

6. Fox       7. Goat       8. Bullfrog

**C. 9.** "The Dog and the Shadow" does not have a moral at the end. Read the fable. Think about the lesson it teaches. Write a moral to fit that lesson.

# The Dog and the Shadow

It happened that a Dog found a piece of meat and was carrying it home. Now on his way home he had to cross a plank lying across a running brook. As he crossed, he looked down and saw his own shadow reflected in the water. He thought it was another dog with another piece of meat. He wanted that meat also. So he snapped at the reflection in the water. But as he opened his mouth the piece of meat fell out, dropped into the water, and was never seen again.

## Apply

**D. 10.** Write your own fable that ends with the moral, "Never give up." Use animal characters. Think of a problem. Make sure the animal does not give up until it finds a way to solve the problem.

## A BOOK TO READ

Title: **Stone Fox**
Author: John Reynolds Gardiner
Publisher: T. Y. Crowell

The day of the big race had arrived. Willy was determined to win. His loyal dog Searchlight would run as fast as his old legs could carry him. They had to travel the tricky 10-mile course faster than the great Shoshone, Stone Fox.

Stone Fox also wanted the five hundred dollar prize at the end of the race. He would use the money to buy land for his people. He had never lost a race in his life.

One hundred feet from the finish line . . . but it would be unfair to spoil a magnificent adventure story. All readers will remember the race and Stone Fox for a long time.

# 7 UNIT TEST

● **Simple Subjects**   pages 240–241

Write the letter of the word in each sentence that is the simple subject.

1. An old bus rumbled along the street.
      a  b  c   d

2. A long line of people waited for it.
     a  b  c   d

3. Suddenly, a blue car crashed into a fire hydrant.
       a       b  c      d

4. Water splashed across the sidewalk.
      a    b    c    d

5. The frightened people stepped away from the hydrant.
       a    b    c       d

● **Simple Predicates**   pages 242–243

Copy each sentence. Draw two lines under the simple predicates.

6. Daurice is fixing the electric toaster.
7. She uses many tools.
8. Now the toaster is working again.
9. Daurice makes two slices of toast.
10. The toaster toasts the bread just right.

● **Subject-Verb Agreement**   pages 244–245

Copy each sentence. Use the verb that agrees with the subject of the sentence.

11. All my friends (meets, meet) at Benny's after school.
12. I (plays, play) tag with Betsy.

**268**   TEST: Unit 7

13. Nick and George (likes, like) to play chess.
14. Benny's mother (makes, make) pizza sometimes.
15. We (helps, help) her clean up before we go.

● **Changing Word Order in Sentences**   pages 246–247

Write a statement for each question by changing the word order.
Begin each statement with the words *yes* or *no*.

16. Is stamp collecting my hobby?
17. Was the third American President Thomas Jefferson?
18. Is a bird's home a nest?
19. Is Mrs. Miller our science teacher?
20. Is the Mississippi the longest river in the United States?
21. Are iguanas lizards?
22. Are Saturn and Pluto planets?

● **Prefixes and Suffixes**   pages 250–253

Copy each word. Underline the base word. Circle the prefix or suffix.

| | | |
|---|---|---|
| 1. unglue | 2. improper | 3. mislabel |
| 4. incomplete | 5. careful | 6. rejoin |
| 7. remake | 8. teacher | 9. helpless |
| 10. prewar | 11. sweetly | 12. unstick |
| 13. director | 14. disappear | 15. lucky |
| 16. nonprofit | 17. passable | 18. indirect |

● **Compound Words**   pages 254–255

Copy these sentences. Underline the compound words.

19. Mr. Smith baited his fishhook.
20. Ms. Rand fished in the afternoon sunshine.
21. The men caught bluefish and sunfish.
22. At sunset it was time for dinner.
23. The men fried their fish and ate cornbread.
24. For dessert they munched blueberries.
25. The men drove to the airport.
26. They watched the afternoon activity on the airfield.
27. Two workers walked out onto the airstrip.
28. They wheeled out a cart containing airmail letters.

## Homophones pages 256–257

Copy each sentence. Choose the correct homophone in each sentence.

29. We're going _____ the park.   (to, too)
30. Will you come _____?   (two, too)
31. When we get_____ we will play ball.   (their, there)
32. Ben and Rhea are coming _____.   (to, too)
33. They will bring _____ ball.   (their, they're)
34. _____ such a beautiful day.   (Its, It's)
35. Perhaps you can bring _____ kite.   (your, you're)
36. Is _____ string long enough?   (its, it's)
37. Then we will have _____ things to do.   (too, two)
38. _____ going to enjoy this day.   (Your, You're)
39. _____ going to meet us at our park.   (Their, They're)
40. I hope we find them _____.   (their, there)

## Combining Subjects and Predicates   pages 258–259

Combine the subjects or the predicates of each pair of sentences using the word *and*. Write the new sentences.

1. Bonnie walked to the grocery store.
   Bonnie shopped for fruit.
2. Apples looked the best.
   Oranges looked the best.
3. Bonnie picked out some fruit.
   Bonnie looked for vegetables.
4. The lettuce appeared wilted.
   The celery appeared wilted.
5. The radishes seemed the freshest vegetables.
   The carrots seemed the freshest vegetables.
6. Bonnie examined the vegetables carefully.
   Bonnie discarded the bad pieces.
7. She chose the best vegetables.
   She walked to the checkout counter.
8. Bonnie purchased the fruit and vegetables.
   Bonnie returned home again.

## ● Writing and Editing Varied Sentences     pages 260–263

Add words to the beginning or end of each sentence. Tell *when,
where, why,* or *how.* Write the new sentences. Be sure they do not
all begin with a subject.

   **9.** I earned some money.   (why)
  **10.** I baby-sat for the Corbys.   (when)
  **11.** I dried dishes.   (when)
  **12.** I shopped for Mrs. Mann.   (where)
  **13.** I raked leaves.   (when)
  **14.** I washed my mother's car.   (how)
  **15.** I ran errands for Mr. Thorpe.   (when)
  **16.** I cleaned out the garage.   (when)
  **17.** I counted my money.   (why)
  **18.** I had earned a lot of money.   (how)
  **19.** I spent it.   (where)
  **20.** I will earn more money.   (how)

## ● Reading a Fable     pages 264–267

Read this fable. Then answer the questions.

### The Fox and the Grapes

   The Fox had gone without breakfast as well as without dinner,
so when he found himself in a vineyard his mouth began to water.
There was one particularly juicy-looking bunch of grapes hanging
on a trellis. The Fox leaped to pull it down, but it was just beyond
his reach. He went back a few steps, took a running start, and
jumped again. Again he missed. Once more he tried, and once
more he failed to get the tempting prize. Finally, weary and worn
out, he left the vineyard. "I really wasn't very hungry," he said, to
console himself. "Besides, I'm sure those grapes are sour."

   **1.** What is the fox doing in this fable?
   **2.** What do we call the lesson a fable teaches?
   **3.** What is the lesson this fable teaches?

# LANGUAGE
## Listening and Speaking
# COMPOSITION
## Writing a Story

# STUDY SKILLS
## Finding Information
# LITERATURE
## Reading a Story

Did you know you spend at least half your time in school listening? You listen for information and to get directions. You listen to your teachers and classmates. You listen to guest speakers.

Do you stop listening when you go home? Most certainly you do not. In fact, you may spend even *more* than half your time at home listening. You listen to your family, to telephone conversations, to TV, and to the radio. It almost seems as if you get most of your knowledge through your ears. Look at the pictures on the opposite page. What kinds of things can these people learn by listening? In this unit you will see how good listening is a way to learn. You will also read about some helpful reference books. You will read and write stories.

# LANGUAGE

## Lesson 1: Making Introductions

Diane is introducing her new friend to her mother. Read what she says.

1. "Mother, I would like you to meet David. He just moved into the Greens' old house."

Diane's mother shakes David's hand. She says a few words to make David feel welcome. Read what she says.

2. "David, I'm glad to meet you. How do you like our neighborhood so far?"

### Think and Discuss

When you introduce people, you always say their names. Who is making the introduction above? Who is being introduced? You should also try to say something about the people you are introducing. If you do, you will help them to start the conversation. What did Diane tell her mother about David?

Notice that Diane introduced the younger person, David, to the older person, her mother. This is the polite way to make introductions.

Sometimes you may forget the name of the person you want to introduce. If you do, talk about the person for a moment. This may help you remember his or her name. If it doesn't, say politely, "I'm sorry, but I forget your name."

## Practice

**A.** Read these introductions. Write the ones that will best help get the conversation going.

1. "Dan, I'd like you to meet my friend, Grace."
2. "Dan, this is my friend, Grace. She just came back from California."
3. "Mom, this is the friend I was telling you about. Her name is Judy and she collects model cars."
4. "Mom, this is Judy."
5. "Steve, meet Betty."
6. "Steve, I want you to meet Betty because you are both going to the same camp this summer."

**B.** Copy and complete these introductions.

7. "Uncle Jack, this is my best friend, Bill. _____."
8. "Janet, this is Mrs. Blakely. Mrs. Blakely is _____ _____."
9. "Deborah has been wanting to meet you for a long time, Aunt Blanche, because both of you _____."
10. "Mom, this is my teacher, Mr. Graham. He _____."

## Apply

**C.** Write these introductions. Then act them out with some classmates.

11. Three friends have come to your house for dinner. Introduce them to your parents.
12. You have just gone backstage after a concert. You know the performer. Introduce him or her to your friend.
13. You have just won a race. The coach is introducing you to the person who will give you the prize. What does the coach say?
14. Introduce someone whose name you have forgotten.
15. Introduce yourself to a new classmate.

# Lesson 2: Using the Telephone

Laura received a telephone call. Read the message she wrote.

> *Saturday, 1:00 P.M.*
> *For Bill. Rosa called. She said there is a problem in the Youth Center. Please call her at the Youth Center as soon as possible.*
> *Laura*

Is Laura's message for Bill clear?

## Think and Discuss

When you take a telephone message, it is important to listen for details. Details that answer *who, what, when,* and *where* are important.

Look at Laura's message. For whom is the message? On what day and at what time did Laura receive the call? It is important to include the day and time of the call. What was the message? Did the caller make any special request? Notice that Laura included important details.

---

**How to Take a Telephone Message**

1. **Write the time and date of the call.**
2. **Write the name of the person called.**
3. **Write the name of the person calling.**
4. **Write the message.**
5. **Write your name.**

---

Always put the note where it will be seen.

When Bill came home, he saw the message and called Rosa. After he spoke to her, he made another call. Read the telephone conversation.

**Bill:** Hello. Is this Steele Plumbing? This is Bill Reynolds. I want to report an emergency. Water is coming into the basement of the Youth Center at 42 Cedar Lane.

**Mr. Steele:** I'll be right over.

Bill made an emergency call. He called about a situation that needed immediate attention.

---

**How to Make an Emergency Call**

1. **Give your name and say that you want to report an emergency.**
2. **State the problem as briefly as possible.**
3. **Give the location of the emergency.**

---

It is a good idea to keep a list of emergency numbers by the telephone. You might need phone numbers for the doctor, the fire department, the ambulance service, and the police department.

## Practice

**A.** Use the five rules on page 276. Take a message from this conversation. Use today's date.

> **Mr. Steele:** This is Mr. Steele. When Barney comes in, please tell him to meet me at 42 Cedar Lane. Have him bring my boots. It's 1:00 P.M. now, so he should be there soon.

**B.** Suppose there is a fire at your house. You must call the fire department. Use the rules on this page to write what you would say.

## Apply

**C.** Make up an emergency situation for which you must call a doctor. Act out your phone call with a classmate.

# Lesson 3: Listening to a Guest Speaker

Ms. Jenner's class is listening to a talk by Mr. Burke. He is an undersea diver. He explores old shipwrecks. He has written many books on the subject of diving. What questions would you want to ask Mr. Burke?

## Think and Discuss

Guest speakers are usually invited to speak about one special subject. After they speak, they often expect to answer questions about that subject.

When you listen carefully to a speaker, you are being polite. You are also being smart. The information they give is not always repeated. If you do not listen, you may miss something important.

Here is how Mr. Burke began his talk.

"I left California in September. I planned to explore a shipwreck off the coast of Mexico. I knew that the ship had belonged to Spanish explorers. There was a good deal of gold aboard."

When he finished talking, three students asked questions. Who listened carefully?

Marie: 1. What else did you find on your dive?
Don: 2. Did you find any gold?
Bob: 3. Where was the shipwreck?

Speakers plan what they are going to say ahead of time. You should also prepare some questions ahead of time. You might plan to ask questions about a person's education, work, or goals. Ask questions that relate to the speaker's subject. You can begin your questions with the words *who, what, where, when, how,* and *why.* If you think of questions as a person is talking, write them down. Do not interrupt the speaker in the middle of his or her talk.

## Practice

**A.** Write the six questions that would be the best ones to ask Mr. Burke.

1. How did you begin your career as a diver?
2. Do you know how to dance?
3. How much do you weigh?
4. How did you feel when you discovered the gold?
5. When are you planning another trip?
6. What did you do to learn how to become a diver?
7. How do you know where to look for shipwrecks?
8. Are you planning to write a book about your discovery?
9. Do you like sports?
10. Do you have any pets?

## Apply

**B.** **11.–15.** Write five additional questions that you would ask Mr. Burke.

## A Challenge

Choose a famous person from history. Write some questions you would like to ask that person about his or her career. Act out your questions and answers with a classmate.

# Lesson 4: Following Directions

Your teacher is going to read a set of directions. Close your book. Take out a sheet of paper and listen carefully. The directions will be read only once.

## Think and Discuss

It is easy to make a mistake if you do not listen carefully to directions. Look at your paper. Did you *print* your name? Did you write the numbers *across* the middle of the paper? Did you circle all the numbers, including the date?

Spoken directions are difficult to follow. You must listen to every word. Written directions may be difficult too. When you read the directions on a form or test, read slowly and carefully. Read the form once to be sure you understand it. Be sure to write down all the information the form requests. Put all the information in the correct place on the form.

Linda went to the library and filled out a form to get a library card. Read her form.

---

**Please print and use a pen.**

**Name:** _Taylor_       _Linda_ _____

            **Last**             **First**

**Age:** _9½_ _____

**Street Address:** _516 East Hudson St._ _____

**City and State:** _New York, New York_    **ZIP Code** _____

**Phone No.:** _555-1231_ _____

**Have you ever had a library card before?**

             **Yes**                      (**No**)

---

Why do you think the form says, "Please print and use a pen"? Did Linda follow directions? Explain.

---

**How to Fill Out a Form**

1. **Read the form over once.**
2. **Write or print clearly.**
3. **Give all the information requested.**
4. **Be sure all the information is in the right place.**

---

## Practice

**A.** Copy this test form. Then fill it out.

Name: (print one letter in each box)

1. ☐☐☐☐☐☐☐☐☐■■☐☐☐☐☐☐☐☐
        **Last**              **First**

2. **Grade:** _____    3. ☐ **Boy** ☐ **Girl (check one)**

4. **Teacher:** _____    5. **Birthday** _____
                                         **(Month)  (Day)  (Year)**

6. **School:** _____

    _____
                  **(Street Address)**

    _____
     **(City)**     **(State)**     **(Zip Code)**

7. **Signature:** _____

---

## Apply

**B. 8.–15.** Close your book and take out a piece of paper. Listen as your teacher reads some directions. Follow the directions carefully. Each will be read only once.

# Lesson 5: Listening Critically

Read these sentences from an ad.

1. This is No-Trouble-Bubble—the soap that has a low-bubble ingredient.
2. Try it and you will agree it is the best soap you ever used.

Be a sincere announcer. Read this commercial as if every word were true.

## Think and Discuss

Now read the ad again carefully. Which sentence states a fact? Which one states an opinion?

Most of the ads you read, see, or hear are a mixture of facts and opinions.

A statement of fact says something about the product that can be proved. A statement of opinion may tell you what you are going to like. It may tell how you are going to feel or look. An opinion does not state something that can be proved.

Which sentences in the following ad state facts? Which one states an opinion?

3. EZ-Put-On Shirts are made of 100 percent cotton.
4. They are sold at all big department stores.
5. If you buy one, you will be glad you did.

## Practice

**A.** Read the following ads. Write *statement of fact* for each sentence that states a fact. Write *statement of opinion* for each sentence that states an opinion.

1. You will love washing your clothes with Cloud 99.
2. It has 10 tested whiteners.
3. Your family will thank you.
4. Dynamite Popcorn is the newest and best.
5. You get 16 ounces in every can.

## Apply

**B. 6.–7.** Write a commercial using facts and opinions. Underline the statements of opinion.

# HOW OUR LANGUAGE GROWS

Where you live has a lot to do with the way you pronounce words. People who grow up in the North and West pronounce both *r*'s in *career,* while those growing up in New England and the South usually do not. Westerners and Midwesterners make *merry* rhyme with *vary.* Easterners say these words quite differently.

A way of using or pronouncing words that is common to a region is called a regional dialect. It is fun to guess where a person is from by listening to the way he or she pronounces words.

1. When you say *Mary* and *merry,* do the words sound alike or different?
2. When you say *dance* does the *a* sound like the *a* in *hat* or *father*?
3. Do you make *greasy* rhyme with *fleecy* or *breezy*?
4. Do you pronounce *Mrs.* with one syllable or two syllables?
5. Do you say *creak* and *creek* in the same way or differently?

# LANGUAGE REVIEW

## Making Introductions   pages 274–275

Which introductions are best? Write them.

1. "Mrs. Halliday, this is Joanne Lupi. Joanne is captain of our soccer team."
2. "Anne-Marie, I'd like you to meet Steven."
3. Dr. Kroeger, I'd like to introduce my son Jerry. Jerry hopes to be a doctor too."
4. "Theodore, meet Anthony Seguira."
5. "Mother, I want you to meet Frances MacDowell. She was my best friend at summer camp."

## Using the Telephone   pages 276–277

6. Take a message from this conversation. Use today's date.

   **Mrs. Lopez:**   This is Anita Lopez. When Ted arrives, please tell him that he has a doctor's appointment at 3:00 P.M. It is 2:00 P.M. now, so he will have to hurry.

   **Benjamin:**   All right, I will tell him.

## Listening to a Guest Speaker   pages 278–279

Write the three questions that would be the best questions to ask a visiting animal trainer.

7. Did you have pets when you were a child?
8. Are there any animals that cannot be trained?
9. What is your favorite color?
10. Have you ever worked with dolphins?
11. How old are you?

## Following Directions   pages 280–281

12. Your teacher will read a set of directions. Listen carefully and follow each direction.

Read this form. Then answer the questions using complete sentences.

**Record Club Membership Form**

1. Name _____
   (print)  last name          first name

2. Street Address _____

3. City _____ State ____ ZIP code ____

4. Amount enclosed _____

5. Bonus record choice _____

**13.** On which line should you write your record choice?
**14.** On which line should you write your ZIP code?
**15.** On which line should you write your street address?
**16.** How should your name look? Write it.

## Listening Critically   pages 282–283

Write the sentence in each pair that states a fact.

**17.** You will love Cool sunglasses. They are made out of colored plastic.
**18.** Tests show that Sweetz cereal gives people energy. Kids always ask for more when you serve Sweetz.
**19.** Frizzola shampoo will change your life. It is made from natural ingredients.
**20.** Hungry Pooch dog food contains 12 vitamins. Your dog will wolf it down.

## Applying Listening and Speaking

**21.** Work in groups of three on this exercise. Pretend to be three famous people. Introduce each other to the class. Then ask the class to repeat one fact about each person introduced.

# STUDY SKILLS

## Lesson 6: Using a Telephone Directory

Mr. Jaro's class is working on a play. The students need to find a carpenter named Bill Dugan to help them build the set. They also need to find a store that rents costumes and wigs.

## Think and Discuss

| DANCER-DWIGHT |
| --- |
| Dancer, Harold 10 Reed Rd.    223-7865 |
| Dover, M. 11 Cannon Ct.    597-0989 |
| Downtown Organization, The |
| 1876 S. Main    907-6785 |
| Dugan, William 42 N. Main    848-3297 |
| Carpentry |

The White Pages is an alphabetical list of names with addresses and phone numbers. The last name of a person is printed first. Under which letter of the alphabet would John Franklin be listed?

Business groups are listed under the first letter of the first important word in their name. Under what letter would the Maple Lumber Company be listed?

Guide words are printed at the top of each page. They help you locate names quickly. Is Bill Dugan's name listed on the page? What is his phone number?

The Yellow Pages is an alphabetical listing of businesses and services. These are listed according to the type of business or service. Examples are: ANTIQUES, BICYCLES, DENTISTS.

The name, address, and telephone number of the business or service is listed. Other information may be listed as well, as you can see in the example.

**COSTUMES**

**Costumes–Supplies**

**ABC Costume Supply**
113 Elm . . . . . . . . . . . . . . 625-3821

**Costumes by Renee**
Rental and Sales
Costumes Made to Order
Wigs and Masks
98 State St.. . . . . . . . . . . 897-0967

**Old Time Costume Company**
Costume Rental
Hours: 9-5, Mon.-Sat.
76 Rte. 1 . . . . . . . . . . . . . 987-8969

## *Practice*

**A.** Look at these guide words from the White Pages:

### Bellew–Bellney

List the names that you would find on that page.

1. Bellinger
2. Bellford
3. Belluci
4. Bellanger
5. Bellomo
6. Bellman

**B.** Use the Yellow Pages pictured on this page to answer these questions.

7. Which business sells wigs?
8. Why is ABC Costume Supply listed first?
9. Which companies rent costumes?
10. What is the address of Costumes by Renee?

## *Apply*

**C. 11.** Make a White Pages page. Make up at least 10 names, addresses, and telephone numbers. List them alphabetically, last names first. Add guide words at the top of your page.

Julian is planning a camping trip with his family. He wants to know if there are any campsites near his home. He looked at a map of his state in a road atlas.

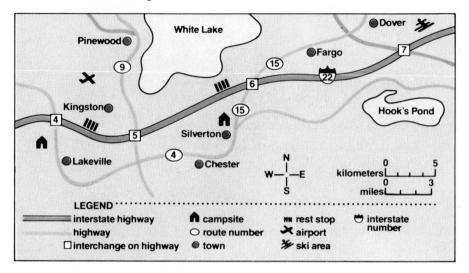

## Think and Discuss

An **atlas** is a book of maps. A **road atlas** contains road maps. It also contains other information travelers need.

Look at the bottom of the map on this page. Find the word **legend.** A legend or key lists and explains the symbols on the map. What is the symbol for a campsite? Where is the campsite nearest Julian's home in Fargo?

The **direction symbol,** or compass, tells you which way is north, south, east, or west on the map. On this map, in which direction is Fargo from Silverton?

The **distance scale** shows the distance on the map in miles and kilometers.

Another kind of atlas is the **world atlas.** It contains maps of all the countries in the world. It also contains information about a country's industries and resources. It may have maps of the moon, diagrams of the ocean floor, illustrations of national flags, and other information.

## Practice

**A.** Write *road atlas* if you would be more likely to use a road atlas to get the information asked for. Write *world atlas* if a world atlas is likely to be used.

1. the kinds of industry in Mexico
2. which road to take to the airport
3. the countries that border Spain
4. the major cities in Canada
5. the distance between two towns

**B.** Look at the map on page 288. Answer the following questions in complete sentences.

6. Between which towns is the airport located?
7. How many rest stops are on the interstate highway?
8. Which town is near the ski area?
9. Is there a road leading directly to Hook's Pond?
10. Does the town of Kingston have a campsite?
11. What is the number of the route that will take you to Pinewood?
12. In which directions does Route 9 go?
13. What direction do you go to get from Chester to Lakeville?
14. Which town is nearest to White Lake?
15. Is Lakeville nearer to Interstate 22 than it is to Route 15?

## Apply

**C. 16.** Use the map on page 288. Write a paragraph telling a stranger the way from Fargo to Pinewood. Remember to tell the direction in which to travel. You might also tell what the traveler will see on the way.

# COMPOSITION

## *Lesson 8: Writing Conversation*

Read this conversation from a story.

"What is that?" asked Darryl.

"I don't know," replied Sue.

Terry mumbled, "It sure is fuzzy. I hope it's not dangerous."

"Watch out! It's moving!" exclaimed Paul.

Name the characters. What does each character say?

### *Think and Discuss*

Characters in stories often speak to one another. The exact words they say are called a **quotation.** The words are always placed inside quotation marks (" "). Look at each sentence of the story. Where do quotation marks appear?

Notice that a new paragraph begins every time a new character speaks. How many paragraphs do you see?

Read the words Sue and Terry said. Their words are separated from the rest of the sentence by a comma.

Now read the words Darryl and Paul said. Questions and exclamations are not separated by commas. What punctuation marks are used? Notice that end punctuation for quoted sentences always comes inside the quotation marks.

Quotations tell what story characters say. It is also important for the reader to know how the characters speak. Read these quotations.

"Wow, it's big too!" <u>said</u> Kim.

"Wow, it's big too!" <u>gasped</u> Kim.

Which gives a better idea of how Kim spoke? Why is the word *gasped* better than the word *said*?

---

**How to Write Conversation**

1. **Place quotation marks before and after a quotation.**
2. **Begin the first word of a quotation with a capital letter.**
3. **Use a comma to separate a quotation from the rest of the sentence unless a question mark or exclamation point is needed.**
4. **Start a new paragraph for each new speaker.**
5. **Use descriptive words to show how a person speaks.**

---

## *Practice*

**A.** Copy each sentence. Underline the quotation. Circle the punctuation mark that separates the quotation from the rest of the sentence.

1. "Why is the dog barking?" asked Lynn.
2. Eddie replied, "Because someone is at the front door."
3. "Will you see who it is?" Mother asked.
4. Eddie answered, "Sure, Mom."
5. "It's Dad. He forgot his keys," shouted Eddie.

**B.** Copy the sentences. Add quotation marks. Put end punctuation marks and capital letters where they belong.

6. i just felt the table move Gloria said.
7. i felt it move too cried Mark.
8. Jean looked frightened. do you think we should go away she asked.
9. we should tell the dog to go away Ben laughed.
10. i wasn't really scared Jean said.

11. yes, you were Mark argued.
12. Ben smiled. you didn't really think a monster was under the table, did you he asked.
13. a monster is under the table Gloria said quietly.
14. i don't understand said Ben with a frown.
15. my dog's name is Monster Gloria smiled.

C. 16. Rewrite this conversation. Make a new paragraph each time a different person speaks. Add punctuation marks.

The children were frightened Gloria told her mother. Why her mother asked. They didn't know the dog was under the table explained Gloria. That dog is too big to be in the house said Gloria's mother sternly. I let him in as a special treat said Gloria.

## Apply

D. 17. Pick two characters from a story you like. Imagine a conversation they might have. Follow the rules on page 291. Write the conversation.

### To Memorize

El mal escribano le echa la culpa a la pluma.
(The poor handwriter always blames the pen for his bad penmanship.)

*A Mexican proverb*

Explain what you think this proverb means.

# Lesson 9: Ordering Events in a Story

Someone once made these statements about writing a story. A story has three parts. In the first part you introduce a cat. In the second part you get it up a tree. In the third part you find a way to get it down. In other words, stories are about problems.

## Think and Discuss

Every story has a plot. The plot tells the action of the story—its beginning, middle, and end.

Read this story beginning.

Stuart and Jack were on a walking trip with their class. As the class hiked along the nature trail, Stuart walked very slowly. He was looking for rocks.

The beginning of a story is called the **introduction.** In it, the main characters and setting are introduced. Who are the characters? What is the setting?

The middle of the story is the **development.** It tells about a problem or challenge for the main characters. Read the development of this story.

Stuart strayed behind the rest of the class. Jack ran back to him. "You're going to get lost," he warned.

"Can't you give me one more minute?" Stuart begged.

"No!" Jack said angrily. "I'm leaving you." He turned quickly. Then he cried out. He had tripped. He reached out for Stuart. Suddenly the two boys were falling. Down and down they went into a deep hole by the side of the trail. Luckily the hole was full of dry grass and leaves.

The boys looked up. The path seemed very far away. "Help! Help!" Jack yelled. But the class was too far away. No one came.

"You and your rocks," Jack said. "Look at the mess they got us into."

"Rocks could get us out of this mess," Stuart said.

"How?" Jack asked.

What is the problem the characters must solve?

The end, or **conclusion,** of a story tells how the problem is solved. How do you think this story will end? Now read, and see if you were right.

Stuart took two small black rocks out of his pocket. He rubbed them together over a small pile of dry leaves. Sparks began to fly. They fell on the leaves. After a moment the leaves began to smoke.

The boys watched the smoke go up out of the hole. Soon their classmates were looking down at them.

"It's lucky you had matches," one of them said.

"Not matches," Jack said with a smile. "Rocks."

The story you read has an introduction, a development, and a conclusion. Review each part. What would be a good title for the story?

---

**How to Write a Story**

1. **Plan your story. Think of characters, setting, a problem, and an ending to solve the problem.**
2. **Write an interesting introduction. In it, introduce the main character and the setting.**
3. **Tell the problem or challenge the main character will face. Then develop the action.**
4. **Write a conclusion. Tell how the main character solves the problem or meets the challenge.**
5. **Use conversation in your story. Begin a new paragraph each time a different character speaks.**
6. **Think of a good title for your story.**

## Practice

**A.** Read these paragraphs from a short story. Copy the story in the correct order. Write a title for the story.

When the bus reached Millville, Sandra got off. She did not see anyone she knew.

Within five minutes Sandra's aunt was hugging her.

Then Sandra spotted the information booth. She asked the attendant to page her aunt.

Sandra was excited. She was on a bus trip to visit her Aunt Ann.

"I waited at the wrong place!" exclaimed Aunt Ann.

**B.** Use this story beginning. Add at least two more paragraphs. Develop the problem. Then tell how the main character solves the problem.

Roberta always went to the zoo with her pockets full of treats. She liked to feed the animals. She did not pay attention to the signs that said, "Please do not feed the animals."

## Apply

**C.** Write your own story. Use one of these topics or one of your own. Follow the suggestions on page 294.

Noises in the Night                An Unusual Ball Game
The Day Nobody Talked to Me   The Lost Pet

PLEASE
DO NOT
FEED THE
ANIMALS

# Lesson 10: Editing a Story

Read the adventure story Sherry wrote.

> "What is moving in that tree?" asked Amy.
> Kate answered, "Let's find out." "I'm too
> scared. you go," whispered Amy.
> Amy and Kate passed a hollow tree.
> Kate tiptoed up to it. As she peered into
> the tree, a flurry of wings beat at her
> face. She ran to Amy.

## Editing Marks

≡ capitalize

⊙ make a period

∧ add something

⋏ add a comma

⌄⋰ add quotation marks

⸒ take something away

◯ spell correctly

⁋ indent the paragraph

/ make a lowercase letter

∿ transpose
tr

## Think and Discuss

When she read her story, Sherry found some mistakes. She forgot to use quotation marks around some conversation. She used this editing mark ⌄⋰ to show where they belong. What word did Sherry need to capitalize?

The biggest change Sherry made was in the order of her story. Which sentence did she move? Why? The abbreviation (tr) means to **transpose,** or change the order. Sherry's new story beginning introduces the characters and the setting of her story.

## Practice

**A.** Copy Sherry's story correctly.

## Apply

**B.** Look back at the story you wrote for Lesson 9. Did you write all the events in the correct order? Did you use conversation and punctuate it correctly? Edit your story. Then copy it again neatly.

# MECHANICS PRACTICE

## Writing Quotations

- Begin the first word of a quotation with a capital letter.
- Use quotation marks before and after a direct quotation.
- Use a comma between a quotation and the rest of the sentence unless a question mark or exclamation point is needed.
- Begin a new paragraph each time a different character speaks.

**A.** Write the sentences correctly. Use capital letters and punctuation marks where they are needed.

1. Mr. Chiu said today we will talk about careers
2. what do you want to be he asked
3. Beverly answered i want to be a doctor
4. José replied maybe I will be an artist
5. i know just what I want to do Tod exclaimed loudly
6. i want to ride racehorses he continued
7. Beth said i want to be a nurse
8. i think I will work in a bank said Marta
9. i really like money she added
10. what a great idea everyone yelled

**B. 11.–15.** Listen while your teacher reads some quotations. Write the sentences correctly.

**C. 16.** Write this conversation correctly. Add quotation marks and capital letters. Begin a new paragraph for each new speaker.

there is nothing to do today sighed Tim. why don't you call Pete asked Molly. pete is not home Tim said. you could help me paint Molly suggested.

# LITERATURE

## Lesson 11: Reading a Short Story

You enjoy reading stories when the author tells you about interesting characters. If you care about the characters, you want to know what happens to them. You want to know how they will solve their problems.

Some of the characters you read about come from the author's imagination. He or she makes them up. Made-up stories are called **fiction.**

### Think and Discuss

This story is about a wise woman and her husband. Their home is visited by a bogle, a sort of goblin who brings bad luck. Read the story. See how Annie solves her unusual problem.

### The Good Luck Bogle

*by Barbara Neelands*

There was a morning when the cow's tail was caught in the door-latch and the chimney crane stuck on its hinge and the downdraft blew ashes into the porridge.

"A bogle must have come to stay," said Annie.

She peeked through the keyhole of the closet. There is no other way to see a bogle. Annie knew that.

Sure enough, there sat a bogle, frowning out, mean as mean.

"That's bad luck for us," said her husband Jamie.

There is positively no way at all to get rid of a bogle. Jamie knew that.

"Oh no, a bogle brings *good* luck!" said Annie, quick

as quick. "Now see, if old Bossie's tail had not gotten caught in the door-latch, she would have strayed off, lost into that fog that's come creeping in while you weren't looking."

And she set a cup of milk by the hearth for the bogle.

"Humph," said Jamie and went about his work.

When he fell from the hayrack and came hobbling back with a turned ankle, he said, "There now. That's the kind of luck that bogle brought!"

"Of course it was," cried Annie, "good luck! Now I've got you here for company instead of going the livelong day talking to myself."

Jamie sat in the cottage with his foot propped up, when Annie went to do the evening chores. While she tossed down the hay and milked the cow, a rainstorm blew up. Back she ran—skirt and shirt and shoes wet through.

"It's lucky I wasn't wearing my woolen shawl," said Annie. "Here it is hanging nice and dry."

She added an oatcake to the bogle's evening meal and peeked through the keyhole at him. He didn't look quite so grumpy now.

The next day the run flooded and carried the pigsty downstream.

"What good luck!" said Annie, after she'd rescued the piglets. "I've gotten every one back again."

That night she skimmed the cream off the milk and saved it for the bogle.

The next night the wind blew away the storm and with it the thatched roof.

"How lucky that your ankle is better so you can mend the thatch," said Annie to Jamie.

Then the teakettle rusted through.

"Good luck again!" said Annie. "The tinkers are due to come by any day now."

She put a dish of honey by the hearth. When she peeked through the keyhole, the bogle looked hardly cross at all.

Every day the bogle ate himself fat and lazy. Every day he heard about all the good luck he'd brought.

Then came a day when the cow calved twins and the wheat ripened early and Jamie found the silver piece he'd lost last fall.

When Annie peeked through the keyhole, the bogle looked a little bit sleepy, and nice as nice.

"And what do you think of our good luck bogle now?" asked Annie.

Jamie pulled her out of the cottage away down to the stile where the bogle couldn't hear. Then he grabbed her around the waist and swung her into the air.

"What I think," said Jamie, "is that I'm ever so lucky to have a wife who's smarter than a bogle."

## *Practice*

**A.** Answer the questions in complete sentences.

1. Write words to describe each of the characters in the story: Annie, Jamie, and the bogle.
2. What is the setting of the story?
3. How did Annie solve her problem?
4. Write a sentence from the story that could be real.
5. Write a sentence from the story that must be fiction.

## *Apply*

**B.** Pick a story you read recently and liked. Answer these questions about it. Use complete sentences.

6. Is the story fiction? How can you tell?
7. Who is the main character in the story?
8. What problem must this character solve?
9. How does the character solve the problem?
10. How does the story end?

# A BOOK TO READ

Title: **The Church Mice Spread Their Wings**
Author: Graham Oakley
Publisher: Atheneum

As a church cat Sampson had vowed never to harm mice. He reluctantly agreed to travel with the church mice on their "return to nature" vacation. Humphrey, the leader of the mice, was in charge of the map. He shouted out the exciting high points of their great voyage.

From wild, storm-tossed seas (really a lake in the park), they went deep into the heart of India (really a dome-shaped bandstand). Through the trackless wastes of the Great Sahara Desert (really the Sand and Gravel Company's sand pits), the mice followed Humphrey and his water-stained map. Just as Sampson thought things were settling down, tragedy struck!

These wild and crazy tales of cats and mice have funny illustrations. When you finish this one, you will want to go to the library and read all the other books in this wonderful series.

# 8 UNIT TEST

● **Making Introductions**   pages 274–275

Write the letter of the words in each set that make the best introduction.

**1.** You are introducing your father to your new friend.
  **a.** "Hi, Dad. I'd like you to meet Kirby."
  **b.** "Dad, I'd like you to meet Kirby Moffett. He just moved here from Florida. Kirby, this is my father, Mr. Dale."
  **c.** "Kirby, this is my father."
  **d.** "Dad, this is Kirby. Kirby, this is my father."

**2.** You are introducing your mother to your teacher.
  **a.** "Mother, this is Mrs. Jackson. Mrs. Jackson, this is my mother."
  **b.** "Mother, I'd like you to meet my science teacher, Mrs. Jackson. Mrs. Jackson, this is my mother."
  **c.** "Mrs. Jackson, this is my mother."
  **d.** "Mother, meet Mrs. Jackson."

● **Using the Telephone**   pages 276–277

Read the telephone conversation. Take a message. Include all the information requested in items 3–7 on page 303.

**Mrs. Tremont:**  Hello, is Jenny Roland there?
**Samuel:**  No, she isn't. This is her brother Samuel. Can I take a message?
**Mrs. Tremont:**  Yes, please. This is Mrs. Tremont, her soccer coach. Will you tell her that soccer practice has been cancelled for Thursday? That's tomorrow.
**Samuel:**  I'll tell her. Good-by.

3. Message for _____

4. Caller _____

5. Date or Day _____

6. Message _____

7. Call answered by _____

## ● Listening to a Guest Speaker    pages 278–279

Which of these questions should you ask a guest speaker who is a taxi driver? Write the three best questions.

8. Do you like dogs?

9. What do you like about your work?

10. Who was your most memorable passenger?

11. How long have you driven a taxi?

12. Wouldn't you rather be a clerk in a store?

## ● Following Directions    pages 280–281

13. Copy this form to apply for a library card. Then fill in the information.

---

**Farmlee Public Library**

Print all information

Name _____

             *last*                *first*            *middle*

Address _____

City/State _____ ZIP code _____

Age _____ Grade _____

School _____

Name of parent or guardian _____

Home telephone number _____

---

## ● Listening Critically    pages 282-283

Read these statements found in advertisements. Write *statement of fact* for each one that states a fact. Write *statement of opinion* for each one that gives an opinion.

14. Bliss Lotion will make you beautiful.
15. Mountain Top ice cream toppings come in two flavors — chocolate and caramel.
16. Huckers' overalls are made of heavy-duty denim.
17. Cracko-Crispee cereal has the crunch you love to munch.
18. Your cat will not scat when you serve Purr Puffs.
19. Vegietime soups are 99 percent salt free.
20. There are 14 styles of Tickety-Tock watches.

## ● Using a Telephone Directory    pages 286-287

Write the names that would appear in a telephone directory under these guide words.

### Duble——Dudra

1. Dubois         2. Duder
3. Dubno         4. Dubovik
5. Dubik         6. Ducern
7. Duda          8. Dufka
9. Ducek        10. Duggle

## ● Using an Atlas    pages 288-289

Copy each sentence. Use one of the words to fill in the blank in each sentence.

atlas        legend        symbols        world
direction symbol        road        maps

11. An _____ is a book of maps.
12. A _____ explains the map symbols.
13. The _____ on a map stand for real things or places.
14. The _____ shows which way north is on a map.
15. A _____ atlas contains maps of roads.
16. A _____ atlas has _____ of the countries of the world.

## ● Writing Conversation    pages 290–292

Write these quotations correctly.

1. look at my new bike said Patty excitedly.
2. Carmen remarked it sure is nice.
3. Mike asked when did you get it?
4. i got it for my birthday boasted Patty.
5. Jeremy exclaimed you are lucky
6. Mrs. Ray asked who does the dishes tonight?
7. It is not my turn replied Carmen.
8. Mike answered I did them yesterday.
9. I did them the day before that added Jeremy.
10. Carmen mumbled i think it is my turn after all
11. Well, I will help you Patty offered.

## ● Writing and Editing a Story    pages 293–297

12. Write a three-paragraph story. It could be happy, sad, exciting, or funny. Make up characters and a setting for the story. Think of a plot. Use conversation to make your story more interesting. Then edit your story to see if it has a beginning, a middle, and an end. Look at the conversation parts of the story. Did you use capital letters and punctuation marks correctly?

## ● Reading a Short Story    pages 298–301

Read this paragraph and answer the questions.

Joe and Lucy had never been far from home. Their favorite game was called *Magic Carpet.* They would sit together on the playroom rug and pretend that they were flying to a new land.
One day, Lucy grew tired of the game. "I wish this rug were really magic," she said. "I wish it would fly us to France!" Without a sound, the carpet began to rise off the floor.

1. Who are the characters in this story?
2. What is the story setting?
3. Is this story fiction? Explain your answer.

# MAINTENANCE and REVIEW

**Complete Subject and Predicate**   pages 10–11

Copy each sentence. Draw one line under the complete subject.
Draw two lines under the complete predicate.

1. Senator Kuri Asato drives to her home.
2. The senator's house is on Highland Boulevard.
3. She meets Doctor Klein for lunch.
4. Mister Jefferson joins them.

**Proper Nouns and Abbreviations**   pages 42–47

**5.–12.** Look back at sentences 1–4. Write the four proper nouns.
Then rewrite each one using abbreviations for titles of people
and for streets.

**Paragraphs**   pages 126–135

13. Write this group of sentences in correct paragraph form. Begin
    with the topic sentence. Leave out the sentence which does not
    keep to the topic.

    Madame Curie won prizes for this work. She discovered a
    powerful element in rocks. This element contained radiation.
    Rocks have many shapes and colors. Marie Curie was a
    famous scientist.

**Adjectives and Adverbs**   pages 162–163, 167–169

Copy the sentences. Underline the adjectives and articles. Circle
the adverbs.

14. The shiny new tractor starts smoothly.
15. It moves evenly in long, straight, and narrow rows.
16. Soon rows of yellow corn are growing.

## Pronouns    pages 202–203

Write the sentences. Underline the pronouns.

**17.** My mother took Rita and me to the store.
**18.** She asked us to find the school supplies.
**19.** We bought notebooks for our science class.
**20.** Their teacher said he would give them paper.

## Simple Subjects and Predicates    pages 240–243

Write each sentence. Draw one line under the simple subject. Draw two lines under the simple predicate.

**21.** The three friends traveled to the Grand Canyon.
**22.** They rode burros into the canyon.
**23.** Colorful rocks lined the canyon walls.
**24.** A muddy brown river was flowing at the bottom.
**25.** Many people floated down the river on rafts.

## Subject-Verb Agreement    pages 244–245

Write each sentence. Use the correct verb.

**26.** Construction workers (build, builds) large buildings.
**27.** One worker (push, pushes) a cart of bricks.
**28.** Another (move, moves) a crane loaded with steel beams.
**29.** The beams (support, supports) the building.
**30.** Ho Choi and Alicia (want, wants) to be construction workers.

## Making Introductions    pages 274–275

Write the best introduction from each pair.

**31. a.** Uncle Fred, this is Steve.
    **b.** Uncle Fred, this is my friend Steve.
       He will be helping me rake your yard.
**32. a.** Ms. Gutierrez is my teacher.
    **b.** Mom, this is Ms. Gutierrez. She is my music teacher.

## Sentences

**GRAMMAR**

**sentence**
- A **sentence** is a group of words that expresses a complete thought. It always begins with a capital letter. It always ends with a punctuation mark. *(page 2)*

**declarative sentence**
- A **declarative sentence** makes a statement. It ends with a period (.). *(page 4)*

This is my best friend.

**interrogative sentence**
- An **interrogative sentence** asks a question. It ends with a question mark (**?**). *(page 4)*

Where are the keys?

**exclamatory sentence**
- An **exclamatory sentence** shows strong feeling or surprise. It ends with an exclamation point (**!**). *(page 6)*

How kind you are!

**imperative sentence**
- An **imperative sentence** gives a command or makes a request. It ends with a period (.). *(page 6)*

Watch your step.

## Practice

Write only the groups of words that are sentences. Add capital letters and end punctuation. Then tell what kind of sentence the word group is.

1. on the very first day
2. what a mess this is
3. dropped a package
4. while I was walking
5. i tripped over the log
6. are you hurt
7. how foolish I felt
8. walked more carefully
9. be more careful
10. writing a letter
11. this blender is broken
12. please fix it
13. in the repair shop
14. can you help me

# Subjects and Predicates

- The **subject** of a sentence is the part about which something is being said. The **complete subject** is all the words that make up the subject  *(page 10)*

  **complete subject**

  <u>Tom</u> told a joke. <u>My cousin Tina</u> laughed.

- The **simple subject** is the key word or group of words in the subject.  *(page 240)*

  **simple subject**

  The small <u>rabbits</u> ran away. <u>Someone</u> saw them.

- The **complete predicate** is all the words that tell something about the subject.  *(page 10)*

  **complete predicate**

  A light <u><u>was shining in her eyes.</u></u>

- The **simple predicate** is the key word or words in the predicate. The simple predicate is an action verb or a linking verb together with any helping verbs.  *(page 242)*

  **simple predicate**

  Lara <u><u>was running</u></u> through the woods.

## Practice

**A.** Write each sentence. Draw one line under the complete subject. Then circle the simple subject.

1. The smaller children were taken by bus.
2. Freshly cut grass was placed in bags.
3. My cousin Freda led the group.
4. Three counselors helped us.
5. I will remember this special day.
6. The tired group hiked in the woods.
7. I rolled down the hill.
8. Matt brought his sleeping bag.

**B. 9.–16.** Write each sentence from Practice A. Draw two lines under the complete predicate. Then circle the simple predicate in each sentence.

# *Nouns*

**noun**
- A **noun** is a word that names a person, place, or thing. *(page 36)*

**common noun**
- A **common noun** names any person, place, or thing. It is a general word that begins with a small letter. *(page 42)*

> child     street     town     rabbit

**proper noun**
- A **proper noun** names a particular person, place, or thing. A proper noun begins with a capital letter. *(page 42)*

> Aunt Sue     Monday     Mexico     California
> Mr. Avila     Flag Day     Asia     October

## *Practice*

**A.** Copy the sentences. Underline each noun.

1. The cowhands tossed the blankets into the wagon.
2. Mrs. Wade yelled to the horses.
3. The wagon rattled out of the gate and across the prairie.
4. The camp was high up in the hills of Iowa.
5. Louise made coffee in a large pot.
6. The sun set as the cowhands ate supper.
7. On Monday the workers will brand each cow.
8. The job will take many days.
9. Dogs help the men and women.
10. New calves will be born next year.

**B.** Write a proper noun for each common noun.

| | | | |
|---|---|---|---|
| 11. country | 12. road | 13. woman | 14. state |
| 15. holiday | 16. day | 17. library | 18. continent |
| 19. dog | 20. city | 21. man | 22. month |
| 23. doctor | 24. street | 25. river | |

# *Noun Plurals*

- To form the plurals of most nouns, add *s.*  *(page 38)*

      chair — chairs      pencil — pencils

- To form the plural of nouns ending in *s, x, ch,* or *sh,* add *es.*  *(page 38)*

      class — classes      box — boxes
      batch — batches      dish — dishes

- To form the plural of nouns ending with a consonant and *y,* change the *y* to *i* and add *es.*  *(page 38)*

      berry — berries      diary — diaries

- Some nouns do not add *s* or *es* to make their plural forms. Some of these nouns are on the chart.  *(page 40)*

| Singular | Plural | Singular | Plural |
|----------|--------|----------|--------|
| sheep | sheep | woman | women |
| deer | deer | man | men |
| elk | elk | child | children |
| moose | moose | foot | feet |
| trousers | trousers | ox | oxen |
| pants | pants | mouse | mice |

## *Practice*

**A.** Write the plural form of each noun.

| | | | |
|---|---|---|---|
| **1.** light | **2.** city | **3.** ranch | **4.** ferry |
| **5.** day | **6.** wish | **7.** puppy | **8.** dash |
| **9.** fox | **10.** needle | **11.** deer | **12.** witch |

**B.** Write sentences of your own using the plurals of these nouns.

| | | | |
|---|---|---|---|
| **13.** fence | **14.** wrench | **15.** crash | **16.** toy |
| **17.** strawberry | **18.** child | **19.** bus | **20.** pass |

# Verbs

**action verb** • An **action verb** is a word that shows an action. An action verb is often the key word in the predicate. It tells what the subject does. *(page 78)*

> The team planned a party.

**linking verb** • A **linking verb** connects the subject with the other words in the predicate. It tells what the subject is or was. The following forms of *be* are often used as linking verbs. *(page 80)*

> am    is    are    was    were
>
> This book was a gift. Carol is my cousin.

**helping verb** • A **helping verb** helps the main verb express an action or make a statement. These words are often used as helping verbs. *(page 82)*

> am    is    are    was    were
> have    has    had    will
>
> I had walked the dog. It was raining.

## Practice

**A.** Copy the verb from each sentence. Next to the verb, write *action verb* or *linking verb* to tell the kind it is.

**1.** I was late.
**2.** I took a cab.
**3.** The drivers were fast.
**4.** The class started late.
**5.** Traffic is heavy.
**6.** The hours are long.

**B.** Copy each sentence. Draw two lines under the main verb and its helping verb. Then circle each helping verb.

**7.** Fran was wearing my gloves.
**8.** She had forgotten hers.
**9.** We are going to a party.
**10.** We will bring a cake.
**11.** Tom has brought his guitar.
**12.** I am singing songs.

# Verb Tenses

- The time expressed by a verb is called the **tense.** *(page 84)*    **tense**

- **Present tense** shows action that is happening now or    **present**
that happens regularly. *(page 84)*    **tense**

> He <u><u>sings</u></u> well. I <u><u>like</u></u> this song.

- **Past tense** shows action that happened in the past.    **past tense**
*(page 84)*

> I <u><u>wrote</u></u> a letter. David <u><u>mailed</u></u> it.

- **Future tense** shows action that will happen in the future.    **future tense**
Verbs that tell about the future have the helping verb *will.*
*(page 84)*

> The game <u><u>will end</u></u> soon. We <u><u>will walk</u></u> home.

## Practice

**A.** Copy each sentence. Draw two lines under the verb.
Then write *present, past,* or *future* to tell the tense.

1. The team plays every weekend.
2. Vera's home run ended the game.
3. I will pitch on Saturday.
4. It rained heavily after the first inning.
5. The coach will announce practice time.
6. Everybody tries very hard.

**B.** Copy each sentence. Use the verb in parentheses ( ) in
the given tense.

7. Henry _____ the floor. (wash, future)
8. I _____ the furniture. (clean, past)
9. Dina _____ the desk yesterday. (paint, past)
10. My parents _____ the books. (pack, future)
11. We _____ late. (work, past)
12. This house _____ very large. (seem, present)

# Irregular Verbs

**irregular verbs**

- **Irregular verbs** are verbs that do not add *ed* to show past tense.  *(pages 90 and 92)*

| Verb | Present | Past | Past with Have, Has, or Had |
|------|---------|------|------------------------------|
| begin | begin(s) | began | begun |
| come | come(s) | came | come |
| do | do(es) | did | done |
| give | give(s) | gave | given |
| go | go(es) | went | gone |
| grow | grow(s) | grew | grown |
| ring | ring(s) | rang | rung |
| run | run(s) | ran | run |
| sing | sing(s) | sang | sung |
| take | take(s) | took | taken |
| write | write(s) | wrote | written |

## Practice

**A.** Choose the correct past tense form of the verb in parentheses ( ). Write the sentences.

1. The music school had _____ a concert.   (gave, given)
2. The chorus _____ well.   (sang, sung)
3. I _____ with my family.   (gone, went)
4. We _____ a taxi to get there on time.   (took, taken)
5. The concert had _____ before we arrived.   (began, begun)
6. My brother _____ up the steps.   (ran, run)
7. He had _____ us our tickets.   (gave, given)
8. Who _____ that piece of music?   (wrote, written)
9. The sounds _____ louder as we approached.   (grew, grown)
10. The concert master _____ a fine job.   (did, done)

11. The chorus had _____ this piece before.   (sang, sung)
12. My brother has _____ piano lessons (took, taken)
13. I _____ my lessons three years ago. (began, begun)
14. My brother _____ well.   (did, done)
15. Many people have _____ to hear him play.   (came, come)

B. Use the correct past form of the verb in parentheses
   ( ). Write the sentences.

16. Several friends had _____ to dinner.   (come)
17. They _____ the bell at six.   (ring)
18. I _____ to the door.   (run)
19. The light had _____ out.   (go)
20. My sister had _____ me a candle.   (give)
21. Carol _____ everyone's coats.   (take)
22. All of us _____ into the living room.   (go)
23. Vera had _____ to tell us a story.   (begin)
24. Someone had _____ her an unsigned letter.   (write)
25. Everyone _____ more curious as she spoke.   (grow)
26. I think I know who _____ it.   (do)
27. Then Mom _____ in to announce dinner.   (come)
28. After dinner we _____ songs.   (sing)
29. I have _____ pictures.   (take)
30. My friends _____ to thank you.   (write)
31. Have you _____ a surprise party?   (give)
32. I have _____ the invitations.   (write)
33. I _____ the invitations to each house.   (take)
34. Then I _____ the doorbell.   (ring)
35. I left the invitations and _____ away.   (go)
36. My friends _____ curious about the party   (grow)
37. They had _____ to many parties.   (go)
38. No one had _____ such an unusual party.   (give)
39. The party _____ at 6:00 P.M.   (begin)
40. All my friends _____.   (come)

# Adjectives

adjective
- An **adjective** is a word that describes a noun. *(page 162)*

    Vanilla cookies are good snacks. An apple fell.

- Adjectives can describe by comparing. *(page 164)*

er, est
- One-syllable adjectives use *er* or *est* to make comparisons. *(page 164)*

    This is the biggest book I've ever read.

more, most
- Adjectives of two or more syllables usually use *more* or *most* to make comparisons. *(page 164)*

    This is the most beautiful flower of all.

a, an, the
- *A*, *an*, and *the* are special adjectives called articles. *(page 167)*

    An owl watched the mouse from a tree.

## Practice

Copy the sentences. Underline the adjectives and articles.

1. The unusual noises were high squeals.
2. Small puppies make strange sounds.
3. The smallest puppy is the brown one.
4. It is the sweetest animal I have ever seen.
5. A large box would be a good bed for them.
6. Bring a soft blanket.
7. The large bowl is for their food.
8. I will choose the brown puppy.
9. The owner of this shop is friendly.
10. A new puppy needs special care.
11. The cutest kitten is white.
12. I would like an orange cat.
13. Have you seen the big parrot?
14. It is a very colorful bird.
15. Is a parrot a smart bird?

# Adverbs

- An **adverb** is a word that tells more about a verb. *(page 168)* **adverb**

- Some adverbs tell *how* an action takes place. Most adverbs that tell *how* end in *ly*. *(page 170)* **how**

  slowly    neatly    smoothly    quickly

- Some adverbs tell *when* an action takes place. *(page 170)* **when**

  then    often    never    yesterday

- Some adverbs tell *where* an action takes place. *(page 170)* **where**

  down    ahead    around    here

## Practice

Copy the sentences. Underline the adverbs. After each sentence write whether the adverb tells *how, when,* or *where.*

1. We visited this museum today.
2. There is a lovely park nearby.
3. We often walk along the paths.
4. The park is neatly kept.
5. Yesterday I spent three hours in the museum.
6. We looked around.
7. Many people were there.
8. We should have come early.
9. Soon we wanted to leave.
10. Fewer people are here in the mornings.
11. We walked quickly through the exhibit rooms.
12. I will plan my trips carefully.
13. Later we had lunch.
14. We ate our pizza outside.
15. Pigeons looked for crumbs nearby.

# *Pronouns*

pronoun
- A **pronoun** is a word used in place of a noun or nouns. *(page 202)*

subject pronoun
- The words *I, you, he, she, it, we,* and *they* are **subject pronouns.** They are always used in the subject part of a sentence. *(page 204)*

pronoun after action verb
- The words *me, you, him, her, it,* and *them* are pronouns that follow action verbs. *(page 206)*

possessive pronoun
- The words *my, your, his, her, our, their,* and *its* are pronouns that are used in place of possessive nouns. They are called **possessive pronouns.** *(page 208)*

pronouns with <u>self</u> and <u>selves</u>
- Some pronouns are formed by adding *self* and *selves.* *Myself, yourself, himself, herself,* and *itself* are singular pronouns. *Ourselves, yourselves,* and *themselves* are plural pronouns. *(page 212)*

## *Practice*

A. Rewrite the sentences. Use a pronoun in place of the underlined word or words.

1. <u>Mario</u> bakes cake for the children.
2. Fran gave <u>Mario</u> the recipe.
3. <u>Fran and Mario</u> are cousins.
4. Mr. Jonas thanked <u>Fran and Mario</u>.
5. This is <u>Fran's</u> cookbook.
6. <u>The cookbook's</u> pages are worn.
7. <u>Fran's and Mario's</u> cakes are famous.
8. <u>Mario's</u> bakery is popular.

B. Use the correct pronouns. Write the sentences.

9. Dad gave Bob and (I, me) these flowers.
10. He gave them (herself, himself).
11. I arranged them in the vase (myself, ourselves).
12. Bob and (I, me) thanked Dad.

# Paragraph

- A **paragraph** is a group of sentences that tell about one main idea. *(page 126)*     **paragraph**
- The **topic sentence** expresses the main idea of the paragraph. The topic sentence is usually, but not always, the first sentence. *(page 128)*     **topic sentence**
- The first line of a paragraph is indented. *(page 126)*

## Practice

**A.** Read the paragraphs. Decide which sentence in each paragraph is the topic sentence. Write it on your paper.

1. Marilyn's day had gotten off to a bad start. Her alarm clock didn't go off, and she missed the school bus. The city bus got stuck in a traffic jam. Marilyn remembered that her math assignment was sitting on her desk at home, and it was due today.

2. When Marilyn got to school, her bad luck continued. She tripped as she got off the bus and got a bad scrape on her knee. After a short and painful trip to the nurse's office, she hobbled off to her history test. Marilyn was not only late. She had studied the wrong chapters for the test.

**B.** Copy the paragraph. Leave out the sentences that do not belong.

Marilyn's luck changed on the way home. Her best friend Sue asked her to a party. Do you like parties? She found the baseball glove she had lost. She even found a good-luck penny on the sidewalk. Marilyn saves all her money in the bank.

# *Friendly Letters*

200 Third Avenue
New York, New York 10003
July 21, 19--

Dear Susan,
    Thank you for the book you sent me. I do love mystery stories. Let me know if you would like to read it when I am finished. Thank you again.

                Sincerely,
                Laurie

- The **friendly letter** and most notes such as **invitations** and **thank you notes** have five parts. *(page 102)*

**heading**
- The **heading** contains the letter writer's address and the date. A comma is used between the name of the city and state and between the day and the year in the date.

**greeting**
- The **greeting** welcomes the person who receives the letter. It begins with a capital letter and is followed by a comma.

**body**
- The **body** of the letter contains the message. Each paragraph in the body is indented.

**closing**
- The **closing** is the end of the letter. The first word of the closing is capitalized. A comma follows the closing.

**signature**
- The **signature** is the name of the letter writer.

## *Practice*

Write a friendly letter to a relative. Tell him or her what you have been doing in school.

# Envelope

*Veronica Penn*
*89 Cranbury Road*
*Clearbrook, NJ 08502*



*Donald Bart*
*40 Horatio Street*
*New York, NY 10014*

- An addressed envelope has two parts.  *(page 104)*
- The **return address** is the name and address of the person who wrote the letter. The return address is in the upper left-hand corner of the envelope.

  **return address**
- The receiver's name and address are written in the middle of the envelope. Postal abbreviations of states' names are written with two capital letters and no periods. Use a ZIP code in all addresses.

  **receiver's name and address**

## Practice

Draw two sample envelopes on your paper. Address the envelopes correctly. Use this information.

**1.** To: Gerry Tano
    366 Henry Street
    New York, NY
10003

From: Kim Lee
    61 Kenmore Drive
Chicago, IL 60611

**2.** To: Mr. Ralph Blake
    Niles, IL 60648
235 Elm St.

From: Mrs. Sara Towne
    1615 East Ave.
Mesa, AZ 85203

# Editing

● It is important to review your work after you write. Here is a checklist to use when you review your work. Use editing marks to show your changes. *(page 22)*

## Editing Marks

≡ capitalize

⊙ make a period

∧ add something

∧, add a comma

ᐦᐦ add quotation marks

ᵍ take something away

◯ spell correctly

�# indent the paragraph

/ make a lowercase letter

∼ transpose
tr

### Editing Checklist

1. **Did I express a complete thought in each sentence?**
2. **Did I write a good topic sentence for each paragraph?**
3. **Did I write detail sentences that support the main idea?**
4. **Did I write detail sentences that keep to the topic?**
5. **Did I begin each sentence with a capital letter?**
6. **Did I end each sentence with the correct punctuation mark?**
7. **Did I use other punctuation marks correctly?**
8. **Did I indent the first line of each paragraph?**
9. **Did I spell correctly?**
10. **Did I write neatly?**

## Practice

Rewrite the paragraph. Make all the corrections shown.

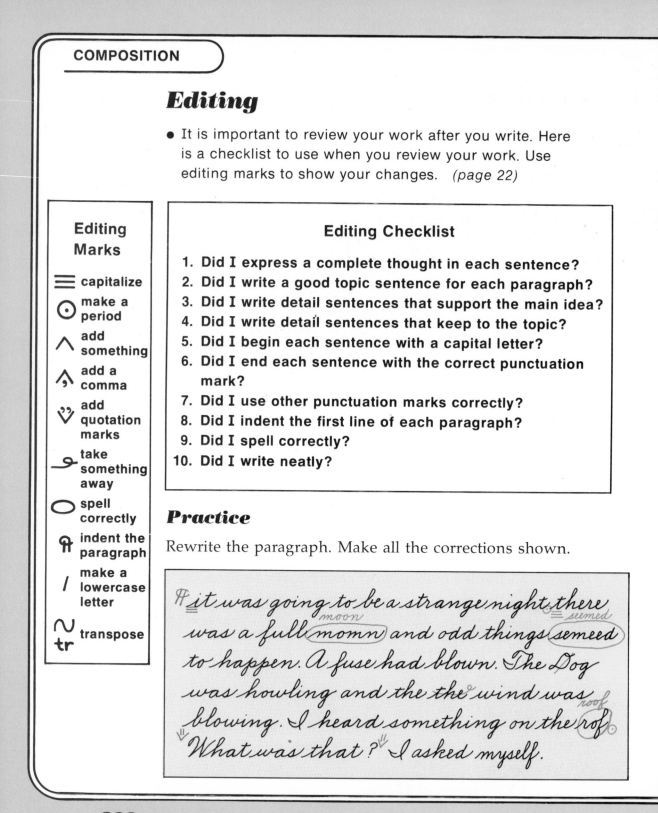

# Names and Titles of People, Names of Pets, and I

- Begin each part of the name of a person with a capital letter. *(page 44)*

  **person's name**

  Robert S. Moro     Alice Sanchez

- Begin titles of people such as *Ms., Mrs., Mr.,* and *Dr.* with a capital letter. *(page 44)*

  **title of a person**

  Dr. Fran Lee     Mr. Allan Layne     Ms. Mary King

- Always capitalize the word *I.* *(page 63)*

  **I**

  I laughed.     Mary and I went home.

- Begin the names of pets with a capital letter. *(page 63)*

  **pet's name**

  Lassie     Benji     Snowflake

## Practice

**A.** Rewrite the names. Use capital letters where they are needed.

1. joanna miller
2. tina lee
3. koko
4. fluffy
5. sen. r.j. howers
6. b.j. thomas
7. dr. jean trotter
8. mr. terry ulrich

**B.** Rewrite the sentences. Use capital letters where they are needed.

9. I wrote a letter to mrs. luisa bogen.
10. My dog hobo was found by dr. kim.
11. sen. arno and mrs. e.j. howard visited us.
12. huey and louie are my pet gerbils.
13. r.g. brown named his cat gino.
14. Sara and i own a goldfish named bubbles.
15. gov. wilcox rode his horse tinker.

# Names of Places

**place name**

- Begin each important word in the name of a town, city, state, and country with a capital letter. *(page 46)*

Mesa, Arizona    New London
North Dakota    United States

- Begin each important word in the names of streets and their abbreviations with capital letters. *(page 46)*

Fifth Street or St.    Park Avenue or Ave.
Dayhill Road or Rd.    Riverside Drive or Dr.

## Practice

**A.** Write these place names correctly.

1. fordham rd.
2. reno, nevada
3. sunset drive
4. london, england
5. newark, new jersey
6. portland, maine
7. suffolk county
8. south america
9. paris, france
10. south street

**B.** Write these sentences correctly. Use capital letters where they are needed.

11. The states of michigan, minnesota, and wisconsin each have a chippewa county.
12. Place names in the united states are interesting.
13. san francisco and los angeles are Spanish names.
14. An old town in wyoming was called hole in the wall.
15. A street in new york city is called columbus avenue.
16. richmond is the capital of virginia.
17. There is a kansas city in kansas and missouri.
18. You can find a zodiac road in nashville, tennessee.
19. zephyr cove is a town in nevada.
20. There is a zebra street in oklahoma city.

# Names of Days, Months, and Holidays

- Begin the name of a day of the week or its abbreviation with a capital letter. *(page 42)*    **day**

    Monday      Wednesday      Wed.
    Tuesday      Saturday      Sat.

- Begin the name of a month or its abbreviation with a capital letter. *(page 42)*    **month**

    January      September      Sept.
    February      October      Oct.

- Begin each important word in the name of a holiday or special day with a capital letter. *(page 42)*    **holiday**

    Halloween      Election Day
    Fourth of July      Flag Day

## Practice

**A.** Write the sentences correctly. Use capital letters where they are needed.

1. School will be closed during july and august.
2. On monday, october 21, it is my birthday.
3. On saturday and sunday I will be in the country.
4. election day always falls on a tuesday.
5. memorial day is celebrated in may.
6. The first monday in september is a holiday.
7. It is called labor day.

**B.** Write the following holidays and special days correctly.

8. martin luther king day
9. washington's birthday
10. columbus day

# Titles of Books, Stories, Poems, and Reports

**titles** Use a capital letter to begin the first, last, and all important words in the title of a book, story, poem, report, song, or television show. *(page 225)*

A Wrinkle in Time (book)
"The Lambkin and the Little Fish" (story)
"Taste of Purple" (poem)

## Practice

**A.** Write the titles correctly. Add capital letters where they are needed.

1. "winter is tacked down" (poem)
2. the tailor of gloucester (book)
3. caring for pet frogs (report)
4. "the juniper tree" (story)
5. ocean dwellers (report)
6. a kiss for little bear (book)

**B.** Write the sentences correctly. Add capital letters to the titles in each sentence.

7. My favorite television show is "the waltons."
8. We memorized the poem "oh have you heard?"
9. Diana titled her report the great whales.
10. I like the drawings in the book benjamin and the box.
11. "the last word of a bluebird" is a lovely poem.
12. My teacher liked my report, dental care.
13. I watched "benjie" on television.
14. I read the book the phantom tollbooth.
15. We played the song "the star-spangled banner" on the piano.

# The Period

- Use a period at the end of a declarative or imperative sentence.  *(pages 4 and 6)*

  **to end sentences**

  > I have picked some flowers for the table.
  > Please hand me that vase.

- Use a period after an abbreviation.  *(page 44)*

  **in abbreviations**

  | | | | | |
  |---|---|---|---|---|
  | Aug. | Ave. | Sen. | Pres. | Sat. |
  | St. | Mr. | A.M. | P.M. | |

- Use a period after an initial.  *(page 44)*

  **after initials**

  > Elizabeth A. Tao

- Use a period after a numeral in the main topic and after a capital letter in the subtopic of an outline.  *(page 220)*

  **in outlines**

  > I. Living things
  >    A. Animals
  >    B. Plants

## Practice

**A.** Write these names and addresses correctly.

1. Mrs Ann T Rossi
2. 23 Clearbrook Blvd
3. Gov James A Furro
4. Dr Barbara A Jonas
5. 6702 Riverside Dr
6. 47 Denver St

**B.** Write these sentences correctly.

7. These cookies are delicious
8. Help me eat them
9. I bought them at the bakery

**C.** Write these abbreviations correctly.

10. Jan
11. Mon
12. Mrs
13. Sept
14. Apr
15. Tues
16. Wed
17. Oct
18. Gov
19. Mar
20. Hwy

# The Comma

**in addresses**
- Use a comma in an address to separate the city and state or the city and country. *(page 102)*

  Portland, Oregon     Paris, France

**in compound sentences**
- Use a comma before the words *and*, *but*, and *or* when two sentences are combined. *(page 18)*

  It rained hard, but I was carrying an umbrella.

**in dates**
- Use a comma between the day and the year. *(page 102)*

  October 29, 1976

**in quotations**
- Use a comma between a quotation and the rest of the sentence. *(page 290)*

  I said, "Let's go."     "It is too late," he said.

**in a series**
- Use a comma to separate three or more words in a series. *(page 182)*

  John, Mary, and Paul are going with us.

**with introductory words**
- Use a comma after the words *yes* and *no* when they begin a statement. *(page 246)*

  Yes, I enjoyed the trip.

## Practice

Copy the sentences. Add commas where they are needed.

1. Did you buy milk eggs and sugar?
2. Yes I bought these groceries.
3. I asked "May I have some money?"
4. Gary Tina and Val gave me some change.
5. We will have guests on July 4 1987.
6. My cousin is coming from Portland Maine.
7. It will be fun but it is such a long time away.
8. "Call me before July" my cousin said.

# The Question Mark and the Exclamation Point

- Use a question mark at the end of an interrogative sentence. *(page 4)*

    **in questions**

    Will you finish on time?

- Use an exclamation point at the end of an exclamatory sentence. *(page 6)*

    **in exclamations**

    What a lovely painting!

# Quotation Marks and Underlines

- Use quotation marks before and after a direct quotation. *(page 290)*

    **in direct quotations**

    "Step into my parlor," said the spider to the fly.

- Use quotation marks before and after the title of a story, poem, song, or television show. *(page 225)*

    **in titles**

    "America the Beautiful" (song)

- Underline the title of a book or report. *(page 60)*

    **in titles**

    Charlotte's Web (book)

## Practice

Write the sentences. Add quotation marks, underlines, and end punctuation marks where they are needed.

1. Is the zoo open I asked.
2. Barbara read a book called Zoo Animals.
3. What an exciting book it was
4. Return the book to the library, her mother said.
5. Barbara watches Animal World on television.
6. A song called Animal Crackers is her favorite.
7. Do you like animals too
8. Barbara said, I draw animal pictures.

# *The Apostrophe and the Colon*

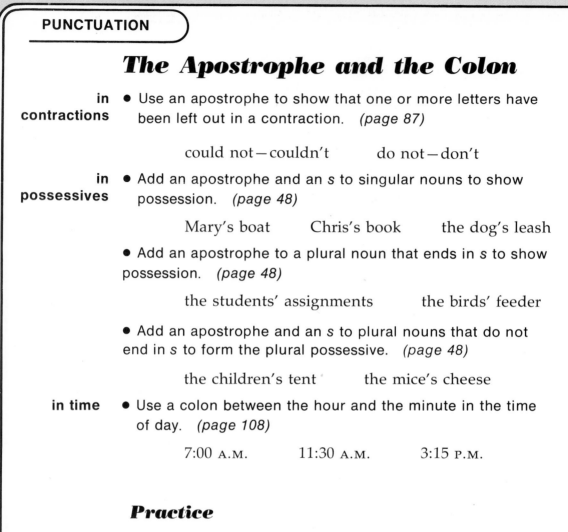

**in contractions** ● Use an apostrophe to show that one or more letters have been left out in a contraction. *(page 87)*

could not — couldn't        do not — don't

**in possessives** ● Add an apostrophe and an *s* to singular nouns to show possession. *(page 48)*

Mary's boat        Chris's book        the dog's leash

● Add an apostrophe to a plural noun that ends in *s* to show possession. *(page 48)*

the students' assignments        the birds' feeder

● Add an apostrophe and an *s* to plural nouns that do not end in *s* to form the plural possessive. *(page 48)*

the children's tent        the mice's cheese

**in time** ● Use a colon between the hour and the minute in the time of day. *(page 108)*

7:00 A.M.        11:30 A.M.        3:15 P.M.

## *Practice*

Write the sentences. Add apostrophes and colons where they are needed.

1. Is the childrens library open?
2. It opens today at 900 A.M.
3. Cant we get in by 830 A.M.?
4. Mats books must be returned so he wont be fined.
5. I havent seen Julies book yet.
6. Isnt this Marthas book?
7. She didnt want it returned.
8. Arent you coming back before 415 P.M.?

# Troublesome Words

- Use *a* before a word that begins with a consonant or a long /u/ sound. Use *an* before a word that begins with a vowel sound other than the long /u/ sound.   *(page 167)*   **a, an**

> a party      a uniform      an apple      an uncle

- The word *I* is always used in the subject part of the sentence. The word *me* follows an action verb.   *(page 210)*   **I, me**

> I had a good time. Sue and I went to a show.
> Carl helped me. He gave Hal and me a lesson.

- The word *good* is an adjective. It describes a noun. The word *well* is an adverb. It tells more about a verb.   *(page 172)*   **good, well**

> We had a good time.      The band played well.

## Practice

Copy the sentences. Choose the correct word to complete each sentence.

1. Mr. Morris is (a, an) artist.
2. He paints (good, well).
3. He did (a, an) painting for us.
4. (I, Me) like the early paintings.
5. My brother and (me, I) saw them in a museum.
6. We also saw some (good, well) sculpture.
7. One statue amazed (I, me).
8. It seemed to stare at Laura and (I, me).
9. My brother showed (I, me) some others.
10. (A, An) open space had a large fountain.
11. It was (a, an) original work of art.
12. The guide told my brother and (I, me) about it.
13. She explained (good, well).
14. Finally we went home on (a, an) bus.
15. We had a (good, well) day.

# Troublesome Words

**their, there, they're**
- Use *their* when you mean "belonging to them." Use *there* when you mean "in that place." Use *they're* when you mean "they are." *They're* is a contraction for *they are.* *(page 256)*

> Their car is in the driveway.
> It is not there.     They're the best I've seen.

**to, too, two**
- Use *to* when you mean "in the direction of." Use *too* when you mean "also" or "more than enough." Use *two* when you mean "one more than one." *(page 256)*

> The children walked to the bus stop.
> They were too late.     Two of them cried.

## Practice

Choose the correct word from the pair of words in parentheses ( ). Write the sentences.

1. (Two, Too) airplanes are overhead.
2. (They're, Their) wings are very large.
3. (They're, There) the biggest I have ever seen.
4. The air terminal is (their, there).
5. (To, Two) pilots walk (to, too) the airport.
6. The flight attendants wear (there, their) uniforms.
7. Porters carry bags and suitcases (too, two).
8. (They're, Their) on line now.
9. Mona and Inéz will get (their, there) tickets.
10. Bring the tickets (to, two) this counter.
11. You can carry (too, two) bags on the plane.
12. Stand in the line over (they're, there).
13. Are you going (to, two) Santa Fe (two, too)?
14. The plane will land (there, they're) at 2:00 P.M.
15. This is (their, there) first visit (two, to) New Mexico.

# *Troublesome Words*

- Use *its* when you mean "belonging to it." Use *it's* when you mean "it is." *It's* is a contraction for *it is.*  *(page 256)*     **its, it's**

> Its paw is hurt.
> It's a beautiful day.

- Use *your* when you mean "belonging to you." Use *you're* when you mean "you are." *You're* is a contraction for *you are.*  *(page 256)*     **your, you're**

> Your books are on the table.
> You're running in this race.

## *Practice*

Choose the correct word from the pair of words in parentheses ( ). Write the sentences.

1. (Your, You're) kite is ready.
2. (Its, It's) the red, white, and blue one.
3. Do you like (its, it's) shape?
4. Have you brought (your, you're) string?
5. (You're, Your) the last one to arrive.
6. (Its, It's) time for the contest to begin.
7. Soon it will be (your, you're) turn.
8. (Your, You're) design is unusual.
9. Do you think (its, it's) going to win?
10. (Your, You're) facing right into the wind.
11. (Its, It's) carrying the kite high overhead.
12. Now unwind more of (your, you're) string.
13. Oh, (its, it's) string has broken.
14. (Your, You're) kite is flying away.
15. (Its, It's) sure to win a prize for flying the farthest!

# MORE PRACTICE

## UNIT 1

**Sentences**    pages 2–3

Copy the groups of words that are complete sentences. If a group of words is not a complete sentence, add words to complete it. Use capital letters and punctuation marks.

1. Lewis Carroll wrote *Alice's Adventures in Wonderland*.
2. One hot summer day Alice and her sister.
3. Suddenly a white rabbit with a watch and a fan.
4. Alice fell down a deep rabbit hole under a hedge.
5. Finally landed on a pile of leaves at the bottom.
6. Smaller and smaller with each passing second.
7. Alice met many odd creatures on her adventure.
8. All the guests at the Mad Hatter's tea party.
9. Found herself lying on the bank of the river.
10. Shaking Alice and telling her to wake up.

**Declarative and Interrogative Sentences**    pages 4–5

Write the sentences correctly. After each one, write *declarative* or *interrogative* to tell the kind of sentence it is.

1. have you read *Alice's Adventures in Wonderland*
2. alice had an unusual dream
3. alice found a little bottle
4. do you think she drank it
5. which is your favorite animal in the story
6. the Queen of Hearts is a character in the story
7. this is a picture of the Mad Hatter
8. a caterpillar gave Alice some advice in a riddle

**9.** would you like to have an adventure like hers

**10.** how did Alice grow larger and smaller

## Imperative and Exclamatory Sentences    pages 6–7

Write the sentences correctly. After each one, write *imperative* or *exclamatory* to tell the kind of sentence it is.

**1.** what a beautiful dive that was

**2.** come with Lauren and me to the edge of the pool

**3.** how deep the water looks

**4.** stand firmly on the diving board

**5.** don't dive until you're sure the pool is clear

**6.** please hurry and help me

**7.** how lucky I am to be here

**8.** wow, our team is doing well

**9.** please tell the coach I will be late for practice

**10.** arch your back to do a swan dive

## Questions and Answers    pages 8–9

Answers are given for each question. Write the answer in a complete sentence. Remember to use words from the question in your answer.

**1.** What is a diatom?   (a kind of tiny plant)

**2.** Where are diatoms found?   (in oceans, ponds, and lakes)

**3.** What shapes are diatoms?   (round and triangular)

**4.** When are diatoms most plentiful?   (spring or fall)

**5.** How large are diatoms?   (very small, or microscopic)

**6.** How can you see diatoms?   (by using a microscope)

**7.** What colors are diatoms?   (golden-brown, red, blue, green, or yellow)

**8.** What do diatoms need to live?   (sunlight)

**9.** What is a large animal that eats diatoms?   (a whale)

**10.** How can diatoms be collected?   (by scraping underwater rocks or weeds)

## Complete Subjects and Predicates    pages 10–11

Copy the sentences. Draw one line under the complete subject. Draw two lines under the complete predicate.

1. The marshy pond lies still in the morning sunshine.
2. Two blue dragonflies dart across its surface.
3. Large bullfrogs croak to each other in the reeds.
4. We watched a mother duck and six ducklings.
5. Many colorful fish swim together in schools.
6. This green water bug skates across the surface of the frozen pond.
7. Many microscopic animals live in pond water.
8. I visit the pond in all four seasons of the year.
9. Mary and I fish in the early morning or in the late evening.
10. These tiny tadpoles become frogs.

## Combining and Writing Sentences    pages 18–19

Combine each pair of sentences. Use the word in parentheses ( ).

1. I like purple. I do not like orange.   (but)
2. Red means danger. It can also mean stop.   (and)
3. You can use purple in your picture. You can use lavender.   (or)
4. Ellen mixed yellow with blue. She made green.   (and)
5. This room is a dull color. It can be painted.   (but)
6. You can draw with chalk. You can use colored pencils.   (or)
7. Yellow is a warm color. Violet is a cool color.   (but)
8. Richard likes brown. He also likes mauve.   (and)
9. People can buy pictures. They can paint their own.   (or)
10. Alicia built a color wheel. Ron painted it.   (and)

**Mechanics Practice**   page 23

Write these sentences correctly. Use capital letters and punctuation marks where necessary.

1. the crowd cheered the winners
2. what a game that was
3. did the players practice for many days
4. everyone is looking forward to the championship
5. bring your friends to the stadium


**Rhyming Words in Poetry**   pages 24–26

Read these lines of poetry. Write the words that rhyme.

> Tommy Jones and Taylor too
> Thought they ought to visit the zoo.
> There were apes in capes and bears in chairs
> A seal on a wheel and squares full of hares.
> Yet Tommy and Taylor said nothing was new
> At this mixed-up, crazy, remarkable zoo!


**Alliteration**   pages 27–29

Copy the sentences in which alliteration is used.

1. Greta's giddy goose gives me the giggles.
2. A whale of a walrus was Wonderful Wally.
3. Penguins love to slide down the ice into the ocean.
4. Is your yak yearning for Yale's yellow yams?
5. Parker's pet pig is pretty, pampered, and petted.
6. Flora found a frog who ferries fleas.
7. Kirby enjoyed watching the antelopes at the zoo.
8. Why does the giraffe have such a long neck?
9. Shaggy Sherlock is a shamefully shabby sheep.
10. Are African anteaters eating average-sized ants?

# UNIT 2

**Nouns**     pages 36–37

Copy the sentences. Underline the nouns. There will be more than one noun in each sentence.

1. Milkweeds are plants that bloom in summer.
2. These plants grow by ponds and in dry, open fields.
3. Their name comes from their milky juice.
4. The purple flowers of the milkweed can be seen all along roads in the country.
5. Some butterflies lay their eggs on milkweeds.
6. Native Americans used to chew the roots of this plant.
7. The pods of the milkweed hold tiny seeds.
8. David and Stanley wrote a report on milkweeds.
9. The boys showed the class some pods and seeds.
10. Camilla asked a question about the silk in the pods.

**Plural Nouns**     pages 38–41

Write the plural form of each noun.

1. valley
2. country
3. tax
4. frog
5. tree
6. woman
7. moose
8. cypress
9. tooth
10. lunch
11. deer
12. bunny
13. donkey
14. address
15. city

**Common and Proper Nouns**     pages 42–43

Use proper nouns for the words in parentheses ( ). Write the new sentences correctly.

1. _____ is coming to visit next week.   (boy's name)
2. Last _____ my sister wrote him a long letter.   (name of a month)
3. She wrote about what has been happening on _____. (name of a street)

4. Our neighbors are visiting _____. (name of a country)
5. _____ lost her cat near my house. (girl's name)
6. She also wrote about our camping trip on _____. (name of a mountain)
7. We followed the _____ that ran alongside our trail. (name of a river)
8. On _____ my father caught fresh fish for dinner. (name of a day)
9. On _____ we will go visit our relatives. (name of a holiday)
10. _____ lives near there. (girl's name)

## Names of People and Places    pages 44–47

Write the sentences. Capitalize the names of people and places.

1. John blackburn and marisa flanders will be married.
2. My Aunt faye and Uncle joshua have been invited.
3. They live on high street in clinton, connecticut.
4. My cousin, kathleen shapiro, will be a flower girl.
5. The wedding will be at a hotel on fifth avenue.
6. John and marisa will take a vacation in utah and colorado.
7. Then they will travel through canada on their way back to east windsor, new jersey.
8. They will live on chambers street.

## Abbreviations    pages 46–47

Use abbreviations for titles and streets. Write each name or place correctly.

1. ms antonia politi
2. high cliff boulevard
3. senator h john heinz
4. hillside street
5. governor james a rhodes
6. doctor susan perkins
7. barrymore place
8. miss amy stanton
9. massachusetts avenue
10. governor jennie denton

## Possessive Nouns    pages 48–51

Write a possessive noun for each group of words. Then use the possessive nouns in sentences.

1. the cups of the baby
2. the paints of Beth
3. the sleds of the children
4. the key belonging to Mother
5. the books of the girls
6. the words of the speaker
7. the pencils of the boys
8. the hat belonging to Rose
9. the toys of the kittens
10. the yarn belonging to Shelley
11. the hats of the models
12. the car of the racer
13. the lights of the men
14. the names of the people
15. the eyes of the cats
16. the machine of the worker
17. the fur of the rabbit
18. the laughter of the clowns

## Main Idea    pages 54–55

Write the sentence that best states the main idea of each selection.

1.    The woodchuck's coloring helps protect it. Its brown, gray, and black fur is just the color of rocks. Often a woodchuck will lie on a stone wall in the sun. Its enemies can't tell it from the rocks.

   a. Woodchucks are brown, gray, and black.
   b. Woodchucks lie on rocks.
   c. Woodchucks have protective coloring.

2. Howler monkeys love to move. In their cages they jump all over. Sometimes they leap from side to side. Often one will jump from the bottom of the cage to the top.

    **a.** Howler monkeys are very active.
    **b.** Howler monkeys live in cages.
    **c.** Howler monkeys make a lot of noise.

### Reading for Details    pages 56–57

Look back at the section called Main Idea. For each selection write two details that you find.

### Writing, Editing, and Presenting a Book Report    pages 60–65

Write a book report about a book you have read recently. Tell about the characters, plot, and setting. Tell your opinion of the book too. After you edit your book report, present it orally to the class.

### Mechanics Practice    page 63

Write the sentences using capital letters and periods correctly.

1. dan is a playful golden retriever.
2. His owner is m j row.
3. Usually dan plays in the den.
4. His veterinarian is dr sidney.
5. i take him for his yearly checkups.

### Reading a Biography    pages 66–69

Read a biography about a famous person you admire. Then answer these questions. Use complete sentences.

1. Who is the main character?
2. Why is the main character important or famous?
3. Who is another character in the story?
4. How does this person help the main character?
5. What have you learned about the main character?

# UNIT 3

### Action Verbs and Linking Verbs    pages 78–81

Copy each sentence. Draw two lines under the verb. Then write *action verb* or *linking verb* to tell the kind of verb each is.

1. Our school is very new.
2. Last Wednesday was the first day of spring.
3. Matthew wrote a report about spring festivals around the world.
4. Todd is the boy next to me in science class.
5. We play chess almost every day after school.
6. My favorite games at recess are tag and dodge ball.
7. My friends and I climb to the top of the jungle gym.
8. Our school's soccer team won five games this year.
9. My best friends at school are Lucy and Laurie.
10. We ride our bicycles to school together each day.

### Main Verbs and Helping Verbs    pages 82–83

Copy each sentence. Draw two lines under the complete verb. Circle the helping verb.

1. This evening I am going on a horseback ride.
2. My three friends have taken the trip already.
3. We were talking about sights and sounds in the night.
4. A barn owl is hooting at us from a hemlock tree.
5. He had heard us from a very great distance away.
6. Small animals are scurrying out of the horses' path.
7. We will canter in the open field in the moonlight.
8. The horses are finding their way in the dark.
9. Angie and Joyce will go on tomorrow night's ride.
10. The stillness of the forest at night will amaze them.

## Verb Tenses  pages 84–86

Copy the sentences. Draw two lines under the verbs. After each sentence write *past, present,* or *future* to tell the tense.

1. This year my family planted a vegetable garden.
2. Grandfather rakes the soil in the garden.
3. My sister waters the seedlings every other day.
4. My parents will build a chicken-wire fence around it.
5. Last year wild animals feasted on most of our vegetables!
6. They visited the garden late at night.
7. Rabbits, skunks, and deer lived in the woods nearby.
8. I will dig another row for the radishes and corn.
9. We will grow 12 different kinds of vegetables.
10. Lettuce and tomatoes make a wonderful salad.

## Contractions  page 87

Change the underlined words to contractions. Write the sentences.

1. The bus has not come.
2. The passengers are not sure.
3. Jeremy will not ride.
4. The express does not stop.
5. Beth did not see me.
6. The schedule was not right.
7. People do not know.
8. They have not arrived.
9. Ed had not stayed.
10. Her bag is not packed yet.
11. I was not sleeping.
12. They were not buying tickets.
13. I will not be coming.
14. Mother did not bring a book.

## Spelling Past Tense Verbs  pages 88–93

Write the past tense form of each verb.

1. ferry
2. trot
3. map
4. copy
5. try
6. bury
7. hum
8. carry
9. stop
10. pop
11. skim
12. worry
13. flip
14. drag
15. reply

## Using Irregular Verbs    pages 90–93

Write the sentences. Use the correct verb form in the parentheses ( ).

1. John has _____ his homework. *(did or done)*
2. Ken _____ his report. *(wrote or written)*
3. Father _____ money to Alicia. *(gave or given)*
4. Jed _____ his report. *(did or done)*
5. Susan has _____ to her aunt. *(wrote or written)*
6. My parents have _____ me a bicycle. *(gave or given)*
7. She _____ flowers and vegetables. *(grew or grown)*
8. We have _____ to the exhibit. *(came or come)*
9. Peter _____ into the store. *(ran or run)*
10. Jill has _____ 3 inches this year. *(grew or grown)*
11. My uncle _____ to our play. *(came or come)*
12. Jeff has _____ a painting class. *(began or begun)*
13. The doorbell _____. *(rang or rung)*
14. The girls _____ home. *(went or gone)*
15. We _____ the rehearsal early. *(began or begun)*
16. The package had _____ last week. *(came or come)*
17. The children _____ to the playground. *(ran or run)*
18. Stan has _____ a song. *(wrote or written)*
19. The child has _____ quickly. *(grew or grown)*
20. Mr. Rice has _____ the bus. *(took or taken)*
21. Jean has _____ the exercises. *(did or done)*
22. Mother _____ an umbrella. *(took or taken)*
23. The circus has _____ to town. *(came or come)*
24. My parents _____ to the theater. *(went or gone)*
25. The puppy has _____ away. *(ran or run)*
26. The mail _____ late. *(came or come)*
27. We _____ our puppy on vacation. *(took or taken)*
28. The boy _____ to the bus. *(ran or run)*
29. Dad has _____ to the airport. *(went or gone)*
30. Have you _____ tulips? *(grew or grown)*

## Alphabetical Order   pages 96–97

Write each group of words in alphabetical order.

1. rice, oats, buckwheat, alfalfa, corn
2. dalmatian, collie, hound, poodle, dog
3. tree, oak, branch, trunk, pine
4. mole, ground, gopher, tunnel, earthworm
5. frog, duck, pond, polliwog, water
6. bug, beetle, butterfly, aphid, caterpillar
7. ocean, cod, crab, coral, octopus
8. catbird, canary, chicken, condor, crow
9. sun, sand, shark, seaweed, salmon
10. walk, wade, warble, wag, wail
11. pilot, pillow, pine, pin, pan
12. sandwich, sand, soap, sash, sat
13. mail, main, lumber, lower, loop
14. lap, land, large, late, less
15. grow, guide, groan, green, grind

## Writing a Friendly Letter   pages 102–103

Rewrite the friendly letter correctly. Use correct
punctuation and capitalization.

2 somerset rd
columbia missouri 65201
february 4 1983

dear Claudine
Have you heard the big news in the neighborhood?
Nicole and Marina von Bergen are moving to England!
Our street won't be the same without them. We are having
a party for them before they go. I wish you lived here so
that you could join us. We'll miss you.

your cousin
Dana

## Writing and Editing an Invitation    pages 108–111

Write an invitation to a party. Pretend you are giving the party. Invite one of your friends. Here is the information you should include in the invitation.

> *date:* February 21, 1983
> *time:* 3:00 P.M. until 5:00 P.M.
> *place:* your address

Edit for correct capitalization and punctuation.

## Mechanics Practice    page 111

Write these sentences correctly. Use capital letters, periods, and commas where necessary.

1. Ted visited washington d c.
2. His cousin lives there on pennsylvania ave
3. Last summer they toured williamsburg virginia.
4. Later they took a boat tour on chesapeake bay.
5. Next spring they will spend a week in houston texas.

## Reading a Play    pages 112–119

Read these lines from a play. Then complete the statements about it.

**Liza** *(Laughing):*   What do you think of your idea now?
**Jonathan** *(Looking at* **Liza** *and smiling):*   Liza, I think I was right. There is something living in this hollow tree. *(He kneels and begins scooping dry leaves from a hollow in the tree.)*
**Troll** *(Angrily):*   What do you mean by disturbing my house!

1. Three characters in this play are _____.
2. An example of stage directions is _____.
3. The setting of this play could be _____.
4. An example of dialog is _____.

# UNIT 4

## Sentence Order in Paragraphs pages 132–133

The sentences in these paragraphs are out of order.
Rewrite them in the correct order. Then underline the
topic sentences.

1. Yesterday we played hide-and-seek. Then Bonita was
   "It." I counted to 100 while the others hid. I found
   Stephanie behind the garage and Roger in a tree. When
   I reached 100, I yelled, "Ready or not, here I come!"

2. The school bus comes at 8:05 A.M. I go downstairs
   when I'm dressed to make breakfast for myself. School
   mornings are busy at my house. Right away I dress and
   make my bed. We all wake up at 7:10 A.M.

3. The floors are put in place. Building a house is a long
   process. When everything is finally built, the house is
   painted. First a basement or crawl space is dug. After
   the floors, frames for walls, doorways, and windows are
   built.

4. My cousins send balloons instead of cards for people's
   birthdays. They blow up the balloons to write messages
   on them. They buy the biggest, strongest balloons. They
   put the deflated balloon in an envelope and send it
   through the mail. When the ink is dry, they let the air
   out.

5. Finally sprinkle some wheat germ on your shake before
   you drink it. I like to make yogurt shakes. Add some
   yogurt and apple juice to the banana. Mix all three
   ingredients well. Cut up a banana and put it in a
   blender.

6. They always do warm-up exercises before they go. The
   exercises stretch their leg muscles. Jennifer runs with
   her parents every morning. Then they run about a mile
   through our town.

**Table of Contents**     pages 138–139

Read the table of contents. Write the answers to the questions that follow it. Use complete sentences.

**1.** Which chapter begins on page 68?

**2.** What is the title of the second chapter?

**3.** Which chapter begins on page 81?

**4.** On what page does Chapter 6 begin?

**5.** Which chapter tells about animals of the plains?

**6.** On what page does Chapter 1 begin?

**Index**     pages 140–141

Use this index to answer the questions.

**1.** On what pages would you find facts about camouflage?

**2.** Where would you look for information about how chimpanzees learn?

**3.** On what page would you find facts about baboons?

**4.** On which subject is there more information, apes or gibbons?

**5.** If you wanted to learn about gibbons, where would you look?

## The Encyclopedia     pages 142–143

Look at the set of encyclopedias on page 142. Write the number of the volume you would use to find information about each topic.

**1.** John Glenn          **2.** Flags
**3.** North Carolina     **4.** Chemistry
**5.** Sailing            **6.** the White House

## Direction Paragraph     pages 146–149

Write a direction paragraph telling how to make or do something. Use words such as *first, second, third, next, last,* and *finally* in your directions. Check to see that the sentences are in the right order. Here are some suggestions.

a recipe                    an art project
a science experiment        an indoor or outdoor game

## Mechanics Practice     page 149

Write these sentences, using capital letters and periods.

**1.** We arrived in the city on tuesday
**2.** Everyone looked forward to the columbus day parade
**3.** We always plan a special event in october.
**4.** The next holiday is in november
**5.** All the family gathers for thanksgiving.

## Reading an Adventure Story     pages 150–153

Find an adventure story in your school or public library. When you have read the story, answer these questions.

**1.** Who is the main character?
**2.** What words describe the main character?
**3.** Where does the story take place?
**4.** What is one problem the main character must face?
**5.** How does the main character solve that problem?

# UNIT 5

**Adjectives**     pages 162–163

Copy the sentences. Underline the adjectives.

1. Our little car was lost in the thick, wet fog.
2. Put on these dark glasses in the bright sunshine.
3. Is the young man swimming on this cold, windy day?
4. The sudden lightning frightened the frisky colt.
5. Fresh white snow blanketed the cozy cabin.
6. Don't those fleecy clouds look like lost sheep?
7. Yellow sunlight poured through the tall window.
8. Heavy rain pounded the dry desert.
9. Carl ran to get a heavy overcoat and warm mittens.
10. Loud thunder and jagged lightning surrounded us.

**Adjectives That Use _er_ or _est_ to Compare**     pages 164–166

Choose the correct adjective. Write the sentences.

1. This stone feels (smoother, smoothest) than yours.
2. Amelia's necklace is the (longer, longest) of the three.
3. Isn't this the (softer, softest) yarn you've ever felt?
4. Which clay figure is the (bigger, biggest) of all?
5. He can work (faster, fastest) than Bradley.
6. I think this color is (lighter, lightest) than the purple.
7. Margo's pot is (smaller, smallest) than Leigh's.
8. This African mask is the (older, oldest) one in the collection.
9. Cammie drew the (sadder, saddest) face I've ever seen.
10. Your mobile is (higher, highest) than mine.

**Adjectives That Use _more_ or _most_ to Compare**
pages 164–166

Use _more_ or _most_ with the adjectives in parentheses ( ).
Write the sentences.

1. Dean is _____ than Crissie on his bicycle.   (careful)
2. This game is _____ than our old one.   (fun)
3. Isn't that the _____ jacket you've ever seen?
   (colorful)
4. The directions were the _____ part of the game.
   (confusing)
5. This is the _____ rule in the game.   (important)
6. Is she _____ than Molly on the tumbling mat?
   (talented)
7. She owns the _____ bike in our neighborhood.
   (expensive)
8. Eddie's paintings are _____ than Herbie's.   (interesting)
9. Mrs. Daley's idea is _____ than yours.   (exciting)
10. Our street is not the _____ street in this area.
    (peaceful)

## Articles     page 167

Choose the correct answer. Write the sentences.

1. (A, The) eye is (a, an) amazing sense organ.
2. (A, An) interesting way to understand (a, the) eye is
   to compare it to (a, an) camera.
3. Like the camera, your eye has (a, an) lens that sharpens
   (an, the) picture you see.
4. Light enters the eye through (an, the) pupil.
5. (An, The) human eye sends thousands of messages to
   (a, an) area in the brain.
6. Someday blind people may be able to "see" with
   (a, an) special machine.
7. The eye of (a, an) owl can see in very dim light.
8. (A, An) eye of (a, an) snake does not have a lid.
9. The eye of (a, an) cat reflects light so the light can be
   used twice.
10. American eye doctors study (a, the) eye for many
    years as part of their schooling.

## Adverbs    pages 168–171

Copy the sentences. Underline the adverbs. Then write whether the adverb tells *how, when,* or *where.*

1. The turtle moved slowly.
2. Soon we will see the seals.
3. They bark loudly.
4. Their pool is nearby.
5. Lions sleep often.
6. They growl hungrily.
7. We arrived early.
8. Tigers pace gracefully.
9. I will wait outside.
10. Look around to find me.
11. The monkeys run inside.
12. They swing freely from trees.
13. Now we will hurry.
14. Watch carefully for the bats.
15. They fly so quickly.
16. They sleep peacefully.
17. It is somewhere.
18. Talk softly near the cage.

## Using good and well    pages 172–173

Choose the correct answer. Write the sentences.

1. Do you think this is a (good, well) play to perform?
2. Madeline acted her part very (good, well).
3. She has studied acting in two (good, well) schools.
4. A (good, well) place to begin is Act III, Scene 1.
5. I think she said those lines very (good, well).
6. Express yourself (good, well).
7. How (good, well) do you know the director?
8. Theodore is a very (good, well) leading man.
9. The orchestra played the music quite (good, well).
10. You have a (good, well) sense of timing as you read.

## Homographs    pages 176–177

Write the meaning of the underlined homographs.

1. Quickly bail the water out of the boat.
2. The count will return to the castle tomorrow.
3. The earthquake will jar the house.
4. If you line this jacket it will be warmer.
5. The page was training to be a knight.

## Synonyms and Antonyms    pages 178–181

Write a synonym (S) or an antonym (A) for each word.

1. near (S)         2. tiny (A)         3. unhappy (A)
4. fearful (S)      5. chilly (S)       6. rich (A)
7. heavy (A)        8. night (A)        9. glad (S)
10. large (S)       11. high (A)        12. inside (A)
13. messy (A)       14. shiny (S)       15. discover (S)

## Sentence Combining    pages 182–183

Combine each set of sentences into one sentence.

1. This coffee is dark. This coffee is strong. This coffee is hot.
2. Their dog is calm. Their dog is smart.
3. The two ducks are mallards. The brown ducks are mallards.
4. The weather is breezy. The weather is warm.
5. Dad's shiny car is new. Dad's green car is new.

## Writing and Editing a Descriptive Paragraph    pages 184–187

Write a paragraph that describes a person, place, or thing you know well. Choose adjectives and adverbs that give the exact meaning you want. Then edit your paragraph.

## Mechanics Practice    page 187

Write these sentences correctly. Use capital letters, periods, colons, and commas where necessary.

1. The circus comes to town in april.
2. We plan to attend the 7 30 p m performance on april 14.
3. The train leaves for the city at 5 00 p m.
4. In the winter the circus stays in dayton ohio.
5. Circus people work long hours beginning at 5 00 a m.

## Comparisons    pages 190–191

Complete the comparisons in column A with the words in column B. Write the complete groups of words.

**A**

1. as quiet as a _____
2. thin like a _____
3. as silly as a _____
4. as cold as a _____
5. as scary as a _____
6. fast like a _____
7. as colorful as a _____
8. as smelly as a _____
9. as dry as a _____
10. busy like a _____

**B**

a. snowball
b. cheetah
c. sunset
d. bee
e. desert
f. clown
g. skunk
h. mouse
i. monster
j. needle

## Exaggeration    pages 192–195

Complete each exaggeration in column A with a choice from column B. Write the sentences.

**A**

1. Tom is so hungry, _____
2. The movie is so scary, _____
3. Wilma is so strong, _____
4. That joke is so old, _____
5. This math is so hard, _____
6. Her eyes are so sharp, _____
7. This meat is so tender, _____
8. Her hair is so long, _____
9. Tex is so thin, _____
10. Alice is so slow, _____

**B**

a. it makes your hair stand on end.
b. he could eat a house.
c. it's like a blanket.
d. it melts in your mouth.
e. the dinosaurs told it.
f. she can lift an elephant.
g. a genius couldn't do it.
h. she can see an ant on the moon.
i. he could walk through the eye of a needle.
j. a turtle could beat her.

# UNIT 6

**Pronouns**     pages 202–203

Write the pronoun from the second sentence of each pair.
Then write the noun for which it stands.

1. Which soup is Andrea's? She made the tomato soup.
2. Tom likes ketchup. This hot dog is covered with it.
3. Matthew washed the dishes. Father dried them.
4. Lorraine makes breakfast. She cooks bacon and eggs.
5. Burt made a sandwich. He gave half to Heather.
6. Mother bought apples. She bought them yesterday.
7. Eric and Wendy ate lunch. They ate outside.
8. Carlos wanted milk. Mr. Elias poured milk for him.
9. Kathy peeled carrots. Frank cooked them.
10. Father saw Carmina. Father gave her the book.

**Subject Pronouns**     pages 204–205

Use subject pronouns to replace the underlined words.
Write the sentences.

1. Leon has skates with bright blue wheels.
2. The skates are new.
3. Leon and Marcy skate down the sidewalk.
4. The sidewalk has many cracks.
5. Doesn't Marcy skate well?

**Pronouns After Action Verbs**     pages 206–207

Use pronouns to replace underlined words after each
action verb. Write the sentences.

1. I asked Lee to play chess.
2. We asked Carol and Chin too.
3. We all played chess for three hours.
4. I taught Carol how to play.
5. Lee beat Carol, Chin, and me.

## Possessive Pronouns    pages 208–209

Use a pronoun in place of the underlined word or words.

1. Tom went on a fishing trip with <u>Tom's</u> brother.
2. <u>The boys'</u> mother packed a picnic lunch for them.
3. She made <u>the mother's</u> best fried chicken recipe.
4. They packed <u>Mother and Tom's</u> car.
5. By the time they finished, <u>the car's</u> trunk was full.

## Using **I** and **Me**    pages 210–211

Choose the correct answer. Write the sentences.

1. Curtis and (I, me) climbed that huge old oak tree.
2. Lesley showed Curtis and (I, me) where to put our hands and feet.
3. Will you please give (I, me) that red toolbox?
4. Lesley, Curtis, and (I, me) are building a tree house.
5. Lesley told (I, me) his sister would also help us.

## Pronouns That End in **self** or **selves**    pages 212–213

Choose the correct answer. Write the sentences.

1. Did you find (himself, yourselves) some bathing suits?
2. Maria pulled (herself, themselves) out of the pool.
3. Jeff taught (himself, hisself) a racing dive.
4. The team practiced by (themselves, theirselves).
5. Bridget and I timed (myself, ourselves) in the relay.

## Report Topics    pages 216–217

Read each pair of report topics. Write the best topic for a short report from each pair.

1. Animals of North America
   How Beavers Build Dams
2. The History of Skiing
   How Skis Have Changed
3. Pedro's Day in São Paolo
   The People of Brazil
4. Bringing Back the Bluebird
   Large and Small Birds

## Writing, Editing, and Presenting a Report   pages 222–227

Study this outline for a report titled "Good Food." Write two paragraphs based on the outline. Edit your report for accuracy. Present the report orally to the class.

I. Why good food is important
   A. Gives you energy
   B. Helps you grow
   C. Helps the body fight off germs
II. Three food groups
   A. Fruits and vegetables
   B. Whole grains, seeds, and nuts
   C. Meat, fish, and poultry

## Mechanics Practice   page 225

Write these sentences correctly. Use capital letters, underlines, and quotation marks where necessary.

1. Have you read the book charlotte's web?
2. I wrote a poem called wilbur and his friends.
3. Jan's favorite story is the mysterious cat.
4. Did you watch underwater secrets on television?
5. My favorite song is the greatest american hero.

## Reading a Magazine Article   pages 228–231

Read this paragraph and write five facts for a report. Write a title for the report.

Toads spend different parts of their lives in water and on land. Toads develop from tadpoles. As tadpoles they live in water. In the spring you may see hundreds of tiny toads near ponds. They begin to travel away from the ponds to dry land. As adults, toads live on land.

# UNIT 7

### Simple Subjects    pages 240–241

Copy the sentences. Underline the simple subjects.

1. Coyotes have been outsmarting humans for centuries.
2. Native Americans respected the coyote's intelligence.
3. The coyote is a very smart animal.
4. A mother takes good care of her pups.
5. She teaches them how to hunt food and avoid traps.
6. Early in life, the pups learn to be very cautious.
7. These clever animals spring farmers' traps.
8. Scientists are studying coyotes in their wild homes.
9. Their discoveries will help the animals in the future.
10. Coyotes are valued for their unusual ability to survive.

### Simple Predicates    pages 242–243

Copy the sentences. Draw two lines under the simple predicates.

1. Coyote pups play outside the den.
2. The three of them tumble in the high, wet grass.
3. Suddenly their ears hear strange sounds.
4. The mother coyote has moved the pups' den.
5. She was disturbed by human voices near her den.
6. I have studied a family of coyotes in Wyoming.
7. Coyotes will eat harmful pests such as rats and gophers.
8. They have helped farmers and ranchers in the past.
9. The coyotes of Yellowstone Park are protected by law.
10. My brother had listened to their night chorus.

### Subject–Verb Agreement    pages 244–245

Choose the correct answer. Write the sentences.

1. She (begin, begins) it.
2. They (take, takes) us.
3. Paul (run, runs) away.
4. The dog (jump, jumps) high.

5. Ed (write, writes) cards.
6. She (grow, grows) flowers.
7. Jay and Ali (talk, talks).
8. George (hike, hikes) home.
9. The wind (blow, blows).
10. Puppies (eat, eats) often.
11. Lea (drive, drives) to work.
12. Two girls (write, writes) it.
13. Soup (taste, tastes) good.
14. Beth (ring, rings) a bell.
15. They (sing, sings) songs.
16. Laurie (come, comes) over.
17. We (write, writes) notes.
18. Do you (hike, hikes)?
19. Jan (take, takes) a snack.
20. The kitten (run, runs).

## Word Order in Sentences    pages 246–247

Change each interrogative sentence to a declarative sentence. Begin answers with the word in parentheses ( ).

1. Is Paraguay a country in South America?   (yes)
2. Does the Amazon River empty into the Pacific Ocean?   (no)
3. Has Brazil increased in population since 1950?   (yes)
4. Are the people of Mexico proud of their history?   (yes)
5. Has Dr. Morales visited Colombia or Ecuador?   (no)
6. Are the Andes Mountains a good place to ski?   (yes)
7. Will the South American jungle be destroyed?   (no)
8. Did Mrs. Weaver tell them about her trip to Peru?   (no)
9. Have they seen the Aztec and Mayan ruins?   (yes)
10. Do many South Americans visit the United States?   (yes)

## Prefixes and Suffixes    pages 250–253

Copy each word. Underline the base word. Circle the prefix or suffix.

1. improper
2. unkind
3. changeable
4. nonstop
5. replay
6. misprint
7. singer
8. incorrect
9. dishonest
10. recharge
11. weightless
12. infirm
13. prisoner
14. unload
15. quickly
16. careful
17. herself
18. safely
19. friendly
20. unhappy

## Compound Words    pages 254–255

Write the sentences. Underline the compound words.

1. The sunlight finally broke through the clouds.
2. The truck raced away from the firehouse.
3. The fire was reported in the newspaper.
4. On a high rooftop gray pigeons cooed.
5. Emily's overcoat is not warm enough for this snow.
6. She made a snowball and threw it at Buster.
7. Have you ever counted the cracks in the sidewalk?
8. She waters the flowers in the flowerpot.
9. At night each streetlight shines on the people.
10. The children are building a snowman with a funny face.

## Homophones    pages 256–257

Choose the correct answer. Write the sentences.

1. Give it (to, too) me.
2. (There, Their) eyes glow.
3. John has (to, two) coins.
4. Here is (your, you're) pen.
5. Find (your, you're) sister.
6. I listen (to, too).
7. (Your, You're) coming now.
8. Go (two, to) my desk.
9. I know (their, they're) here.
10. (Their, They're) missing.
11. (There, They're) glad to see us.
12. (Its, It's) song is cheerful.
13. Bring me (its, it's) cover.
14. (Your, You're) lunch is ready.
15. (Its, It's) paw is hurt.
16. I hear (your, you're) elected.
17. She lives (their, there).
18. (Its, It's) a fine day.

## Combining Subjects and Predicates    pages 258–259

Combine the subjects or predicates in each pair of sentences. Use the word *and*. Write the new sentence.

1. Alice plays the violin. Penny plays the violin.
2. Bill beats the drums. Ann beats the drums.

3. Jean kicked the ball. Jean ran to first base.
4. George sings in the chorus. Ivan sings in the chorus.
5. He caught the ball. He tagged her as she ran.
6. The coach saw the play. The coach blew her whistle.
7. Karl blows on the sax. Joseph blows on the sax.
8. Ted stood at home plate. Ted kicked the ball far.
9. The ball sailed into left field. The ball landed.
10. Jack conducts the group. Abby conducts the group.

## Varying and Editing Sentences    pages 260–263

Write a paragraph of five sentences about a subject. Begin
your sentences in different ways. Edit your sentences.
Here are some suggestions.

> my day at school          what I do on Saturday
> dinosaurs                 animal homes
> a description of a friend, a pet, or a story character

## Mechanics Practice    page 263

Write these sentences correctly. Use commas where
necessary.

1. It was a cool crisp sunny day.
2. Beth Leo and I planned a hiking trip.
3. We packed sandwiches fruit and lemonade for lunch.
4. During our hike we saw rabbits deer horses and
   squirrels.
5. Yes it was a day to remember.

## Reading a Fable    pages 264–267

Read a fable. Then answer the questions.

1. What is the title of the fable?
2. Who are the characters in the fable?
3. What is the moral of the fable?
4. Why is this moral a good lesson for people?

# UNIT 8

### Giving and Getting Information    pages 276–277

Mrs. Smith calls Pam's mother. Read what she says. Write the information Pam needs to tell her mother.

"Hello Pam. This is Mrs. Smith. Isn't it a lovely day? I'm so glad the rain has ended. Now we'll have good weather for our bake sale. We'll need two dozen cupcakes. Your mother should bring them to my house by two o'clock. I'm making a cake."

### Critical Listening    pages 282–283

Write the sentence from each pair that states a fact.

1. Dart-Quik Fish Food will "put wings" on your tropical fish. It is made from brine, shrimp, and seaweed.
2. Tests show Dr. Fang's Toothpaste helps prevent cavities. You'll have the whitest teeth in town.
3. Greezy Motor Oil makes your car's engine happy. It is blended from high-grade oils.
4. MOOOO Ice Cream contains the most cream of any brand. It is everyone's favorite.
5. Cheapo Toys are built to last. They are made out of unbreakable plastic.
6. McSwamp's Coffee has that down-home taste. This coffee is made from Brazilian coffee beans.
7. Ever-Stick bandages will help heal you fast. They are used in many hospitals all over the country.
8. Dodo Doughnuts are made from natural ingredients. You'll want to buy all nine varieties.
9. Suzy Stand-Up is the doll you'll want by your side. She comes with a carrying case.
10. Sky-High Popcorn is made with vegetable oil. Pop it into your mouth for a super taste treat!

## Using a Telephone Directory   pages 286–287

Study these two guide words from a page in the telephone directory. Write the names you would find on that page.

### Gonzalez—Goodyear

| | | |
|---|---|---|
| **1.** Goodridge | **2.** Goodman | **3.** Gonsher |
| **4.** Gould | **5.** Goodney | **6.** Goodzeit |
| **7.** Gonzaga | **8.** Gomez | **9.** Goodnough |
| **10.** Goorland | **11.** Goodall | **12.** Goodwin |
| **13.** Gootenberg | **14.** Goodsmith | **15.** Gonzer |

## Using an Atlas   pages 288–289

Study this map and legend. Then answer the questions using complete sentences.

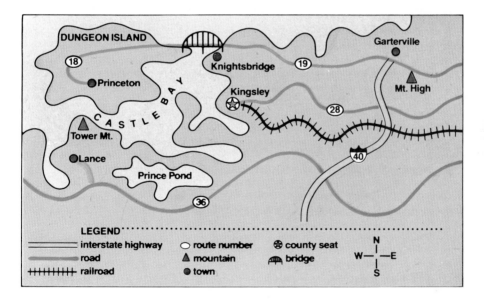

1. On what island is Princeton located?
2. From Kingsley, in what direction does the railroad go?
3. What is the name of the county seat?
4. What is the symbol for a mountain?
5. What town is near Prince Pond?

### Writing Conversation    pages 290–292

Write the sentences correctly.

1. Nicholas said I am reading a book about first aid.
2. what have you learned so far asked the teacher.
3. the first chapter is about safety Nicholas replied.
4. I know ways to carry a swimmer back to shore he said.
5. I know what to do for sunburns and small cuts he added.

### Writing and Editing a Story    pages 293–297

Write a story about a character or characters you make up. Describe the setting. Tell the events in the right order. Edit your story for interesting sentences. Use one of these topics or choose one of your own.

Teacher for a Day            The Mystery at the Zoo
Journey Through Space        A New Student at School

### Mechanics Practice    page 297

Write these sentences correctly. Use capital letters and punctuation marks where necessary.

1. where is the gerbil's cage steve asked
2. we keep it in the den said lori
3. what is your gerbil's name asked maria
4. i named him jumper said lori
5. what an unusual name said rick

### Reading a Story    pages 298–301

Read a story that is fiction. Then answer the questions.

1. What is the title of the story?
2. Who are the main characters in the story?
3. What is the setting of the story?
4. What is one challenge the main character faces?
5. How does he or she solve the problem?

# INDEX

A and *An*, 167, 174, 196, 237, 331, 351
Abbreviations
    in addresses, 46–47, 53, 71, 102–103, 111,
        306, 324, 339
    of days and months, 149
    in names and titles of people, 44–45, 53,
        63, 158, 306, 323, 327, 339
    of state names, 104–105, 123, 321
    in times of day, 108–109, 187
Action verbs, 78–79, 94, 120, 158–159, 236,
    312, 342
    using pronouns after, 206–207, 214, 232,
        318
Addresses, 46–47, 53, 71, 102–103, 104–105,
    111, 123, 320–321, 324
Addressing an envelope, 104–105, 123, 321
Adjectives, 162–163, 172–175, 182–183, 196–
    197, 237, 306, 316, 350–351
    that compare, 164–166, 174, 196, 316,
        350–351
Adventure story, 150–153, 157, 349
Adverbs, 168–169, 175, 197, 237, 306, 317, 352
    that tell *how, when,* and *where,* 170–173,
        175, 237, 317, 352
Aesop, 264
Agreement, subject and verb. *See* Subject-
    Verb agreement
Alliteration, 27–29, 33, 337
Alphabetical order, 96–97, 122, 345
    in book parts, 140–141
    in a card catalog, 16–17
    in an encyclopedia, 142–143, 156–157,
        349
    in a telephone directory, 286–287, 304
A.M. and P.M., 108–109, 187, 330
Answers to questions, forming, 8–9, 13, 31,
    246–247, 269, 335, 359
Antonyms, 178–181, 198, 353
Apostrophe
    in contractions, 87, 95, 121, 330, 343
    in possessives, 48–51, 53, 71, 158, 330,
        340
Articles, 167, 174, 196–197, 237, 331, 351
Articles, magazine. *See* Magazine articles
Atlas, 288–289, 304, 363
Author card, 16–17, 32

Bacmeister, Rhoda W., 33
Baruch, Dorothy W., 28
Belting, Natalia M., 191

Biography, 14–15, 32
    *Jane Goodall,* 66
    reading a, 66–69, 73, 341
Boiko, Claire, 117
Book, parts of a
    glossary, 140–141, 156
    index, 140–141, 156, 348
    table of contents, 138–139, 155–156, 348
    title page, 138–139, 155–156
Book to Read, A
    *All About Mud,* 231
    *American Tall Tales,* 195
    *Arthur Mitchell,* 69
    *The Church Mice Spread Their Wings,* 301
    *Ed Emberly's Great Thumbprint Drawing*
        *Book,* 153
    *Encyclopedia Brown Carries On,* 119
    *Stone Fox,* 267
    *Where the Sidewalk Ends,* 29
Book report
    editing a, 62–63, 73, 341
    writing a, 60–61, 73, 341
Book talk, 64–65, 73, 341
Books, kinds of, 14–15, 32

Capitalization
    of abbreviations, 44–45, 323
    of addresses, 46–47, 53, 71, 102–105, 111,
        123, 321, 324
    of A.M. and P.M., 108–109, 187, 330
    to begin sentences, 2–7, 12, 20–23, 74,
        308, 334–335
    of direct quotations, 290–292, 297, 305,
        329, 364
    of *I,* 63, 323
    of initials, 44–45, 53, 63, 158, 323, 339
    of names of days and months, 42–43, 52,
        71, 149, 325, 338–339
    of names of holidays, 42, 149, 325, 339
    of names of pets, 63, 323
    of names of places, 46–47, 53, 71, 324,
        339
    of names and titles of people, 44–45, 63,
        71, 323, 339
    of outlines, 220–221
    of titles of books, reports, stories, poems,
        and television shows, 60–61, 225
Card catalog, 16–17, 32
Challenge, A, 7, 47, 101, 131, 177, 207, 257,
    279
Characters
    in plays, 112–119
    in stories, 68–69, 150–153, 192, 264–267,
        293–295, 298–301

Coerr, Eleanor, 66
Colon, in times of day, 108–109, 187, 330
Comma
    in addresses, 102–103, 123, 328, 345
    in compound sentences, 18–19, 32–33, 328, 336
    in dates, 102, 149, 187, 328
    editing mark for, 110, 186
    in greetings and closings, 102–103, 106–107, 320, 328, 345
    in a series, 182–183, 198, 263, 328, 353
    with *yes/no* when they begin statements, 246–247, 249, 263, 269, 359
Common nouns. *See* Nouns, common
Comparisons, adjective
    *er* and *est,* 164–166
    *more* and *most,* 164–166
Complete predicates, 10–11, 13, 31, 74–75, 158, 236, 306, 336
Complete subjects, 10–11, 13, 31, 74–75, 158, 236, 306, 336
Composition. *See* Writing
Compound words, 254–255, 269, 360
Conjunctions, 18–19, 32–33, 182–183, 198, 258–259, 270, 336, 353, 360–361
Contractions, 87, 95, 121, 330, 343
Conversation, writing, 290–292, 297, 305, 329, 364
Coordinating conjunctions, 18–19, 32–33

Dates, 42, 102, 149, 187, 325, 328
Declarative sentences. *See* Sentences, declarative
Description, in poetry. *See* Poetry, description in
Descriptive paragraphs. *See* Paragraphs, descriptive
Details, reading for, 56–57, 72, 341
Dictionary
    alphabetical order in, 96–97, 122
    boldface in, 98–99
    definitions, 98–99, 122
    entry words, 98–99, 122
    examples in, 98–99, 122
    guide words, 96–97, 122
    parts of speech in, 98
    pronunciation in, 98–101, 122
Direction paragraphs. *See* Paragraphs, direction
Directions
    following, 280–281, 284–285, 303
    giving, 144–145, 157

Editing
    book reports, 62–63, 73, 341
    descriptive paragraphs, 186–187, 199, 353
    direction paragraphs, 148–149, 156
    letters, 110–111, 346
    marks, 22, 62, 110, 148, 186, 224, 262, 296, 322
    reports, 224–225, 235
    for sentence variety, 262, 271, 361
    sentences, 22–23, 33
    stories, 296, 305, 364
Emberley, Ed, 153
Emerson, Ralph Waldo, 26
Encyclopedia, 142–143, 156, 349
Entry words, 98–99, 122
Envelope, addressing an, 104–105, 123, 321
Exclamation point, 6–7, 20–21, 23, 31, 308, 329, 335
Exclamatory sentences. *See* Sentences, exclamatory

Fables
    "The Boastful Bullfrog and the Bull," 265–266
    "The Dog and the Shadow," 267
    "The Fox and the Goat," 264–265
    "The Fox and the Grapes," 271
    reading, 264–267, 271, 361
Fact, statements of, 56–59, 72, 282–283, 285, 304
Fallis, Edwina, 199
Fiction, 14–15, 32. *See also* A Book to Read; Fables; Short Stories
Field, Rachel, 190
Figures of speech, 166
Fisher, Aileen, 25, 188
Fogel, Julianna A., 150
Frost, Frances, 189
Future tense, 84–86, 94, 121, 159, 313

Gardiner, John Reynolds, 267
Gilbert, Alice, 28
Glossary, 140–141, 156
*Good* and *well,* 172–173, 316, 331, 352
Guide words, 96–97, 122

Helping verbs, 82–83, 94, 120, 159, 312, 342
Henniker-Heaton, Peter J., 89
Hoberman, Mary Ann, 33
Homographs, 176–177, 197
Homophones, 256–257, 270, 332–333, 360

Verbs *(continued)*

> helping, 82–83, 94, 120, 159, 312, 342
> irregular, 90–93, 95, 121, 159, 314–315, 344
> linking, 80–81, 94, 120, 158–159, 236, 312, 342
> main, 82–83, 94, 159, 342
> spelling past tense, 88–89, 95, 121, 313
> subjects and, agreement, 244–245, 249, 268–269, 307, 358–359
> tense, 84–86, 94, 121, 159, 313, 343

Wadsworth, Wallace, 192
Warner, Mark, 228
*Well. See Good* and *well.*
Word order. *See* Sentences
Words, troublesome

> *a* and *an,* 167, 174, 196–197, 331, 351
> *good* and *well,* 172–173, 175, 197, 237, 331, 352
> *I* and *me,* 210–211, 215, 233, 331, 356
> *its* and *it's,* 256–257, 270, 332, 360
> *their, there* and *they're,* 256–257, 270, 332, 360

Words, troublesome *(continued)*

> *to, too,* and *two,* 256–257, 270, 332, 360
> *your* and *you're,* 256–257, 270, 332, 360

Writing. *See also* Capitalization

> book reports, 60–63, 73, 341
> commercials, 283
> conversation, 290–292, 305, 364
> fables, 267
> introductions, 274–275, 284
> letters, 102–111, 123, 209, 320, 345–346
> paragraphs, 126–137, 146–149, 155, 157, 159, 184–185, 199, 203, 261, 295, 306, 349, 353
> poems, 26, 189
> questions and answers, 8–9, 13, 335
> riddles, 26, 257
> reports, 216–225, 235, 357
> stories, 293–295, 364

*Yes,* comma after, 246–247, 249, 269, 328, 359
*Your* and *you're,* 256–257, 270, 332, 360

Zip code, 105, 321